"Every business owner should know how to properly structure their affairs. Kathleen Spitzer has written an excellent book detailing the secrets of why Wyoming is the state for asset protection structures."

Blair Singer
Best-selling author of
Sales Dogs and *The ABCs of Building a Business Team That Wins*

AF877961

"Many Americans are victims of litigation that could be avoided by using the strategies outlined in Kathleen Spitzer's book. If you are an investor, entrepreneur, or business owner, this is required reading. Entity formation and maintenance may save you a small fortune in litigation costs."

Jessica Rutzick
Trial Lawyer
Jackson, Wyoming

"The Wyoming Corporate Handbook provides clearly written tax and legal advice every investor and business owner can utilize to their benefit."

James C. Reed, CPA
President
Teton Tax Strategies, LLC

"Kathleen Spitzer provides excellent legal advice for the entrepreneur starting a business."

Ron Sacchi
Business Coach and Author,
Design/Build Your Business

The Wyoming Corporate Handbook

By Kathleen Spitzer, Esq.

A Corporate Direct Nonfiction Book

Copyright 2005 by Kathleen Spitzer. All rights reserved. No part of this publication may be reproduced, stored in a retrieval system, or transmitted in any form or by any means, electronic, mechanical, photocopied, recorded, or otherwise, except in the case of brief quotations embodied in critical articles or reviews, without the prior written permission of the publisher. For more information, write Corporate Direct, Inc., 2248 Meridian Boulevard, Suite H, Minden, Nevada, 89423 or visit www.corporatedirect.com.

Cover design by MeshCreative, Inc. www.meshcreative.com

Corporate Direct, Inc.
COPYRIGHT © 2005, Kathleen Spitzer
All Rights Reserved
Printed in the United States of America
10 987654321

Library of Congress Control No: in progress
ISBN No. 0-9746844-7-3

This publication is designed to provide general information regarding the subject matter covered. Because each individual's legal, tax, and financial situation is different, specific advice should be tailored to the particular circumstances. For this reason, the reader is advised to consult with his or her own attorney, accountant and/or other advisor regarding that individual's specific situation. The author has taken reasonable precautions in the preparation of this book and believes that the information presented in the book is accurate as of the date it was written. However, neither the author nor the publisher assume any responsibility for any errors or omissions. The author and publisher specifically disclaim any liability resulting from the use or application of the information contained in this book, and the information is not intended to serve as legal, tax, or other financial advice related to individual situations.

Dedication

To my family.

TABLE OF CONTENTS

Introduction

Because you are reading this book I am going to assume two things: (1) You are thinking about setting up and maintaining an entity either for investment or business activities; and (2) You are considering setting your entity up in the great State of Wyoming. Let me congratulate you on both interests and for making a move in the right direction by picking up this book. Entity formation is a relatively simple and very necessary step that, when done correctly, can save you untold headaches and money. But it is important to enter the creation phase with knowledge – knowledge of how your entity is formed, how it is maintained, and overshadowing both these considerations, the knowledge that your entity can be formed and maintained in any state.

Corporations, limited partnerships and limited liability companies are entities separate and apart from you, their originator. When one of these entities is formed a legal existence is created. This legal existence may in whole or in part be controlled by you, but it is very important to keep in mind that it is separate. Because it is not a part of you, the entity in which you are a shareholder or member of does not have to live in the same state as you reside. But you want it to live in a place where the laws are kind to it. So, don't limit your company to the choices you have made for yourself. It is a big country out there with 50 different states to choose from. Of course, that is a lot of research ... but wait! You've bought this book so look no further. We have done the research for you.

The decision of where to form your entity depends on several factors. Sometimes it does turn out that the best place to form your entity is indeed the state where you reside. But for those businesses that are better off being formed elsewhere, the question "Where?" is a very important one. After all, every state has different rules, laws and idiosyncrasies governing their domestic entities.

Wyoming is the state of choice for entity formation. Yes, the Cowboy State! It is a beautiful place of open plains and dramatic mountains that only about half a million people get to call home. It may be the Old West but it is the new frontier for corporations, limited liability companies and limited partnerships. With the passage of important legislation in 1989, Wyoming has become a true corporate haven offering the most liberal corporate laws in America, with minimal government involvement and maximum corporate flexibility.

This book was written as a basic guide for those interested in the advantages of setting up an entity in Wyoming. I set out to cover the fundamentals of entity formation – the how, when, why and where – not to write a book for experts. Laws are organic and complex. Do not use this handbook in place of a good attorney and CPA – but read it for background so you will have enough knowledge to speak intelligently to your attorney and CPA.

Chapter 1: Should I Form An Entity?

Four Basic Reasons

It seems that everyone you talk to these days is a member, partner or shareholder of at least one entity. This is because every year, tens of thousands of corporations, limited liability companies (LLCs) and limited partnerships (LPs) are formed in the United States. Why is everyone so entity-happy these days? Individual reasons can vary, but there are four main reasons to form an entity.

1. Asset Protection

"The law provides incredible financial incentives to seek out a victim with deep pockets, drag him into court, ruin his reputation, wear him down with endless discovery demands, pay a fortune to defend himself, and then extort a settlement from him. This is not justice in any sense of the word." - ***The Tort Informer***

The best way to protect your assets is to separate them from each other and from yourself. The limited liability concept arose in the 1500s as a means of encouraging wealthy individuals to invest in maritime ventures. Before the establishment of corporations, investors in a ship that was lost at sea not only lost their investment, they were financially ruined. Creditors of the venture could personally sue the investors. The English Crown had the foresight to limit the exposure of investors through the corporate charter. As a fictitious entity created and chartered by the Crown, a corporation became a creature separate from its owners and employees. As such, the corporation's debts were not extended to investors, providing investors the protection of limited liability. By allowing a group of investors to safely pool their resources in a corporation, the Crown enabled voyagers to explore the seas and seek profit. With the addition of a few new limited liability vehicles, governments today continue to allow those willing to risk money in economic activity to limit their exposure.

Face it -- we live in a litigious world. Spending your time looking over your shoulder is no way to live. The best way to avoid losing your hard won assets is to shield them from each other. Placing your business and your assets into limited liability entities protects them from exposure to each other. Imagine that there was a shoebox available that held potential liabilities rather than shoes. By purchasing and maintaining these shoeboxes your personal assets would be safe from the threat of a suit arising from your business ventures and investments. All liability associated with the investment or venture would be stuck within the six walls of the shoebox. Imagine further that each of these shoeboxes were very affordable to purchase and maintain.

Each entity you form operates to protect your assets in roughly the same manner. When properly maintained, an entity says, "Hey, I'm not that guy – sure you can sue me, but only me. The guy who formed me, and all of his other assets, are separate and protected." If you are a shareholder, member, or limited partner of a business entity and that business later is sued, only the assets of that business are liable for any judgment. Any equity that you may have in the business entity is thus exposed, but your personal assets such as your house, car, savings, investments and other businesses would not be part of that entity and thus not liable for any judgments. Your other assets are protected.

Concentrate on the word "entity" for a moment. Webster's Dictionary defines the word "entity" as an "existing thing, to be separate, or self-contained existence; the existence of a thing as contrasted with its attributes; something that has separate and distinct existence and objective or conceptual reality." In other words – NOT YOU! Sure, you are either a member or a shareholder or possibly a limited partner, director, officer or manager of the entity, but you are not the entity. So long as you always respect your entity as something separate and apart from yourself and follow the rules, you and yours will remain separate and distinct – i.e. limited in liability. Limited to what? Your ownership interest. That's it.

Asset protection is achieved through the use of entities.

2. Tax Incentives and Fringe Benefits

*The trick is to stop thinking of it as "your" money. - **IRS Auditor***

In most forms of ownership, you and your business are one entity for income tax purposes. By contrast, if you form an entity separate from yourself, you have a choice of tax treatment. In Chapters 2 and 3 we explore the different tax choices in greater detail. For now, just be aware that entity selection can enable you to minimize taxes in the following ways:

- If you are taxed as a corporation you can decide when to distribute dividend income. For instance, if you've had a good monetary year in other aspects of your financial life, you may choose to hold on to some of the corporate profit at the corporate level.
- Profits, other than salary, taken out of an S Corporation are not subject to payroll taxes.
- Medical insurance for you and your family may be fully deductible.
- Retirement plans may be set up using pre-tax dollars.
- Losses are fully deductible for a corporation whereas an individual must prove a profit motive before deducting losses.
- Different levels of estate planning can be accomplished through entity selection. Limited partnerships in particular are great tools for estate planning because the IRS actually allows you to reduce the taxable amount gifted to Limited Partners.
- If you are taxed as a C Corporation you can choose your fiscal year, for example, June 1st or October 1st instead of January 1st. Not being hemmed into a calendar year allows for some creative tax planning. You may also use accounting methods that are best suited to your needs.
- Single-member LLCs are disregarded entities for tax purposes; thus an LLC that owns real estate can still gain the tax benefits of sole ownership while, in most states, enjoying limited liability status.
- So long as certain treasury requirements are met, an LLC can make special allocations of profits and losses among its members.
- Money borrowed by an LLC can increase the tax basis of the members.
- Property contributions to an LLC by members are not taxable events.
- LLCs may increase their asset basis if a member's interest is purchased.
- LLCs can distribute certain property to their members tax free.

(As always, laws are subject to change. Please consult with your advisor as to current regulations.)

3. Perpetuity

"Simply the thing that I am shall make me live." - ***Shakespeare***

Because you are creating an entity that exists apart from you, it can live forever. So if a corporate founder passes away, business can go on as usual. Even with LLCs and LPs you can be sure that there won't be a break in stride through a properly written Operating Agreement or Limited Partnership Agreement. This continuity of existence and its natural extension of ease of transferability are other bonuses associated with entity formation. An entity's assets and accounts may be transferred by an assignment of stock or membership/partnership interest. With a sole proprietorship, each individual asset, license, permit, etc. must be transferred individually. And unlike a corporation, LLC or LP, when the sole proprietor dies, the sole proprietorship dies with him or her, offering no business continuity.

4. Privacy

"The greatest misfortune that ever befell man was the invention of printing."
– Benjamin Disraeli

And now we have the internet! Privacy is one of those quirky things - many people aren't sure when or why they'll need it. Unfortunately for most of us, it's the old umbrella rule – the sky was blue when you left home and had you taken an umbrella it probably would not have rained. If you had taken some steps to keep your name private, then Mr. X would never have bothered you. There are certain classes of people for whom privacy is a no-brainer. If you are well known as an individual with some backing, in a profession where people automatically assume that you have deep pockets, or if you are an easy target for a lawsuit, then privacy is essential. There are many sources of information available to the want-to-be litigant. The less your name appears on public records, the greater the chance that you will be left alone. Entity formation allows a measure of privacy because the name of your entity, not your own, is used. Through the use of a nominee officer, director, or manager, you can achieve a much greater level of privacy in that the nominee's name, and not yours, appears on all state filings and on the internet. Wyoming is one of the few states that allows nominees for your important privacy.

Chapter 2: Which Entity Do I Form?

Before we jump into the benefits of the various limited liability entity choices, let's talk a bit about that other kind of entity, the one that provides **un**limited liability.

Sole proprietorships and general partnerships both provide the same amount of asset protection -- none, zero, zip. But, general partnerships go a step further in the asset exposure arena -- you have another person or several persons (your partners) whose actions you could be held responsible for. Both are bad entities.

Sole Proprietorship

People often get caught in sole proprietorships because becoming one takes little effort. No formalities are necessary to form a sole proprietorship. As I mentioned above, a sole proprietorship provides the proprietor with no asset protection. Meaning that she owns the business in her own name and therefore everything else she owns is exposed to any liability arising from the sole proprietorship. Sole proprietorships are also bad for estate planning purposes. As mentioned, when the sole proprietor dies, the business dies with her, preventing business continuity for any heirs.

Sole proprietorships are also a poor choice for tax planning strategies. Although sole proprietorships are taxed at ordinary income levels, the proprietor himself is subject to self-employment taxes on all income. The right entity can avoid this expensive (and less than beneficial) withholding. Additionally, recently published statistics indicate that the Internal Revenue Service is more likely to audit sole proprietorships than any other form of business. This may be because the IRS is more suspicious of deductions claimed by sole proprietors. While the threat of an audit may be a relatively minor consideration when deciding which business entity to use, it is one that should be added to the list of factors weighing against the use of sole proprietorships.

General Partnerships

General partnerships are similar to sole proprietorships in many respects. No paperwork is necessary to create a general partnership. The partnership does not pay taxes as an entity. Instead, the individual partners pay regular income tax on their share of the partnership's income. The company's funding comes directly from the partners. The partners retain control over the company, and are each entitled to act to bind the partnership. Partners may be personally liable for a general partnership's debts and obligations.

While a written partnership agreement outlining the partners' relationship can be prepared (although certainly not by our firm) it is important to know that a handshake can also create a general partnership, resulting in unlimited personal liability. This is called "innocent formation" and it can lead to a lifetime of liability. You must be careful when casually entering into a business relationship.

Taxation and contributions differ slightly between sole proprietorships and general partnerships. While neither a sole proprietorship nor a general partnership pays taxes as an entity, a general partnership must report income separately to the IRS.

Unlike a sole proprietorship, control of a partnership is not consolidated in one person. Compare the level of control exerted by the sole proprietor, who can make all decisions unilaterally, to the control exerted by a partner, who owes fiduciary duties of loyalty and care to the other partners and shares control with the other partners. Even though a partnership agreement may require all partners to approve before certain actions are taken, realistically, one partner may act on his or her own to bind the partnership. This may have devastating consequences if a rogue partner acts against the partnership's interests. The threat of a rogue partner reveals an important consideration about the liability exposure of general partnerships. That is: you are personally responsible whether you agreed to it or not.

Entity Selection

So, you've decided that you want to form a limited liability entity to shield your personal assets from your business ventures and to shield your business assets from each other. Which entity do you choose? It's probably the most frequently asked question that I hear from entrepreneurs, both experienced and those just getting their feet wet. And it is an important question, a keystone question. And in answering it, a number of important considerations to keep in mind include the following:

- Do you plan on doing active business?
- Do you plan to have partners?
- Do you plan on using your entity primarily for asset protection?
- Do you plan on using your entity primarily for transferring assets, or estate planning?
- What size business to you intend on starting?
- Do you foresee heavy start up costs?
- Do you foresee a loss in the first few years?
- Do you foresee the need for a number of investors or shareholders?
- Do you intend to go public someday?
- Do you intend on setting up benefits packages?

These are just a few of the questions that need to be analyzed in choosing the correct entity form. As with many decisions in life, your choice of entity is not written in stone, at least in the State of Wyoming. Pursuant to Title 17, Chapter 26 of the Wyoming Statutes, you can convert your entity into another form. Thus, if you form an LLC and later decide that a corporation is better suited to your needs, Wyoming would allow you to make that conversion. That said, be sure to discuss such a move with your tax advisor as there could be some tax consequences with such a conversion. Below, the advantages and disadvantages of each form are discussed in further detail.

Regular, or "C" Corporations ("C Corp")

A C Corp is a great entity for a beginning business that:

- Wants to retain earnings, rather than disburse them each year;
- May have large start-up costs and expects to have losses in the first few years;
- Wants to look for outside investors, and may even plan on going public;
- Wants to have multiple classes of stock and sell stock to anyone, anywhere in the world;
- Wants the option of providing its owners and its employees with tax-free benefits;
- May have very high-income owners.

As mentioned previously, corporations came of age in England in the 1500s, as the Crown's answer to Fate and Mother Nature. At that time, most business ventures were operated as general partnerships. As general partnerships, these business ventures also featured unlimited liability of each partner, one of the key reasons general partnerships should be avoided. So, that new schooner you and your partners purchased, outfitted and sent on a trade mission to China for silk and pepper had better not sink. If it does, you and your partners would be personally answering to the bank that loaned you the money to buy the ship and the creditors that provided you with trade goods to outfit your ship.

Unfortunately, both Fate and Mother Nature intervened frequently, and the losses were so large that it kept people from taking business risks. In an attempt to encourage entrepreneurs, the English government devised the Corporation, which existed as its own entity, distinct and separate from each shareholder who had invested in it. The partners (now called shareholders) were liable only for the money they invested, not the entire loss that may be suffered. Creditors now had only the Corporation to sue, and not the shareholders. So if the Corporation had no assets (or if it did, but they were resting at the bottom of the ocean) those creditors were out of luck.

Because corporations exist as separate, independent entities, they file their own tax returns. The S Corporation, as we'll discuss, is the same as a C Corporation. Both are corporations according to state law. The only difference is that the S Corporation is permitted by the IRS to use flow-through/partnership taxation and the C Corporation is taxed at the corporate level and then shareholders are taxed at their individual rate when distributions are made. A C Corp's earnings will be taxed at a relatively low rate on the first $50,000 in taxable income. But you must be aware that forming two or more C Corps and allocating a portion of your profits into two or more entities to split the profits for the lower 15% tax bracket won't work. If you own more than 50% of one or more of those C corporations, the IRS will tag all of those companies as being part of a control group, and ramp their taxation rates back up toward a 38% rate. Control group status realistically applies to C Corps though, so be careful to plan a proper mix of entities into your wealth-planning structure.

A C Corp has the widest range of deductions and expenses allowed by the IRS, especially in the area of employee fringe benefits. A C Corp can set up medical reimbursement, disability life insurance, and other employee benefits, and deduct the costs of running these programs, including all premiums paid. The employees, including you as the owner/shareholder, do not pay taxes on the value of those benefits. This is not the case in a flow-through entity, such as an S Corp, LLC or LP. In each of those cases the entity may write off the costs of the benefits, but any employee/shareholder who owns more than 2% of the entity will pay taxes on the value of their benefits received. Medical insurance premiums are the exception to this rule. So, if having the maximum deductions and all of the employee fringe benefits on a tax-free basis is important to you, a C Corp may be your ideal entity choice.

C corporations are great for a business that sells products, has a storefront and employees, and may or may not have a warehouse where it keeps its inventory. C Corps do not work well for businesses that want to hold appreciating assets, such as real estate, because of the tax treatment on the sale of these assets. The taxes on the sale of appreciated real estate held in a C Corp will be much greater than if held in an LLC or LP. You won't use a C Corp to hold real estate.

The most often-cited disadvantage of using a C Corp is the "double taxation" issue. Double taxation happens when a C Corp has a profit left over at the end of the year and wants to distribute it to the shareholders as a dividend. The C Corp has already paid taxes on that profit, but once it distributes the profit to its shareholders, those shareholders will have to declare the dividends they receive as income on their personal tax returns, and pay taxes again at their own personal rates.

There are many things you can do to avoid the double taxation scenario. Structure the C Corp so that there are no profits left over -- use all of the write-offs and deductions allowed by the IRS to reduce the C Corp's net income. Offer great benefit plans! Pay higher salaries to yourself and the other owner/employees than you would if you were using a flow-through entity such as an S Corp. Yes, you will have to pay payroll taxes and personal income taxes on those monies, but you would pay personal taxes on dividends paid to you anyway. And it may be that in the big picture, the savings on one side outweigh the additional taxes paid on the other side.

Choosing the best entity is a decision that really does, in so many cases, hinge on taxes. Therefore, with any corporate-related decision, you are wise to seek the advice and assistance of a good CPA.

Sub-Chapter "S" Corporations ("S Corp")

An S Corp is a great entity for a beginning business that:

- Will provide a service;
- Does not have significant start-up costs;
- Will not need to make major equipment purchases before beginning operations;
- Will make a sizable amount of money without a great deal of effort an expense;
- Will expect having no more than 100 shareholders, who will live in the United States or will file a U.S. Resident tax return.

An S-Corp is structurally the same as a C corporation (i.e., it has officers, directors and shareholders, and files articles of incorporation in its state of formation), but with one key difference. An S Corp files an election with the IRS, called a Form 2553, that provides it with a flow-through tax structure like those found in partnerships and limited liability companies. This means the company's net income or loss will flow through to its shareholders, and be split among them according to each shareholder's ownership percentage. The S Corp's taxes will actually be paid by its shareholders, at their individual tax rates, and in proportion to their individual ownership percentages.

From a taxation standpoint, an S Corp is a great fit for a company that offers a service, because in many cases the revenues can be split and paid to the shareholders in two categories: salary and passive earnings. A flow-through tax structure means that the profits and corresponding losses, deductions and expenses are divided up among the shareholders, in proportion to their ownership percentages, and reported on each shareholder's personal income tax return.

Therefore, if your income from an S Corp is split into two streams, salary and passive, each stream will be taxed differently. Your salary stream will be subject to both income tax and payroll taxes such as Medicare and social security. However, the passive income stream will be subject only to income tax. So, by taking a reasonable salary from the S Corp and the rest as dividends, your tax payments would be lower than if you were to take your entire share of the earnings as salary.

Now be careful here. If you do not take a reasonable salary you will likely be subject to an audit and could end up losing this tax advantage. For instance if you are the CEO of an S Corp which grosses $5,000,000 a year, then $30,000 annually is not a reasonable salary. The IRS view is that you could not hire someone on the open market to run the business for such a low salary. So it will challenge an owner who takes such a low salary to avoid payroll taxes. It would be wise to consult a good accountant to determine what would qualify as a reasonable salary for your position.

An S Corp is also a great entity for businesses with low start-up costs that do not have to purchase a significant amount of assets to begin operations. For example, buying a working laundromat would be an excellent choice for an S Corp. You are purchasing a turnkey business -- it's already operating, and you aren't going to be laying out significant cash to get it up and running. You will have a pretty good income stream immediately, and that income stream can best be disbursed to you and your partners, if any, through the S Corp structure. Two other great matches for an S Corp are network marketing and Internet-only businesses. In each case, the business is likely to have no storefront, low operating costs, and probably doesn't maintain a warehouse. Most network marketing and Internet-only businesses drop-ship from their suppliers directly to the consumer if they even deliver products at all. Because these can be high-income, low-cost operations, an S Corp structure can be useful. But again, these scenarios and the entities presented are not one-size-fits-all. There may be other reasons why a C Corp, LLC or LP may be beneficial.

Here's another reason we suggest S Corps for many service-oriented businesses: to avoid being characterized as a Personal Service Corporation, or "PSC" by the IRS. PSCs are C corporations that are classified by the IRS as providing a service, such as consulting, to the general public. Now, as you may know, the United States government, in an effort to boost the economy and keep business working, assesses C corporations with a pretty low initial rate -- 15% on profits up to $50,000. That's quite a bit lower than you would pay personally if you were receiving that same $50,000 as salary. And, that 15% rate is also lower than you would pay if your business were an S Corp. So, to head off the anticipated revenue drain, the IRS closed that loophole by designating C corporations that provide services to be PSCs. The additional tax rate for PSC earnings can be a flat 35% plus 15% of the corporation's undistributed personal holding company income. That may be higher than you would pay through your S Corp if you took a reasonable salary and the designated the rest as dividends. And, it's enough, in many cases, to make the difference between going S Corp and C Corp.

A downside to S Corps is the limitation on who can be a shareholder and what kind of shares it can issue. There can be no more than 100 shareholders in total, and no one may take their shares in anything other than their personal names (or in their living trust). So forget transferring your S Corp shares into an irrevocable trust, limited partnership or children's trust. You cannot have any non-U.S. resident shareholders, either. Everyone who holds shares in an S Corp must file a U.S. resident tax return. You are limited to only one class of shares, which can be confining, especially if your plans include taking your company public or looking for outside investors. If you breach any of these requirements, the IRS will strip your company of its S Corp status, and automatically turn it into a C Corporation, which may have negative tax consequences.

Another downside is asset transfer treatment. Both C and S Corps are not great vehicles if your business will hold appreciating assets, such as land, buildings, stocks, bonds, and the like. Transferring assets out of a C or S corporation can have tax consequences and trigger an immediate tax. On the other hand, transferring assets out of an LLC or LP will not trigger a tax.

The steps to create a C or S corporation are the same. Articles of Incorporation are prepared and filed, Bylaws are drafted, directors are elected by the shareholders, officers are elected by the directors, and shares are issued to the shareholders. In this sense, a C Corp and an S Corp are identical. It is only in their taxation that they differ.

To initiate the different tax treatment, the S Corp declaration, a.k.a. Form 2553, should be filed within 75 days of the incorporation date. Do not delay if this is how you see your company proceeding. If you do not file within that 75-day period, the IRS can deny you S Corp status for a full year, meaning that your first year of operations will be conducted at C Corporation tax rates.

For both S and C corporations, the shareholders, directors and officers of the company must remember to follow corporate formalities. They must treat the corporation as a separate and independent legal entity, which includes holding regularly scheduled meetings, conducting banking through a separate corporate bank account, filing a separate corporate tax return, signing all documents related to the business in their official capacity, and filing corporate papers with the state on a timely basis. If these steps are not followed, a business creditor may be allowed to "pierce the corporate veil" and seek personal liability against the officers, directors and shareholders. Adhering to corporate formalities is not at all difficult or particularly time consuming. In fact, if you have someone handle the corporate filings and the preparation of annual minutes and direct your accountant to prepare the corporate tax return, you should spend minimal time at it and have only a slight increase in cost. The point is that if you spend the extra money to form a corporation in order to gain limited liability, it makes sense to spend the extra time and money to ensure that protection.

Limited Liability Companies (LLCs)

An LLC is a great entity for a beginning business that:

- Wants to invest in assets that will appreciate over time;
- Is intended to be an estate-planning vehicle to transfer wealth to the next generation;
- Wants its owners to hold their interests in the names of other entities or trusts;
- Wants to be able to sell ownership interests all over the world;
- Wants to provide its owners with flow-through taxation;
- Wants to divide up the profits and losses in ratios other than strict ownership percentages;
- Wants to protect its assets from creditors.

Of the entities discussed in this chapter, limited liability companies (LLCs) are the youngest. Prior to 1977, LLCs were not recognized in the U.S. Over a hundred years ago, Germany was the first to provide for such an entity that exhibited characteristics of partnerships and corporations. But Wyoming was the first state in the U.S. to allow the formation of such an entity. Now, all states have adopted laws that allow for the formation of LLCs, but each state's treatment of LLCs varies. LLCs provide both the limited liability protection found with corporations and the flow-through taxation of a partnership. They allow you to divide up profit and loss allocations among the owners in varying ways -- and not based strictly on ownership percentages, as is required in C and S Corps. Ownership may be held by individuals, corporations or trusts, and there are no restrictions on where owners live either inside or out of the United States. Annual meetings are not required but are strongly recommended, both as a good method of communication between the managers and the members and as a way to establish that the LLC is a distinct, stand-alone entity. That last point is important, because when formalities are not followed, creditors may attempt to pierce the veil of protection.

An LLC is formed when one files a document titled the Articles of Organization with a state's Secretary of State. The Articles provide general information about the LLC as required by state law. The internal documents, such as the Operating Agreement, provide the LLC's operating details and the nature of the relationship among the LLC's members. Whenever a dispute arises as to voting rights, distributions, or other internal operations, the Articles and Operating Agreement should provide a clear solution or a procedure for resolving the dispute. Operating Agreements are discussed further in Chapter 5.

The LLC offers flow-through taxation, flexible management, limited liability for all owners, and flexible distributions. One of the desirable characteristics of an LLC is that income "passes through" an LLC and is not taxed at the entity level. Income earned by the LLC is taxed to the LLC's members as ordinary income. That income can be distributed or retained by the LLC. In order to be taxed like a partnership, the IRS initially required that an LLC exhibit three of the following four corporate characteristics: perpetual existence, freely transferable interests, centralized management, and limited liability. If an LLC exhibited all four characteristics, the IRS would treat the entity as a corporation and would tax income once at the entity level and again when distributed to the entity's owners, as with a C Corp. However, the limitations on LLC characteristics have now largely been removed, allowing the LLC to exhibit the characteristics traditionally attributed to corporations.

In an LLC, the owners are called "members" instead of shareholders. They receive "membership interests" instead of shares based on the value of assets or services contributed by each member. Adding members to an LLC has the effect of reducing the holdings of existing members.

To illustrate, compare LLC ownership to slices of a pie. Each partner has a slice based on his or her initial contribution (or some other basis set forth in the Operating Agreement). To invite another member into the LLC, one or all members must give up some of his or her interest in the LLC, thus diminishing their piece of the pie. Accordingly, LLC members generally must approve the admittance of a new member to the LLC. This differs from a corporation, where the corporation may have retained some of the pie for later distribution to new shareholders. Accordingly, shareholders need not always approve the corporation's sale of stock to new shareholders. This distinction may be confusing for those who are familiar with corporations and the effects of issuing shares, so caution should be exercised to differentiate between LLC membership interests and shares of corporate stock.

Special Features of a Single-Member LLC

If your entity will be owned by you and used as a vehicle to hold assets, then the simplest way to do that is by using a single-member LLC. In Wyoming, a single-member LLC is referred to as a flexible limited liability company or FLLC. LLCs in Wyoming generally must have two or more members. However, if you elect in your articles to be a flexible limited liability company, you may have only one member.

The IRS favors the single-member LLC for homeowners (a one-member LLC, an LLC owned solely by husband and wife as community property under the laws of a state, or an LLC whose sole member is a living trust, all qualify in the eyes of the IRS as a single-member LLC). At the end of 2002, the IRS introduced a treasury regulation (Treasury Regulation Section 1.121), allowing those who form a single-member LLC and transfer their home into that LLC to retain the mortgage interest deduction. Prior to December 2002, this deduction was lost, making homeowners choose between a tax deduction and extra asset protection. As well, the IRS allows taxpayers who hold their primary residence in a single-member LLC to receive the tax-free gain upon sale of the house. As you may know, the first $250,000 in gain for singles and $500,000 in gain for married couples is tax-free on the sale of property used as a primary residence for two out of the last five years. This now applies to primary residences held in a single-member LLC.

In addition, the IRS considers a single-member LLC a disregarded entity for tax purposes. This means you do not have to file a separate LLC tax return. Instead, the LLC's tax obligations flow directly onto your personal return. You don't lose the limited liability protection, but you do save on the expense of preparing an LLC tax return. That said, court cases in some states (including California and Colorado) have denied asset protection benefits to single-member LLCs. So be sure to work with your advisor on the best strategy for you.

Member-Managed LLC

LLCs can either be governed collectively, by all of its members, or by one or more managers who are voted in by the members and who carry out the day-to-day functions and business of the LLC.

A member-managed LLC is just that -- operated by all of its members, or by a committee of members selected by the other members. Remember, in an LLC, shareholders (or owners) are referred to as members.

The member-managed LLC is the most democratic of the three structures and is a great vehicle in situations where you have only a few members who will all be participating equally in the daily operations of your business.

If your entity will be used as a business vehicle by unrelated parties, then a member-managed LLC may be a good option. You will each have an equal share in how the business is operated, yet you will each remain insulated from personal liability with respect to your involvement in the business. Keep in mind, however, that too many hands in the pot can make it difficult to run day-to- day operations and thus a manager managed LLC may be beneficial depending on the type of activity the LLC is involved in.

Manager-Managed LLC

A manager-managed LLC is run by a manager, who is initially appointed by the members. The manager may be a person, more than one person, or a corporate entity. A manager does not have to be a member and hold ownership interests in the LLC, although it certainly can do that.

A manager usually has control over all of the day-to-day operations of the LLC, and the members are involved peripherally, on actions such as voting to acquire or dispose of major assets, or possibly voting to remove a manager from office.

If your entity will be owned by your family and used as a vehicle to amass and manage family wealth, then either a manager-managed LLC or an LP is a safe bet. Both of these methods will allow you to maintain control over the daily management of your assets, and to move ownership gradually over to your children, without potentially losing control.

LLCs are excellent entities for use in connection with real estate investing. Properties held in an LLC are easy to transfer, and incur less tax on a subsequent sale than would be assessed if that same property were held in a corporation. LLCs work well for family asset based entities, where the goal is to increase the family wealth, plan for the future, and maximize tax savings. You can put other things into an LLC, such as day-trading accounts, stocks and bonds, insurance policies and annuities.

Limited Partnerships (LPs)

Like LLCs, LPs are a great entity for most of the same reasons. They are particularly excellent for use as an estate planning vehicle, because when properly structured, they allow parents to transfer wealth to their children tax-free, while maintaining complete control over the assets and the day-to-day operations of the LP. This control continues even after majority ownership has passed on paper to your children.

This is because an LP has two types of partners: (1) a general partner who is actively and personally responsible for managing the partnership and (2) limited partners who are passive owners, with no management rights. The general partner can be an individual or another entity, and has broad powers to obligate the LP and manage its daily operations. However, unlike any of the other entities we have discussed, a general partner remains personally liable for the debts incurred by the LP. So, for protection purposes it is recommended that you use a C Corp, S Corp or an LLC to serve as the general partner, thus insulating you personally from liability.

A limited partner is restricted to ownership of his or her limited partnership interests only, and has absolutely no control over how the entity operates. Limited partners receive passive profit distributions from the LP. The distributions are taxed at each limited partner's individual personal income tax rate, unless an asset sold has been held for over a year, in which case the profit will be taxed at the long-term capital gains rate (15% as of this writing).

LPs can be a great way for parents to transfer their assets to their children. By using an aggressive gifting strategy, parents can pass along ownership of assets to their children and provide their children with an income stream that will be taxed at their children's usually lower individual tax rate. Because of the inherent lack of control of the limited partner, the IRS allows you to gift value in the limited partnership to the limited partners at an accelerated rate. This is also true for Wyoming Close LLCs as the powers of certain members can also be limited. With

LLCs one must be cautious, however, not to grant children a greater than 49% interest or it would be possible for them to wrest control of the LLC. This is not a possibility with Limited Partnerships in that general partners with as little as 2% ownership of the LP may control the entity. How to employ gifting strategies is discussed in detail in Garrett Sutton's book, *How to Use Limited Liability Companies & Limited Partnerships,* available through www.successdna.com.

LPs can be an excellent choice for a family with children who may not be mature or capable enough of making prudent financial decisions. Because limited partners cannot interfere in the daily LP operations, even though they may have majority ownership of the LP assets, the children cannot remove or sell assets from the LP. Again, even though the general partner may have as little as 2% of the LP interests, it can still retain complete control over the LP's operations. This can be a great way to save your kids from themselves.

Another good reason to use LPs in an estate planning situation has to do with the law. Because LPs have been around much longer than LLCs, the laws surrounding their operation are much more settled. It is very difficult for limited partners to wrest control from the general partner, no matter how high their ownership percentage. Generally speaking, for a general partner to be removed from control it takes a finding of fraud or serious misdoings by the general partner.

An LP is governed by a formal Limited Partnership Agreement. Because an LP provides a great deal of flexibility, the written limited partnership agreement can be drafted to suit the business and family planning requirements of any situation. There are very few statutory requirements that cannot be changed or eliminated through a well drafted limited partnership agreement.

In addition to the entities provided in these paragraphs, some states offer hybrid entities that share characteristics with some of the entities provided. For example, Texas allows for the formation of limited liability partnerships. These partnerships provide limited liability for partnership debts arising from negligence and similar misconduct. They do not, however, provide limited liability for contractual relations. A partner may not be held liable for the misconduct of another partner or an agent. Texas enacted laws to allow for this form of entity after lawyers voiced concerns about legal malpractice liability. Another form of hybrid is the limited liability limited partnership, which is similar to a limited partnership, but provides the general partner with limited liability in most circumstances. As always, consult a professional before making any decisions about using these types of entities. The following chart helps illustrate the entity types we have discussed:

ENTITY CHART

	Limits on the Entity's Life Span	Owner's Financial Rights and Responsibilities
SOLE PROPRIETORSHIP	Formed when individual enters into business. Dissolves upon the owner's death or bankruptcy.	Owner responsible for all capital contributions, but entitled to all profits after expenses.
GENERAL PARTNERSHIP	Formed when two people or businesses enter into a partnership agreement or agree to share profits. Dissolves upon any partner's death, bankruptcy, or withdrawal.	Partners may contribute equally and divide profits equally, but this is flexible. Partners may be required to make subsequent contributions or assessments.
LIMITED PARTNERSHIP	Formed when a certificate is filed with a state official. May dissolve under the same conditions as a general partnership, depending on the partnership agreement.	Partners may contribute equally and divide profits equally, but this is flexible. Partners may be required to make subsequent contributions or assessments.
LIMITED LIABILITY COMPANY	Formed when the articles of organization are filed with a state official. States differ regarding whether the LLC dissolves upon a member's death or withdrawal.	Members may base contributions and representative interests as they desire. Members may be required to make subsequent contributions.
S-CORPORATION	Formed when the articles of incorporation are filed with a state official. Has perpetual existence.	Shareholders have right to dividends, if issued, in proportion to their ownership interest. No additional contributions are required.
C-CORPORATION	Formed when the articles of incorporation are filed with a state official. Has perpetual existence.	Shareholders have right to dividends, if issued, but this is not an absolute right. No additional contributions are required.

Control and Authority to Act	Transferring Ownership Interests	Owner Liability to Outsiders	Entity and Owner Taxation
Owner has absolute control and may delegate authority to act on proprietorship's behalf.	Ownership can only be transferred through a sale of the business's assets. Securities laws generally do not apply.	Owner subject to unlimited liability.	Income taxed only as income to the owner. No taxes applied at the entity level.
Each partner has shared control but has unrestricted authority to act on the partnership's behalf. One partner may be liable to other partners for breach of fiduciary duties under some circumstances.	Partnership interest may not be sold without the automatic dissolution of partnership. Remaining partners may enter into a new partnership agreement to continue the business.	Each partner subject to unlimited liability and threat that one partner's actions will result in liability for all other partners.	Income taxed only as income to the partners. No taxes applied at the entity level. Partnership must report partnership income.
General partner has control over daily management and is the only partner authorized to act on partnership's behalf.	Partnership interest may not be sold without the automatic dissolution of the partnership. Partners may choose to enter into a new partnership agreement to continue the business. Securities laws apply to interests.	General partner is subject to unlimited liability. Limited partners are protected by limited liability unless they engage in management of the limited partnership.	Income taxed only as income to the partners. No taxes applied at the entity level. Limited partnership must report partnership income.
Members may structure control and authority as they desire, including management by members, by a member, or by a hired manager.	States differ and some allow members to provide for transferable membership interests. Securities laws apply to membership interests.	Members are protected by limited liability, regardless of role in limited liability company's management.	Income taxed as income to the members. Some states apply entity level taxes as annual fees or based on income. Generally, pass-through taxation. LLC must report income.
Shareholders elect Directors, who act as senior management. Directors appoint Officers for daily management.	Shares are freely transferable, but are subject to securities laws. No more than 100 U.S. residents, or resident aliens may hold shares.	Shareholders are protected by limited liability, regardless of role in corporate management.	Income taxed as income to the shareholders. No taxes applied at the entity level (except in California). State fees vary.
Shareholders elect Directors, who act as senior management. Directors appoint Officers for daily management.	Shares are freely transferable, but are subject to securities laws.	Shareholders are protected by limited liability, regardless of role in corporate management.	Income taxed as income to corporation. Dividends taxed as income to shareholders. Double taxation. State fees vary.

Chapter 3: The Wyoming Advantage Taxes and Wyoming

Why incorporate in Wyoming? It is simple: Wyoming offers great liability protection, has incredibly low fees and an uncomplicated incorporation procedure. Additionally, Wyoming has:

- ✓ No personal income tax
- ✓ No corporate income tax
- ✓ No gross receipts tax
- ✓ No inventory tax
- ✓ No intangibles tax
- ✓ Low retail sales tax
- ✓ Low property taxes
- ✓ Favorable inheritance tax
- ✓ Favorable unemployment tax

In this Chapter we will discuss how you can take advantage of Wyoming's lack of corporate income tax by forming an entity.

Entity Taxation in General

All C corporations have to pay a federal tax on the income earned by the corporation. Similar to the individual income tax that we all must pay to the federal government, the corporate income tax is based on a percentage of the corporation's earnings. The federal corporate tax is a graduated tax based upon earnings. Personal service corporations are an exception to the graduated tax base as all are subject to a flat tax of 35% regardless of their income. In addition to this federal tax, many states charge their own corporate income tax. One of the advantages of Wyoming is that it charges no corporate or personal income tax at the state level.

But what about the federal tax? By forming an entity you gain some tax choices. There are two basic ways in which entities are taxed – at the corporate level or with a flow-through tax that goes directly to the shareholders. Both have distinct advantages. Below is a brief explanation of these tax methods.

- Corporate Taxation. You can choose to have your business treated as a separate entity for income tax purposes. If you form a corporation or LLC and make that choice, the entity will pay its own taxes on its profits. As a member of the entity, you won't pay individual taxes until you receive money, usually in the form of a distribution. Notice that two levels of taxation have been outlined here. The money earned by the corporation is taxed first at the corporate level, and again if money is distributed to the shareholders. Corporate income taxes are generally lower than personal income taxes, as illustrated by the federal tax figures below. However, keep in mind that once money is distributed to shareholders, a tax is paid once again. (And note that the tax is assessed twice on the same dollar of profit, thus double taxed.)

Corporate Tax Rates*

Corporate tax of 15% on the first $50,000 of taxable income

Corporate tax of 25% on the next $25,000 of taxable income

Corporate tax of 34% on the next $25,000 of taxable income

Corporate tax of 39.5% on the next $235,000 of taxable income

Corporate tax of 39.5% on taxable income in excess of $335,000

* As of this writing.

Individual Tax Rates

Single filers	Married filing jointly or qualifying widow/widower	Married filing separately	Head of household	Tax Rate
Up to $7,000	Up to $14,000	Up to $7,000	Up to $10,000	10%
$7,001 - $28,400	$14,001 - $56,800	$7,001 - $28,400	$10,001 - $38,050	15%
$28,401 - $68,800	$56,801 - $114,650	$28,401 - $57,325	$38,051 - $98,250	25%
$68,801 - $143,500	$114,651 - $174,700	$57,326 - $87,350	$98,251 - $159,100	28%
$143,501- $311,950	$174,701 - $311,950	$87,351 - $155,975	$159,101 - $311,950	33%
$311,951 or more	$311,951 or more	$155,976 or more	$311,951 or more	35%

- Flow-Through Taxation. Flow-through taxation allows your entity to be taxed like a partnership with each individual owner reporting their share of LLC or corporate profits on their own tax returns, whether or not the money has been distributed to them. This means there is only one level of tax, your own personal income level. With corporations, you have the choice of electing to be treated as a subchapter S corporation by filing Form 2553. LLCs are given a similar choice, reflected in IRS form 8832, which allows you to check the box indicating whether you want income to pass through directly to members or be taxed like a corporation.

The choice of how to be taxed can be made at the beginning of your entity's existence or at the beginning of a new tax year. The only caveat is that if you switch from "S" status (flow-through taxation) to "C" status (corporate taxation), you have to wait five years before you can re-elect "S" corporation status.

One of the advantages of corporate taxation is that fringe benefits such as health, accident and life insurance are deductible <u>directly from corporate income.</u> With flow-through entities, if you are a 2% shareholder/member (or greater) some of these benefits, such as health insurance, are not deductible by the corporation, but flow-through to the shareholder/member. Shareholders in a high tax bracket may also appreciate corporate taxation because they have the option of leaving money in their company for expansion or other activities. This will save money in taxes because these company profits will only be taxed at the lower corporate rate. Also, shareholders on the corporation's payroll are allowed to take a "reasonable" salary and thus avoid double taxation. (There are rules requiring that payment to shareholders be reasonable in relation to his or her job. If a shareholder's salary is too high, it may be considered a dividend and thus be subject to double taxation.)

There are different advantages to flow-though taxation. The most obvious one, discussed above, is the fact that you are only subject to taxes at one level. Additionally, because you are electing to be treated as a partnership, shareholders who "materially participate" in the business can share in any losses that the business might experience due to start-up costs and other factors. Salaries and other expenses of the corporation are also deductible because you are only taxed on the corporation's net earnings. Plus, like shareholders who are employees in a C corporation, employee shareholders of an S corporation can also take a "reasonable" salary. But, in contrast to the C corporation, the employee may want be paid at the lower end of the reasonable scale and take the rest of their share of profits as a distribution. Remember, distributions are only taxed at personal income levels -- no corporate tax and no payroll tax is tacked on beforehand.

Piggy Banking or Upstreaming

Obviously, you are going to be able to take the most advantage of Wyoming's lack of taxes by moving yourself and your business into this State. For those of you who do not want to up and move to cowboy country, there are still ways in which you can gain the Wyoming advantage.

One method is called "piggy banking" or "upstreaming." If you choose to operate a business in a state that does have a corporate income tax, you could form two entities, one in your state and one in Wyoming. The entity that you operate in your state could elect flow-through tax treatment, or corporate taxation, whichever you and your tax professional decide upon. The Wyoming entity, however, may elect to be taxed as a corporation so that its earnings do not flow through to your personal return in your tax-fettered state.

Your objective would be to "upstream" as much income as possible to the Wyoming entity and leave the Wyoming entity's earnings in Wyoming. The term "piggy banking" is used because your corporation in Wyoming could be conceptualized as a piggy bank. Bear in mind that both of these goals rely heavily on various state tax regulations. You do not want your Wyoming entity's acts to be considered "doing business" in another state that has a corporate tax. This would require your Wyoming entity to register to do business in that state and potentially subject it to that state's taxes. All states have their own definition about what they consider to be doing business in their state. Generally, owning vacant land in another state without more (such as renting it out) is not considered doing business. Loaning money is also generally not considered doing business. The more passive an activity is, the less likely it is to be labeled as doing business. So the trick for you is to find a passive activity that your Wyoming corporation can engage in that justifies payment from your other entity. The best way to accomplish this is to meet with a local tax specialist to discuss your state's treatment of various activities related to your business.

Once you have the Wyoming entity in place and it is earning state tax-free dollars, the next step is to figure out what you want to do with that money. Obviously, distributing it to you would subject it to your state taxes and defeat the whole purpose. One popular idea is to have your Wyoming corporation loan money to your Wyoming LLC that then purchases real estate. Most likely your Wyoming entity is a C corporation and if you are an employee or officer or director of this corporation, you could also put the reserve cash toward retirement and insurance benefits for yourself and your family. There are many ways to utilize the money earned by the Wyoming entity, but again it is important to consult with a tax specialist about what methods are best for your particular situation.

The following example shows how asset protection strategies can be created for each individual scenario.

Jim

Jim owned a restaurant in Los Angeles. It was the place to be seen: actors, politicians, entrepreneurs and wannabes all flocked to dine on expensive cuisines and sip on fine wines priced at the level of liquid gold.

Life was good for Jim. Except for one irony. The energy and abundance of California which helped fuel his success was accompanied by an expensive and over zealous state tax regime that limited his success. Jim could not believe how much he had to pay in California state taxes and fees for the privilege of doing business there. His restaurant operated as an S corporation and with state and federal taxes he was losing almost 50% of what he made to the government.

Jim was determined to do something to modify this situation and began reading. He learned about the Wyoming piggy bank strategy. Working with his new CPA and attorney, he set up a beneficial strategy.

First, Jim set up a Wyoming C corporation with offices in Jackson Hole. Jim liked to ski and the thought of a business travel expense to Jackson Hole appealed to him. Of course, such travel was voluntary. Jim didn't have to go to Wyoming to hold meetings but he thought he might do that in the future.

Jim and his advisors discussed the issue of privacy. This was important to Jim. He had been sued by two disgruntled employees in the last three years. The juries bought the lies and nonsense presented under oath. It was an expensive and emotionally draining experience. Additionally, the judgments entered against him for damages allowed the plaintiff's lawyers to start looking into his financial affairs. Jim did not want his confidential dealings made public to even a small group of legal vultures.

So Jim readily agreed to using a nominee officer and director for the Wyoming C Corporation. For a cost of $650 per year, his advisors used an individual other than Jim to serve as officer and director of the company, thus keeping Jim's name off the Internet and other filings. Jim still owned the Wyoming C Corporation, but by using a nominee officer and director, his involvement was more confidential and private.

Jim's advisors then told him that for the piggy bank strategy to work, Jim had to have a legitimate office presence in Wyoming. He could not just have a resident agent there for $125 a year, a strategy that worked well for many passive-holding entities. Instead, Jim's C Corporation was actually going to be doing business. He needed to have a receptionist answering the phone and his company name on an office reader board. His advisors said this was necessary in the somewhat unlikely event

California (or any other state) came calling. But Jim and his advisors didn't want state scrutiny. To that end, his advisors relayed to him the old adage "Pigs get fat, hogs get slaughtered." Jim was not going to send every last dollar of profit to Wyoming to avoid California taxes. He would pay his fair share in California, but he would not pay more than his fair share, which was why he was setting up this strategy. Besides, the U.S. corporate tax rates went up at higher profit levels, as Jim was about to learn.

Jim followed his advisor's advice and arranged for an office package in Jackson, Wyoming. The cost was approximately $2,000 a year and offered a telephone receptionist, fax, conference room, mail forwarding and the like. For just $250 a month, it was much cheaper than setting up his own office.

His advisors indicated that the other costs of doing business were not expensive. They suggested Jim could allocate another $1,500 for a business trip to Jackson and other miscellaneous expenses. Jim decided to allocate $2,500 for other expenses.

Next his advisors explained that the Wyoming C corporation had to perform a service for Jim's California S corporation. There were many types of services that could be performed including real estate trend studies, research and development, location analysis, market research and economic reports. Jim indicated he was considering opening a second restaurant and a location analysis report would be very useful.

The advisors explained that the report would have to be prepared outside of California for the piggy bank strategy to work. The reason, of course, was that any work performed in California (or any other high-tax state) would be subject to state taxes. However, if Jim's California S Corporation hired the Wyoming C Corporation, which stayed out of California, to perform the work in Wyoming, then California taxes were legitimately not due on the Wyoming work. As well, the Wyoming work was an expense to the California Company, this reducing its profits and correspondingly its taxes.

Jim's advisors noted that this was the essence of upstreaming income. They used the chart below to explain:

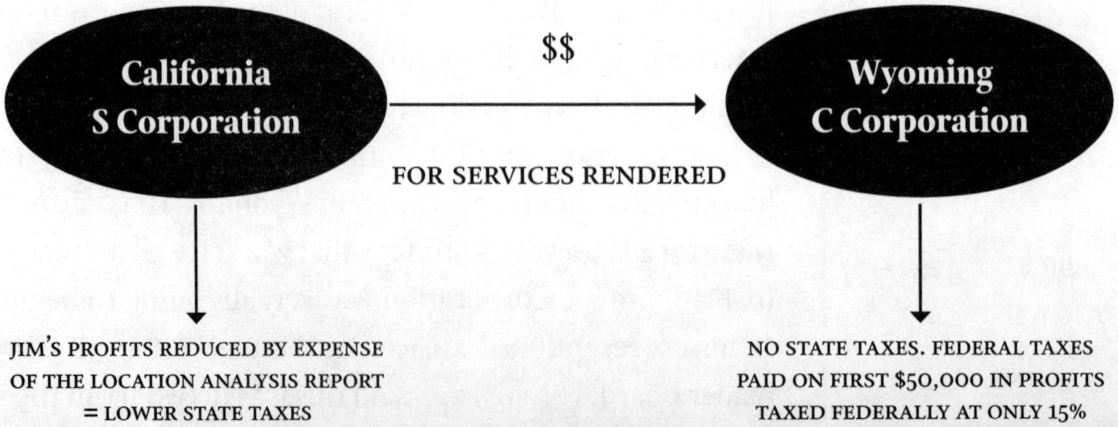

The advisors explained that it didn't have to be an S corporation contracting with a C corporation. The strategy worked for LLCs, LPs and C and S corporations.

The advisors then cautioned that a C corporation contracting with another C corporation may lose the lower federal tax rate. The advisors explained that the IRS, in order to prevent people from using two or more C corporations to achieve the 15% tax rate on the first $50,000 of profits, had instituted a rule called control group status. If you owned two (or more) C corporations, the IRS lumped them together to assess a higher corporate tax rate. But the advisors noted that controlled group status didn't apply to Jim's situation. He had one S corporation and one C corporation. The S corporation was a flow-through tax entity taxed at Jim's state and federal rates, so the corporate tax rates did not apply. As long as Jim had only one C corporation (which he did) the lower corporate tax rates would apply for the one C corporation.

The advisors then went on to discuss how the Wyoming C Corporation would prepare the location analysis. The company would hire a qualified individual or company in Wyoming (or another state outside of California) to draft the report. The advisors noted it was important for the report to actually be prepared and in the file. Jim agreed that he really did need such a report. The advisors noted that they had an excellent referral source for him.

Jim liked this strategy. The advisors detailed how it would truly benefit Jim.

The California S Corporation was going to pay for the location analysis report. The Wyoming C Corporation would make a nice profit, the first $50,000 of which is taxed at 15%. Jim's after tax profit far exceeds the money he would have had left over had it not been expensed but rather flowed through his California S corporation. The advantage is that Jim took a nice expense-paid business trip, had an important report prepared and saved thousands in taxes.

But his advisors noted there was one more huge advantage. Jim now had money in his Wyoming piggy bank. With the nominee officer and director in place, no one knew Jim was associated with the company. By filing just a standard corporate return and not making any shareholder distributions, the IRS did not know who owned the corporation. Like Nevada, Wyoming does not disclose (or even collect) shareholder information. Jim's piggy bank was a private matter.

Jim's advisors noted that if he wanted to distribute the money to himself as a shareholder, then he could do so. He would pay a federal tax and a California tax if he distributed all the money. But they had an alternative strategy.

First they warned that the IRS did not like to see monies accumulate in a C Corporation. They want it distributed or used somehow so they can tax it again. So the IRS instituted an accumulated earnings tax of 39.6% on top of corporate tax rates for companies with $250,000 or more in accumulated earnings.

Jim did not like the sound of this but his advisors allayed his concerns. In the first year with the money he had in earnings or in the fifth year when the after-tax monies reached $250,000 (or anytime in between) Jim could have the C corporation loan the money to an LLC or LP he created to buy real estate.

Jim liked this idea. He was putting his money to work by buying real estate. Better yet, the loan from the corporation to the LLC could be used to create a favorable encumbrance of the property.

For example, after five years Jim decides to use the $250,000 in his piggy bank to buy a new restaurant location for himself in Southern California. The $250,000 is placed into a new Wyoming LLC qualified to do business in California. The money is 20% down on a $1,250,000 building. A mortgage of $1 million is obtained and the title to the restaurant real estate is taken in the name of the Wyoming LLC. Jim's California S corporation leases the location from Jim's Wyoming LLC. Thus, Jim is using pre-tax dollars (rent) to buy himself a good piece of property.

With 20% down, there is now $250,000 in exposed equity on the property. But remember where the money came from. It was a loan from Jim's Wyoming C corporation, his piggy bank entity. Isn't the Wyoming C corporation entitled to some security on the loan? Of course it is, Jim's advisors argue.

And so once the property closes and the first deed of trust for the $1 million mortgage is in place, a second deed of trust for the $250,000 loan is recorded. In this way the property is fully encumbered, which reduces it as an attractive target for a lawsuit. Jim's Wyoming C corporation remains a private entity and Jim's name is not publicly associated with it. Jim has used the piggy bank strategy to his great advantage.

Chapter 4: The Wyoming Advantage Asset Protection in Wyoming

It cannot be denied that we live in a litigious country. Everyday thousands of lawsuits are brought and many of these are groundless attempts to take advantage of our justice system to better one's lot in life. Business owners and investors that are not protected by limited liability could be putting themselves out on a very weak, very long limb. If that bough breaks, your personal assets do not have to go along "cradle and all." Set up an entity and plant yourself firmly on the ground.

Privacy Benefits of a Wyoming Corporation

In the fight to protect your assets, keeping the public ignorant about what you own is a key step. It is important to keep a low profile. Wyoming's minimal reporting and disclosure requirements can help you gain maximum privacy.

A corporate principal or shareholder in Wyoming has a great deal of privacy from the prying eyes of government agencies and outsiders. Although all states require that Articles of Incorporation be filed with their secretary of state, the level of information that is required to be disclosed in those articles varies. The only information that Wyoming asks you to reveal in the articles is the name and address of the registered agent and the name and address of the incorporators. A list of shareholders and their addresses is not required to be filed in the Wyoming Articles. Additionally, the address of the incorporator can be a P.O. Box. Thus, you can keep your name and association with your entity private.

Attorneys often act as incorporators and registered agents, but there are numerous services available that serve these functions. Either way, the names you are required to provide on your articles can be largely unconnected to your entity. Because the incorporator and registered agent can be a service or person apart from you or other investors, disclosing the name of the incorporator and registered agent in no way impedes your privacy.

All states require that an annual report be filed with the secretary of state. The form requests that you inform the secretary of state of any changes to your contact address or address of your principal office and that you provide them with the names of the current officers and directors. The data provided on this report is the only information available on officers and directors of a Wyoming corporation.

If you would prefer to not have your name appear on your corporation's annual report, Wyoming provides a solution. Wyoming permits the use of nominee officers and directors. Nominee services are available to provide you with a nominee officer and/or director. (Our firm charges $650 per year for this service.) Because in Wyoming one person can serve as director and officer, you can get by with just one nominee. The nominee's name appears on the annual report instead of your own. A simple corporate resolution allows you to have signatory power so that your need for the nominee's services remains minimal.

Lifetime Proxies

Also important is the fact that Wyoming is the only state which allows lifetime proxies. Lifetime proxies allow you to keep a low profile while maximizing your control over the corporation and minimizing your risk. Proxies allow you to vote shares that you don't own. Thus, if you are ever sued your shares are safe because no one can take from you what you don't own. The problem is that most state laws do not allow lifetime proxies, thus you run the very great risk that the "owner" of the shares won't renew your proxy once it expires. Because Wyoming allows you to have a lifetime proxy you can take advantage of control without ownership sans the renewal risk.

Wyoming also does not have an information sharing agreement with the IRS, nor does it have a corporate commission, as does Delaware, California and so many others, which heavily regulates the transfer and issuance of stock. Shares of stock in a Wyoming corporation can be easily transferred to another person, corporation or trust without a government agency granting permission or even knowing the identity of the shareholders.

Bearer Shares and Bearer Scrip

Bearer shares and bearer scrip can provide the ultimate in privacy as they provide a shareholder ownership in a corporation without any record of that ownership. While ownership comes from possession of the shares or scrip, there is no other documentation which would tie the individual to the entity. The bearer becomes the registered shareholder and possession of the stock certificate makes that party the legal owner.

Bearer scrip is specifically provided for in Wyoming's laws. Scrip permits capitalization by stockholders in increments less than the fixed par value. It is fractional stock. A shareholder can hold as much scrip as he wishes, thus a scripholder could have more stock in a corporation than a shareholder, as illustrated in the example below.

ABC, Inc. stock is valued at $1,000 per share. Sherrie Shareholder purchases 100 one-quarter shares, or scrips, of ABC, Inc. for $250 per scrip. Shad Shareholder purchases 20 shares of ABC, Inc. for $1,000 per share. Sherrie owns more stock in ABC, Inc. than does Shad, but the stock is in scrip form.

In Wyoming, if the scrip so provides, the holder of fractional stock is entitled to exercise all the rights of a shareholder, including the right to vote, to receive dividends, and the right to participate in the assets of the corporation upon liquidation.

Bearer shares differ from bearer scrip only in that they represent whole shares rather than fractional shares. Although not specifically provided for in the Wyoming Statutes, they are permitted if a corporation continues or domesticates into Wyoming with bearer shares. Therefore, there is a strong argument that you could hold bearer shares if you initially start a corporation in Wyoming.

The anonymity provided to the bearer is a benefit used by many promoters to encourage people to form their entities in states offering bearer shares or scrip. However, there may be more risk than benefit associated with this means of stock ownership. Ownership of non-bearer stock is documented on a corporation's internal paperwork. As mentioned above, Wyoming does not require public disclosure of its shareholders. Thus, only those with access to your corporate paperwork, and possibly any taxing authorities, will have knowledge of your ownership interests.

Of course, if your corporation is sued, the internal paperwork will be examined by the plaintiff and your interest will be exposed. If your shares were only evidenced by bearer stock and your corporation is sued, to remain anonymous you would have to pass the bearer shares onto someone else. Yet this transfer will have tax consequences and you will lose control of your ownership. Additionally, this transfer could easily be considered fraudulent and could expose you to further liability. It is difficult to envision a scenario where bearer shares will truly benefit the holder. There have been many cases where this type of ownership has proven useless and even problematic. Unless one has a definitive reason for choosing this type of ownership, bearer shares are best kept a choice not taken.

Privacy Benefits of Nominee Managers

As mentioned in Chapter 2, LLCs can be either member managed or manager managed. The difference can be insignificant or substantial depending upon who acts as a manager. If you and a partner are the only two members of an LLC and both want to be managers, then you have the choice of electing yourselves as co-operating managers or electing to be member managed. The end result is the same because a member-managed LLC is managed by its members. It may be inefficient, however, to have an LLC with numerous members be member-managed. It would be prudent in this case to elect one manager (or a few managers) to run daily operations. The managers could be the LLC's members or an outside individual with no interest in the LLC.

If privacy is your concern, you will want to be manager managed. In Wyoming, the Articles of Organization that are filed with the secretary of state do not ask for the names of the members of an LLC *unless* that LLC is member managed. If an LLC is manager managed, then the members can remain anonymous. If privacy is important to you -- be manager managed and have a nominee manager. If you choose to utilize a nominee manager, the nominee will be manager in name only. You can still run your company's day-to-day operations. And later, perhaps when you don't need a nominee, you can then become the manager, leaving the other members' names off the record and preserving their privacy.

The Charging Order

One of the greatest things about using a limited liability entity is protection. All the risks inherent to your business activities can be contained within that entity. Thus, a well-managed entity protects personal assets from creditors of the entity. If a judgment is awarded against the entity itself, it may be levied, and only the entity's (not your own) property seized or sold in payment. But what about protecting your business assets from yourself? Wyoming takes asset protection one step further with charging order protection for LLCs. The majority of states follow the Revised Limited Partnership Act (RUPLA). RUPLA provides charging order type protection for Limited Partnerships. So a limited partnership in any state provides some extra protection. However, if you want to set up an LLC and also have that extra protection you will need to set up your LLC in Wyoming. Wyoming provides LLCs as well as LPs with charging order protection. As illustrated below, charging orders essentially keep outside liabilities from affecting your business.

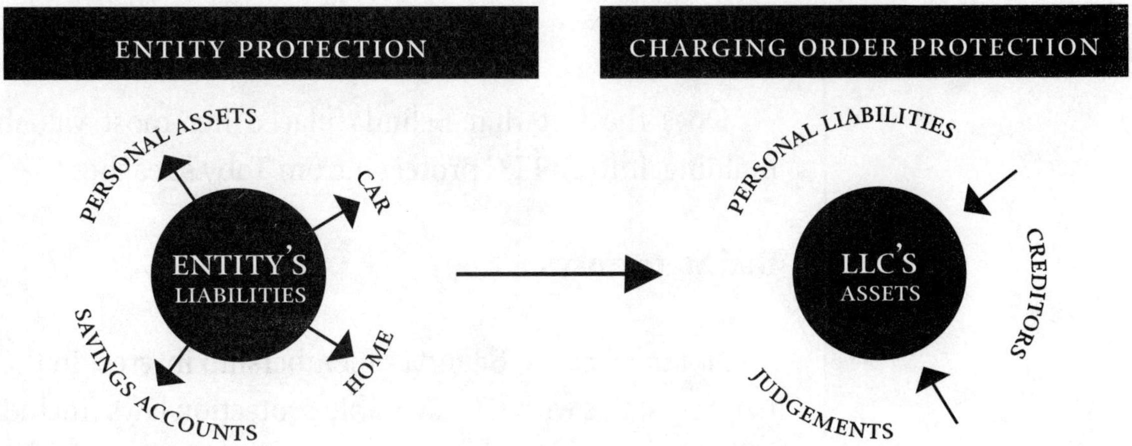

The charging order rule provides that if a judgment is awarded against a Wyoming LLC member in a multi-member LLC or an LP partner, distribution of equity usually cannot be compelled to satisfy the judgment. Under a charging order, a creditor receives the right to collect distributions from the Wyoming LLC or LP when (and if) profits are distributed. But that creditor does <u>not</u> receive the right to vote, or have any impact or control over the daily operations of the Wyoming LLC or LP. That makes you a much smaller target for litigation-minded individuals.

<u>Belinda</u>

Belinda felt very secure. She had done so well with her investments over the years that she and her partner, Max, were recently able to purchase a brand new apartment building in Home State worth over two million dollars. It generated enough passive income that Max and Belinda could look forward to retiring in another year. Because they were intelligent businesspeople, Max and Belinda knew that they should place their apartment building in a limited liability entity. They formed Sunpartments, LLC in Home State and deeded their interest in the apartment building to the LLC. The members ran their LLC by the book: they maintained a separate bank account, never commingled funds, held annual meetings, documented all major decisions, and generally instituted good business practices. One day, Belinda was eating a low-carb burger while driving. It was very messy and she spilled some ketchup on her favorite blouse. She stared down in dismay at the big red splotch a moment too long and rear-ended the car in front of her that had stopped to make a left turn. Toby, the driver was pretty shaken up. Hot coffee had spilled all over his lap and he had banged his head on the steering wheel. He insisted on calling an ambulance and was taken to a nearby hospital. Belinda had good car insurance, but her policy limits would not be enough if Toby were truly injured. Toby decided to sue Belinda for everything she was worth.

Question

Does the fact that Belinda placed her most valuable asset, the apartment building, into an LLC protect it from Toby's reaches?

Bad State Answer

Not in all cases. Belinda's membership interest in the LLC is one of her assets. In many states with less favorable protection laws (including California) a creditor will be able to attach that asset and gain control of Belinda's 50% interest in Sunpartments LLC.

As a 50% owner of Sunpartments, LLC, the creditor is now Max's partner. Because a creditor won't be interested in a passive income partnership with Max, the creditor will use his 50 % ownership interest to vote for a sale in order to pay off the judgment. If possible, Max will want to try to buy the creditor out of his half and thus retain his investment. Or if Max cannot find the funds to purchase the 50% interest, he would have to submit to a sale. If he fought the sale, the LLC would be in deadlock and the creditor could apply for judicial dissolution of the LLC and the building would be sold as part of the dissolution process.

In all of these scenarios the result is the same and Belinda and Max's retirement plans will have to be significantly revised.

Wyoming Answer

If Belinda and Max had formed their LLC in Wyoming and qualified it to do business in Home State, the result would be different. Wyoming law specifically provides that a charging order is the exclusive remedy by which a creditor may satisfy a claim against a member's interest in an LLC. According to the charging order rule, a creditor has no right to participate in the management of the business and affairs of the LLC and cannot become a member. The creditor is only entitled to receive the share of profits or other compensation to which the member charged would have been entitled. The reality of this situation is that a creditor can receive nothing from the LLC except a tax bill. How is this possible? Well, the Wyoming rule says that Max and Belinda are still in control of the LLC, so the creditor is only entitled to any distributions that the LLC might give. Belinda and Max make over $100,000 profit that year but choose to not make any distributions to the members. Belinda gets nothing so the creditor gets nothing. Nothing except Belinda's tax bill. Her fifty percent membership interest in the LLC earned $50,000. The IRS doesn't care if Belinda actually received this money. LLCs have flow-through tax, so Belinda's portion of the profit flowed right through to her tax return, received or not. But wait! It isn't Belinda's responsibility anymore -- it is the creditor's because he is the one who is entitled to the payment, if they had chosen to make a payment. So, the creditor not only does not receive any cash, he has a tax bill for the phantom income.

The phantom income result for creditors is one of the many reasons Wyoming is an excellent state in which to form your LLC. It is a huge deterrent to litigation. Foreclosing on a member's interest in an LLC takes time and money -- time and money a creditor won't be willing to spend when he knows the end result will likely be a tax bill for his effort.

It is important to understand, however, that Wyoming law is not always going to be there to help you. You need to have a multi-member LLC and the problem must arise outside of the entity with the creditor trying to attach your interest in the entity. Belinda's situation arose outside of the LLC interests. Remember, Toby's claim arose from the auto accident and had nothing to do with her real estate. What happens when liability arises from operation and ownership of the apartment building?

Joe Tenant

Joe Tenant rented apartment 2B on the second floor of Belinda and Max's apartment building. Joe had been down on his luck lately and was about to be late with his rental for the sixth time, an offense for which he could be evicted. Joe Tenant resented Belinda and Max, as well as everyone else he thought had it better than him. One day while watching reality TV, Joe got the idea that a simple injury could solve all his problems. That night he snuck out to the outside stairway of the apartment building and loosened the railing enough so that with the right amount of pressure it would break off. The next morning he picked up his television set and stood leaning lightly against the railing until his neighbor Loretta walked out of her apartment. "Hi Loretta," Joe called. "I gotta take my TV in to be repaired." As Joe uttered these words he leaned hard against the railing, causing it to break free, with him and the TV falling behind. Due to the television breaking into pieces on top of him, the crash caused Joe more injuries than he had anticipated. He also received a higher damage award from the jury in Home State than he thought. Injured but happy, Joe, (not Belinda or Max) was able to retire early from the profit he made selling the apartment building.

What happened? Why didn't the charging order step in and save the day as it had for Belinda previously? The reason is that in the second scenario, the liability for Joe's injuries did not rest with Belinda personally. The liability was the LLC's. Charging orders apply to protect your entity and its members from liability arising from and assessed against the individual acts of a member. Charging orders do not protect your LLC from itself. In the first scenario, Toby wasn't suing the LLC, he was suing Belinda personally and trying to obtain her rights to a Wyoming entity. In this case, Wyoming charging order rules apply. In the second scenario, the liability arose against the LLC – the entity that held and managed the apartment building. As such, charging orders do not offer protection.

It is important to keep in mind that while the charging order does not apply, Belinda and Max's other personal and business assets were shielded from suit because the apartment complex was held in an LLC. Had they owned it in their own names as sole proprietors, everything else they owned, including their homes, cars, bank accounts, other investments, etc., could have been taken by Joe Tenant. So, the limited liability nature of the LLC protects all the assets you hold outside the LLC. Wyoming law protects your LLC from liability arising out of your other activities.

A Note on Equity

Belinda and Max's situation would not have been as unfortunate if they held secured notes against their apartment building for the equity they had contributed. Say they had each put $75,000.00 into the LLC for the down payment on the building. Instead of contributing the money to the LLC they should have loaned it to the LLC. So long as they maintained proper insurance coverage courts should not find the LLC undercapitalized and they would be in line to be paid back their equity if the building were sold.

Continuance

Do you like the benefits offered by Wyoming? Are you interested in moving your entity to Wyoming? You can by using "continuance."

Continuance is unique to Wyoming. Through the process called continuance, Wyoming allows a corporation or limited liability company to domicile in this state as if it had been organized there initially, so there is no break in corporate status. By filing Articles of Continuance with the state of Wyoming, an entity can easily take advantage of this legal fiction. To the author's best knowledge, Wyoming's continuance laws are unique.

If you have formed an entity in a state whose laws you now realize are not advantageous, continuance provides an easy remedy. The filing fee for the Articles of Continuance is $100, the same as for filing articles of organization or incorporation for a new entity. Yet you will not have a new entity, but one with history because you will retain your original date of existence. This is especially important if your existing corporation has a good credit history. By continuing in Wyoming, your good corporate credit can also be continued.

There are many advantages to being able to relocate your business to a friendlier state. One important benefit that many business owners do not consider has to do with the statute of limitations. All lawsuits have time limits. The statute of limitations refers to the legal deadline by which a lawsuit must be filed. These deadlines vary based upon the type of claim being asserted. For instance, the statute of limitations in many states is ten years for asserting a claim on a written contract, and eight years for an oral contract. So if your business made a blunder, you could hear about it and be held accountable for it, several years after the fact. Thus, it is important to maintain your entity for at least as long as the longest applicable statute of limitations. So, if you are thinking of closing shop, go ahead, but keep your entity active in a low annual fee state such as Wyoming.

180-Degree Construction, Inc.

Mike had owned and operated 180-Degree Construction, Inc. in California for nearly twenty years and he was ready to retire. He knew that with a corporation there were some steps he needed to take before he closed shop, so he made an appointment with his attorney to ask about the best way to wind things up. Among the recommendations his attorney gave, Mike was informed that the statute of limitations in California for construction issues was ten years. Thus, Mike needed to keep his corporation active for ten years after he stopped working. Because it was a California corporation, this was going to cost Mike $800 per year in state filing fees. Mike was understandably aggravated about this – after all, he was trying to retire. Mike, however, had a good attorney. After explaining the situation to Mike, he offered a solution to the financial drain of California fees. Mike could continue his company into Wyoming. By continuing 180-Degree Construction, Inc. into Wyoming, Mike could maintain his limited liability status without a break and get away from California's high rates. Wyoming would charge him only $50 annually. That means Mike could leave his corporation intact for ten years for $500 rather than $8,000! Mike gave his attorney the go-ahead to complete the necessary paperwork and retired a much happier man.

The Wyoming Close LLC

Another major attraction to Wyoming is the Wyoming Close Limited Liability Company Supplement. Wyoming is the first state to have a Close LLC, one of the latest developments in the area of asset protection and estate planning. The Wyoming Close LLC offers the same asset protection and discounted gifting benefits that a limited partnership does, but it is cheaper and easier to create and manage. A Wyoming Close LLC has all the asset protection benefits of a Wyoming LLC and a limited partnership, creditors of members of a Close LLC can only obtain a charging order and thus gain no right or control over the LLC or Close LLC. In addition, a Wyoming Close LLC provides tax savings similar to a limited partnership, but without the complexity inherent to the limited partnership .

By statute, the Wyoming Close LLC Supplement places restrictions upon the rights of a member to withdraw from the LLC, all members must consent to the withdrawal. Return of a member's capital from the property of the LLC is also very restricted, and, unless the articles of organization state otherwise, or all members consent, no member has the right to receive anything but cash in return for a capital contribution of whatever nature. Although these restrictions may not seem beneficial to the naked eye, it is because of them that the IRS will permit the value of the LLC interests to be discounted, making the Wyoming Close LLC a great wealth preservation tool.

Similar to a Limited Partnership, the Close LLC is as effective in avoiding judgment creditors yet less burdensome to operate. Remember, a limited partnership has a flaw – the general partner is completely exposed. To correct that flaw the limited partnership has to encapsulate the liability exposure of the general partner by creating a second entity to serve as the general partner. Thus, you have to pay for two entities to be formed, you have to pay annual fees on two entities, maintain two EIN numbers, two bank accounts, two tax returns. With a Close LLC only one entity needs to be created and maintained! If you are looking for simplicity as well as asset protection and tax savings, the Wyoming Close LLC could be the answer. But, be sure to check with your advisors – this is new law that we are talking about. The benefit of the history and certainty of the law surrounding partnerships is a benefit in itself. Always make sure your advisors are up to date on any changes.

Dynasty Trusts

Wyoming Dynasty Trusts not only provide extraordinary estate tax savings, they also offer the bonus of asset protection for the assets placed in trust. In a typical dynasty trust a person transfers assets to a trustee who holds and invests the assets for the beneficiaries. As long as the assets stay in the trust they can pass from generation to generation without estate or generation skipping taxes. Additionally, a Wyoming Dynasty Trust is not liable for any state income tax, nor does it pay any federal income tax on assets distributed to beneficiaries. Please note that beneficiaries must pay taxes on the distributions received from the trust. You do not have to live in Wyoming to set up a Dynasty Trust in Wyoming, you just need a trustee, or trust company, that is located in Wyoming. With Wyoming's strong asset protection laws and lack of personal and corporate income tax, it is the perfect place to set up a Dynasty Trust.

Because of the Rule Against Perpetuities, Dynasty Trusts do not exist in many states. The Rule Against Perpetuities states that "no future interest is valid unless it can be shown that it will necessarily vest, if at all, no later than 21 years after some life in being at the creation of the interest." The rule has existed for centuries because the common law disfavored property being held forever in trust, so it was created to advance the marketability of property. The Rule acted to void any agreement which does not conclude 21 years after a life in being or one generation after those lives presently in being, plus 21 years. In many states you cannot place property in trust for more than 90 to 120 years. Because the Rule Against Perpetuities is state law, states have the option of relaxing or eliminating its constraints. While Wyoming has not abolished the Rule Against Perpetuities, it does allow Trusts to last one thousand (1,000) years. Because of this 1,000 year duration, the Wyoming Dynasty Trust exists as one of the most dynamic estate planning tools available today.

John D. Rockefeller believed that the secret of his success was to "own nothing and control everything." This concept is at the heart of asset protection and a key tenant of Dynasty Trusts. The assets in a Dynasty Trust are protected because you don't own them. The beneficiaries can enjoy the income from the trust assets without fear of losing them to a judgment creditor, your ex-spouse in a divorce, or medical bills and costs (outright distributions of wealth will likely make you ineligible for state or federal medical programs). Tax free growth of assets combined with asset protection, what else could you ask for!

If you are the grantor of the trust you can control the assets for generations by leaving specific instructions with the trustee. If you do not want your grandchildren and their children and your future descendants to just kick back and collect money, the dynasty trust enables you to dictate how and when the beneficiaries can receive income. This kind of "control from the grave" may not please everyone, but it is a good way to assure that your wealth provides for and encourages generations of productive descendants.

You can also take advantage of discounted gifting through the use of a Wyoming Close LLC or a Limited Partnership to fund your Wyoming Dynasty Trust. Because it is possible to limit the control of certain members in a Wyoming Close LLC and because limited partners by definition have no control over the assets of a limited partnership, it is possible to superfund your dynasty trust through the use of these entities and the discounts allowed by the IRS.

Chapter 5: Entity Paperwork

An amazing number of people try to incorporate themselves in order to save money. Others go online and choose from the thousands of incorporation services available on the Web. The cheapest service providers will not even have an attorney on staff and therefore cannot perform any acts considered to be the practice of law. So what do you receive from these companies? For a fee they will send you an incorporation document, have you fill it out and they will file it with the secretary of state. Because they are not lawyers, they cannot perform anything other than the most ministerial of functions. And if they do more, they could be guilty of practicing law without a license. They do not tell you about the need for a resident agent, bylaws, operating agreements, minutes or other necessary paperwork. They will lead you down a rosy path replete with thorns. You will think you are protected, but you will be as exposed as ever.

Unfortunately if you go in this direction you will not save any money. On the contrary, you are setting yourself up for:

- Tax pitfalls that will come as a result of not receiving any advice on the tax consequences of your entity choice;
- Legal ramifications, the worst being that you, in reality, have no liability protection;
- Management problems because you will not know to properly run your entity; and
- Logistical issues as you try to open accounts, borrow money, gather investors.

And this is just skimming the surface. The choice is yours, but using a competent attorney and CPA, or a full service incorporation firm is strongly recommended. Spending several hundred dollars at the start will save you several thousand dollars down the road.

State Fees

The costs associated with organizing your entity vary greatly depending upon the state in which you decide to domesticate. All states charge an initial filing fee for filing your articles. Methods for determining this fee vary among states. While many states apply a flat fee, some base the initial incorporation fee on the par value or number of shares the corporation is authorized to issue.

When forming a corporation, most states require that the articles of incorporation provide the number of shares of stock the corporation will be authorized to issue. This is an arbitrary determination that the incorporator initially makes, based on the corporation's expected financing needs and a determination of how ownership will be allocated. The number of authorized shares should include a cushion to account for future sales of stock. In states where the corporation is required to pay a fee or taxes based on the number or value of shares issued, it may be appealing to simply authorize few shares. However, authorizing only a limited number of shares may present problems for the corporation in the future if it wants to offer stock incentives to key employees or if it needs to raise additional funds by selling shares of stock.

One of Wyoming's many benefits is that it allows you to authorize an unlimited amount of shares and it doesn't charge you for them. So if you incorporate in Wyoming you will never have to worry about authorizing additional shares. Additionally, Wyoming charges you $100 to file your articles, whether you choose to authorize ten shares, a million shares, or unlimited shares. State filing fees that are based upon number of shares can be a trap for the unwary. For example, Nevada starts charging for additional shares over 75 million. Ohio starts charging you a fee per share if you authorize more than 1,500 shares of stock. Wyoming also has no par value requirement so incorporators do not have to come up with an arbitrary, and for many, confusing value for their stock.

Besides filing fees, many states have annual fees that must be paid when the annual report is filed. This annual tax is often based upon the number of authorized shares or par value of authorized shares. Wyoming has a license tax that is pretty unique. Because Wyoming authorizes unlimited shares with no par value, it cannot base its tax upon these numbers. Rather, Wyoming bases its tax upon the values of the entity's assets "located and employed in Wyoming." The tax is $50 or two-tenths of one mill on the dollar ($.0002) for assets located and employed in Wyoming, whichever is greater. Thus, an entity with $250,000 or less in assets located and employed in the state of Wyoming pays an annual fee of only $50! If all of your assets, or all assets over $250,000 are located outside of Wyoming, then you will only pay this low $50 fee. And remember, there is no requirement that you have a bank account located within Wyoming. You could set up your bank account in, say, Nevada, and do all your banking online. But, consider this, even if you have $2 million in assets at work in Wyoming, your annual fee will be just $400. That is half of what California charges for every entity, whether they have assets or not.

Articles of Incorporation, Articles of Organization and Certificates of Existence

The Articles of Incorporation for a corporation or Articles of Organization for an LLC, often referred to simply as your "articles," as well as the Certificate of Existence for a limited partnership are the first documents to be prepared in the process of gaining limited liability protection.

Articles of Incorporation

The Articles of Incorporation are used to form a corporation. Wyoming requires minimal information to be disclosed in your articles:

- The name of your corporation;
- The number of shares the corporation is authorized to issue, which may be unlimited. If there will be more than one class of shares, the articles must include a designation for each class as well as any preferences, limitations and rights of the class;
- The street address of the corporation's initial registered office and the name of its initial registered agent at that office; and
- The name and address of an incorporator.

You may mention other matters in your articles, but nothing other than the above is required. Some corporations have detailed articles that list various powers and purposes, but this can be unnecessary. Corporate powers are spelled out in Wyoming law and Wyoming assumes a general purpose of engaging in any lawful activity. Privacy is the main reason to keep your articles short. You don't want the internal workings of your entity to be part of the public record, which articles are. But there is a practical reason as well – you avoid having to amend them later. The Bylaws can contain all the specifics -- these are kept private because they are internal documents that are not filed. They can be amended without notifying or paying the Secretary of State.

Once your articles are filed at the office of the Secretary of State, your corporation has been chartered and officially exists. However, it is crucial for liability protection to maintain your active status with the Secretary of State by paying annual fees and completing annual reports. It is also important that you draft and maintain internal documents such as bylaws and minutes.

Articles of Organization

The Articles of Organization are used to form an LLC. The following information must be included in articles for LLCs filed in Wyoming:

- The name of the LLC;
- The period of its duration (may be perpetual but you are defaulted to a 30-year period if you do not specify a duration);
- The purpose for which the limited liability company is organized;
- The name and address of its registered agent in Wyoming;
- The amount of cash or property initially contributed to the LLC and a description and agreed value of that property;
- The total additional contributions, if any, agreed to be made by all members and the times at which they shall be made;
- The right, if given, of the members to admit additional members, and the terms and conditions of the admission;
- The right, if given, of the remaining members of the limited liability company to continue the business upon the death, retirement, resignation, expulsion, bankruptcy or dissolution of a member or occurrence of any other event which terminates the continued membership of a member in the limited liability company;
- If the limited liability company is to be managed by a manager or managers, the articles of organization shall so state. They shall set out the names and addresses of such manager or managers who are to serve as managers until the first annual meeting of members or until their successors are elected and qualify. If the management of a limited liability company is reserved to the members, the names and addresses of the members shall be set out in the articles of organization; and
- If the LLC elects status as a flexible limited liability company (having only one member) it must state this in the articles with express reference to the statute.

As with the Articles of Incorporation, the Articles of Organization need not contain any information other than the requirements listed above. It is best to keep the important internal issues private. The LLC's operating agreement can and should detail the specifics of your company's policies.

Certificate of Existence

The Certificate of Existence is used to establish a limited partnership. The following information must be included in certificates sent to Wyoming:

- The name of the limited partnership which must contain, without abbreviation, the words "limited partnership;"
- The name and address of the registered agent in Wyoming;
- A mailing address for correspondence;
- The name and address of any general partners;
- The amount of cash or the value of services or other property contributed or to be contributed in the future to the limited partnership;
- The latest date upon which the limited partnership is to dissolve, and this date can be perpetual or a fixed date of any duration.

Articles of Incorporation, Articles of Organization and Certificates of Existence must be accompanied by a written consent signed manually by the registered agent. The filing fee for all three forms (Articles of Incorporation, Articles of Organization, Certificate of Existence) is the same -- $100 in Wyoming.

Bylaws and Agreements

Bylaws

All corporations should have bylaws that are adopted by the incorporators or the board of directors. Bylaws are internal documents that are not on the public record. They are not filed with the secretary of state but are instead kept with your company records. At minimum they spell out how your company or partnership is managed, organized and operated. They should not be drafted and then tucked away, but referenced and adhered to. If there are matters addressed in them that are out of date or no longer desirable, you need to formally amend them. Some of the issues that your Bylaws should address are:

- Head office location;

- Shareholder meetings, annual meetings (location and time and date), special meetings, notice, quorum, voting;
- Directors and Officers for corporations: offices, elections and terms, duties and powers, meetings (regular and special), notices, resignation, removal, salary, committees, actions, liability;
- Shares of stock, transfer, assignment, certificates, value;
- Dividends;
- Fiscal year for corporations;
- Company seal;
- Indemnification provisions; and
- Amendments.

The above is just a sample of the issues that should be addressed in your Bylaws and many of the noted items should be covered in depth.

Shareholder or "Buy-Sell" Agreements

Corporations should have Shareholder or "Buy Sell" Agreements in addition to bylaws. In Wyoming, any corporation that is not publicly traded may have a Shareholder or "Buy Sell" Agreement. This agreement documents certain understandings among shareholders. It can be fairly complicated and should be drafted by a competent corporate attorney. Generally, shareholder agreements anticipate problems among the shareholders and spell out what is to happen in the event of a disagreement or change in circumstances. They may include such matters as:

- Deadlocks
- Divorce or death of shareholder
- Dispute resolution procedures
- Rights of minority shareholders
- Restrictions on share transfer
- Buy-out provisions
- Purchase price formula and payment provisions
- Control of ownership
- Guaranteed purchaser
- Cumulative voting
- Exit strategies
- Preemptive rights

In Wyoming, shareholder agreements may also:

- Restrict the powers of the board of directors or entirely eliminate the board of directors;
- Subject to certain legalities, may authorize distributions that are not in proportion to ownership of shares;
- Establish who will serve as officers and directors, and outline provisions for their selection and removal;
- Govern the voting power of shareholders, including use of weighted voting rights or director proxies;
- Establish the terms and conditions of any agreement for the transfer or use of property or the provision of services between or among the corporation and any shareholder, director, officer or employee of the corporation;
- Transfer to one (1) or more shareholders or other persons all or part of the authority to exercise the corporate powers or to manage the business and affairs of the corporation, including the resolution of any issue about which there exists a deadlock among directors or shareholders;
- Dictate any power or relationship not contrary to public policy.

If a shareholder agreement is entered into in Wyoming, it must be noted conspicuously on all stock certificates, or if stock certificates are not issued, an informational notice must be prepared.

Some entities lend themselves to needing a Shareholder Agreement more than other entities do. A well drafted Operating Agreement or Partnership Agreement usually, but not always, has "built-in" Buy-Sell provisions. So, if your business is operating through either a Limited Liability Company or Limited Partnership and the proper language is included, you may not need to use a Shareholder or Buy-Sell Agreement. If your LLC or LP documents do not contain such provisions or if you are starting, or already part of, a corporation, you will want to have a Shareholder or Buy-Sell Agreement drafted. For more information on these arrangements, see Garrett Sutton's *Buy Sell Agreements: Drafting a Will for Your Business* (Corporate Direct, 2005).

Operating Agreements and Partnership Agreements

LLCs and LPs are the perfect vehicle for anyone wanting to safely hold assets that are expected to increase in value. Because LLCs and LPs can be long-term entities, careful planning needs to be done ahead of time to stave off problems down the road. Most states have few, if any, rules about how these entities are governed. Indeed, in Wyoming, often repeated words in the LLC statute are "unless the articles of organization or the operating agreement of that limited liability company provide otherwise." Or in the LP statute: "except as provided in the partnership agreement." Thus your operating agreement or limited partnership agreement is very important.

In many states, there is no legal requirement for either entity to have a written agreement. However, by not doing one you leave yourself entirely at the mercy of your state's laws or at the mercy of a judge trying to figure out the oral ambiguities of "he said/she said." And, in many cases, whatever default laws do exist may not necessarily be written to your benefit, or to the benefit of your entity. Generally speaking, state laws provide for an LLC or an LP to be run along the lines of a traditional corporation, which is likely to be much less flexible.

For example, without a written agreement providing otherwise, by default you could not allocate profits and losses in any way other than a straight pro-rata basis. So, if you had one member who contributed the cash, and another member who contributed the sweat, you could not redistribute the profit and losses to provide extra losses and write-offs to the cash contributor in early years. Another example would be a voting deadlock between members. Without a written formula to break ties and move forward, some state laws require that the entity be dissolved in the event of a deadlock.

Do not leave these important decisions unaddressed so that you, by default, become subject to general, often unfavorable, state laws. Think about it -- if the whole point of setting up your own LLC or LP is to take control over your business, then why would you immediately give that control over to someone or something else, especially a government?

You can have tremendous flexibility in how you structure your company. Do you want to have different classes of ownership interests with different rights? You can do it. Do you want interest to be valued based on services or cash depending upon the circumstances? Go ahead. Do you want to use common terms, such as President, Secretary and Treasurer to describe your managing members or managers (in the case of an LLC) or your General Partner (in the case of an LP)? No problem. Do you want to be able to split profits and allocate losses on a formula other than straight ownership percentages? Consider it done, of course with the help of your CPA.

The downside to this incredible flexibility is that you, as the owner, need to have some forethought and careful planning before you draft your entity's operating agreement or limited partnership agreement. This is the operating structure for your entity, and it needs to be comprehensive enough to handle all sorts of issues that may come up now, or well down the road into the future.

Another important thing to think about if you are considering running an LLC or LP without an agreement is whether that could be used as evidence to show that you are not really operating a business, but using a business name as a front to try to avoid liability. One of the things that a potential litigant's lawyers will look at is whether you keep entity (LLC or LP) records, and whether these records are up to date. If you do not keep at least minimal LLC or LP records, you can expect an argument in court that you are not really operating as a protected entity, but rather as an unprotected sole proprietorship or general partnership.

The following are several questions and areas to think about when formulating your operating agreement or limited partnership agreement. Most of these questions are interchangeable between the entities and are equally applicable.

- Will your LLC or LP be owned by a single person, a couple, a family, or by unrelated parties?
- Will your LLC be operated as a member-managed LLC or a manager-managed LLC? If manager-managed, must your manager(s) also be member(s)?
- If you decide to go with a member-managed LLC, what percentage of membership votes will be required to make decisions?
- If you decide to go with a manager-managed LLC, most of the day-to-day decisions will be made by the manager. What decisions do you want made by the full membership?
- Will everyone be contributing equal amounts of (a.) time and (b.) money or assets?
- What are the expectations of the members? Will some be actively operating the business while others are passive?
- How will the LLC be taxed? As a partnership or as a corporation?
- How will you handle profit distributions? Do you want a standard percentage ratio, or do you need to make some special arrangements, to take into account varying member contributions and performance expectations?
- How will members be able to leave the LLC? Will outsiders be permitted to buy in?
- How will you handle situations in which the LLC needs money?
- Do you want the LLC to have a buy-out provision in the case of the death or divorce of a member?
- Do you want the LLC to have a buy-out provision in the case of a member who is not performing to assigned expectations?

- What happens if you and the member fight among yourselves? Do you want the LLC to have some type of buy-out provision of one or more members in case of a disagreement? If so, how will you choose who gets to stay and who is bought out?
- What happens if a member is in financial or legal trouble and a creditor attacks that member's interest in court? Do you want to allow creditors to attach a member's interest through the use of a charging order, or do you want a lawsuit to trigger a member buy-out?
- If your LLC or LP is to be used by your family as an estate planning vehicle, have you thought about how to manage the transfer of power and control from one generation to the next, as well as what to do in cases where the next generation isn't quite ready for the challenge?

These questions are intended to get you thinking. You should be aware of the various elements that go into these types of agreements in order to help you determine what needs to go into yours. But, under no circumstances should you consider this sufficient advice and not also seek counsel from your own attorney, CPA or tax advisor.

Resolutions and Minutes

Organizational Resolutions

Shareholders, directors, members, managers, limited partners, and general partners all need to adopt organizational resolutions. The organizational resolutions set out the beginning structure of your new entity, name your management and shareholders or members, select a banking institution and appoint signatories, adopt the operating agreement or bylaws, and document various other administrative functions.

Minutes

Every corporation, LLC and LP must hold meetings and maintain a set of minutes of its meetings. Because meeting minutes are the primary paper trail of an entity's legal life, it is important to know when and how to prepare these minutes. While you do not need to document routine business decisions, you should prepare written minutes or consent resolutions for events or decisions that require formal board of director or shareholder participation, or member or manager participation for an LLC. These include, but are not limited to, the following:

- The proceedings of annual and special meetings;
- The issuance of stock or member certificates;
- The decision to amend or modify any corporate paperwork;
- Large purchases – a good example is the purchase of real property;
- The authorization of a significant loan amount or substantial line of credit;
- The sale of most or all of the company's assets;
- The adoption of a stock option or retirement plan; and
- In general, the making of any significant decision.

You will help protect your limited liability status by documenting important corporate decisions through formal written minutes or consent resolutions. You'll also have adequate records if key decisions are later questioned by creditors, the courts or the IRS. In addition, documenting decisions allows you to note the reasons for making critical decisions; this can prevent future disputes among fellow shareholders, officers or directors.

Meg

Meg was a do-it-yourselfer and she hated to spend money on expenses she considered unnecessary. She prepared her own taxes, she sewed her own curtains, she had recently painted her family room and stained her deck. When she started her own business she thought she could just incorporate herself. She went online and read everything she could about incorporation. There was a lot of conflicting information that just ended up confusing her. She also found a lot of online advertisements for incorporation services. One company promised to incorporate her for just $49. "Bingo!" She said to herself. "That I can afford." Or so she thought. Meg filled out the short questionnaire, handed over her credit card information, and several weeks later received a copy of her filed Articles of Incorporation in the mail. She operated her business happily and without too many hitches for a few years. During those years Meg made several important business moves such as moving her office to a higher rent area, spending thousands on new computer equipment, starting a retirement plan and borrowing money from a local bank.

One day the local sheriff appeared to serve Meg with a summons. Her company was being sued and she was also named personally in the lawsuit. Meg was scared, but felt confident that her personal assets were protected – she had incorporated, after all. Unfortunately, the lawyer that she was forced to hire disagreed. He explained that her single piece of paper entitled "Articles of Incorporation" was just one step of the process. All the other pieces of corporate protection were missing. She did not have bylaws, nor did she have organizational minutes. In fact, she had no minutes, resolutions or agreements of any sort for any of the significant decisions that she had made over the years. And this was just the missing paper trail.

The online incorporators charged $49 for the simple act of filing the Articles, but they did not provide Meg with any other documentation or knowledge of how to operate her corporation and maintain her limited liability. The poor and incomplete state of her corporate books left her open to having the corporate veil pierced and personal liability imposed. She now stood to lose a lot of money.

A Word on Registered Agents

I often am asked, "Why do I need a registered agent?" Every state requires the name of the registered agent and address of the registered office to be provided in or along with the company's articles. Some states, including Wyoming, require a manually signed consent form to accompany the Articles whereby the agent consents to serve the entity. The reason for this is that the resident agent is there to accept service of lawsuits, legal documents and other notifications from the state or other persons or entities. If you are authorized to transact business in a state, then that state wants to be able to find you or your agent within its borders. Thus, a physical presence is required. There are many companies that perform registered agent services. Corporate Direct, for example, can serve as your registered agent in all fifty states for the low fee of $125 per year. Others perform the service for more or less. The key is that you have a professional registered agent.

When the sheriff shows up to serve a lawsuit on your entity, you want your resident agent to be open to accept it and knowledgeable enough to know its importance. If the agent has closed its doors, the plaintiff can publish notice of the lawsuit in a local paper. You won't get the notice and can lose the case to a default judgment. If the agent doesn't appreciate the timeliness of a lawsuit, you can, quite fatally, miss the deadline to answer. In either case you lose. You are better off using a professional resident agent to handle this important task.

Chapter 6: Getting Started

Business License

The type of license that you will require depends largely upon the state you live in and the type of business you operate. You may also need more than one license because the state, county and municipality in which you are located may each have different rules. In Wyoming, business licensing and registration requirements are dependent on a variety of factors including one's legal formation, the business location and the nature of the products or services to be offered.

Regulatory oversight of businesses exists at three bureaucratic levels: federal, state and local. Unless the start-up business has employees, or is engaged in a few highly selective activities, federal regulations can be the least intrusive from a compliance standpoint. Local licensing requirements in Wyoming vary. Some areas have registration obligations and some do not. City or county clerks are good contact sources, as is the local planning office. Regulation of business activity in Wyoming is largely dependent upon the product sold, and most licensing of professions is conducted at the state level. If you are operating a business in Wyoming or through Wyoming, helpful information can be found by contacting the Wyoming Business Council at 307- 777-2800 or 800-262-3425. You may also visit their website at www.wyomingbusiness.org. Other state and local agencies will have their own websites and points of contact.

EIN Number

A company's employer identification number (EIN number) is akin to an individual's social security number. However, it is issued by the IRS rather than the Social Security Administration. The EIN is also known as a federal taxpayer identification number or TIN, and is used to identify a business entity. An LLC of which you are the sole member and that has no employees is not required by the IRS to have an employer identification number. However, most banks require you to give them either an EIN or social security number in order to open a bank account.

S-Election

If you set up a corporation and want to elect to be treated as an S corporation by the IRS, you must file an S-election within 75 days of the initial incorporation. The form used to achieve this is called Form 2553 and can be obtained from the IRS. It is best to consult with your attorney or accountant about the process and ramifications of this election. Basically, by electing S corporation status, the corporation will have the flow-through taxation of a partnership.

Bank Accounts

After you have completed your internal paperwork, obtained your tax ID number and any necessary business licenses, the next step is to open a business bank account in the name of your company. Most banks will want a copy of your articles of incorporation or organization, or certificate of existence if you are a limited partnership. All banks will need a copy of your Tax ID or EIN number. Don't waste your time and that of the bank officer unless you have these copies with you. You will also have to provide signature samples for all individuals who will be authorized to sign on behalf of the company (i.e. write checks). Be careful to whom you give this privilege. Common sense dictates the imprudence of having too many authorized check signers. However, beyond common sense it is important to know that the bank will run every signer's name through their database to check for red flags, such as bounced checks and other financial missteps. If any of the signers has a less than optimal financial history, your account could be denied. Another potential roadblock comes from the Patriot Act. Introduced after 9/11, the act makes it difficult for foreign residents to open bank accounts. For these reasons we recommend using a heightened level of discretion when authorizing signers.

Qualifying to Conduct Business in Another State

It is important to note that, although you can form your entity in Wyoming, if you will be transacting business in another state, you must qualify your entity to conduct business in that state. What constitutes "transacting business" varies slightly from state to state. Wyoming excludes the following activities and allows you to perform them in this state without obtaining a certificate of authority:

- Maintaining, defending or settling any proceeding;
- Holding meetings of the board of directors or shareholders or carrying on

other activities concerning internal corporate affairs;
- Maintaining bank accounts;
- Maintaining offices or agencies for the transfer, exchange and registration of the corporation's own securities or maintaining trustees or depositaries with respect to those securities;
- Selling through independent contractors;
- Soliciting or obtaining orders, whether by mail or through employees or agents or otherwise, if the orders require acceptance outside this state before they become contracts;
- Creating or acquiring indebtedness, mortgages and security interests in real or personal property;
- Securing or collecting debts or enforcing mortgages and security interests in property;
- Owning, without conducting a trade or business, real or personal property;
- Conducting an isolated transaction that is completed within thirty (30) days and that is not one in the course of repeated transactions of a like nature; or
- Transacting business in interstate commerce.

Additionally, an entity that serves as the organizer, manager or member of a company in Wyoming is not required to obtain a certificate of authority in order to fulfill these duties.

W.S. 17-16-1501

If you are transacting business in another state, qualifying to conduct business in that state is a relatively simple process that usually requires the following steps: (1) register the corporation's name with the foreign secretary of state, (2) retain a registered agent for service of process in the foreign state, (3) obtain a certificate of qualification or good standing from the Wyoming Secretary of State (or whatever state you are incorporated or organized under), and (4) pay filing fees to the foreign state. Keep in mind that the entity will also be subject to taxes and fees in the state where it conducts business. Your entity name must also be available in the state in which you are registering as a foreign entity, otherwise you will have to adopt a fictitious name in order to conduct business in that state.

While it is a rule of every state that a foreign entity (foreign is what you are called if you were organized or incorporated in a different state) must obtain a certificate of authority to transact business in that state, the failure to do so will not likely impair the validity of your corporate acts in that state. At least, that is the rule in Wyoming. However, if you are found to be conducting business in Wyoming without being registered you will be subject to a fine of $5,000 plus expenses and any fees or license taxes that you would have incurred with an interest rate of 18% tacked on. Additionally, your entity cannot maintain any lawsuits in the state, which is not a favorable position to be in.

Prudence dictates that you qualify your Wyoming corporation in any state in which you conduct an active trade or business. Beware of promoters who claim that by incorporating in Wyoming you can avoid, for example, California's minimum $800 franchise fee and all of California's business taxes. If you do business in California, that advice will get you into trouble. If your Wyoming entity does business in another state, you are best advised to qualify in that state. That said, by forming in Wyoming and qualifying in your home state, you still have the benefit of Wyoming corporate law and are not paying any extra Wyoming taxes (since there aren't any) for this benefit.

Chapter 7: Issuing Stock, Entity Ownership and Raising Money

An important thing to think about when you start your company is how it will be funded or capitalized. Capitalizing your company refers to the amount of money, services, insurance or assets you put into your company. Some states have a minimum capitalization requirement -- meaning you need to put a minimum amount, such as $1,000 for Texas corporations, into a corporate bank account. Wyoming does not have such a rule. However, some courts, most notably California, use inadequate capitalization as a contributing factor in piercing your company's limited liability protection. In other words, if your company is sued and it is under-capitalized, courts may look to your personal assets to compensate plaintiffs. So, how do you fund your company at the beginning?

There are two main ways to fund the company. You can either loan money to the company or pay money into the company in exchange for stock. This is known, respectively as debt or equity.

Many people will do a blend of the two. For example, Johnny and Debbie need $100,000 to start a franchise cleaning business. They could each buy 50,000 shares at $1 per share to raise the needed capital, which is the equity route. Or they could each loan $50,000 to the company, which is the debt route. The benefit of the debt route is that when profits are earned, Johnny and Debbie could each receive their $50,000 loan back without paying taxes. They are simply having their loan paid back, a non-taxable return of principal. Of course, any interest received on the loan will be taxable to them. And the monies used by the corporation to pay them back would be after-tax corporate dollars. But the return of principal strategy is an excellent means to get start-up monies back to the owners.

This is especially true when compared with trying to get money back to founders who only bought stock in the company. Any payment to shareholders is a dividend and a taxable event. So by paying back initial debt instead of initial equity, the founders receive better tax treatment.

But the problem of capitalizing the company with only debt is that it does not result in any shares in the company being issued, which is a necessary corporate formality.

Using a combination of debt and equity is one way that stock can be issued and monies can be advanced via loans and paid back tax-free.

Suppose Johnny and Debbie purchase 50,000 shares at $.10 per share. Note that the same amount of shares (50,000), are still being purchased, albeit at a lower price. A total of $5,000 is used as an equity purchase. The remaining $45,000 is then loaned to the Company. With the total $90,000 loaned to the company by Johnny and Debbie, the first $90,000 in corporate profits can be paid to them tax-free as a return of principal. Many investors have used this combination of debt and equity strategies successfully.

Wyoming allows you to exchange stock for current or future services. However, keep in mind that if you receive stock in exchange for services, it is still considered income for tax purposes as to the value of those services. So if you decide your services are worth $50,000 and you grant yourself an equivalent amount of stock in return, you will have to pay taxes on that amount. Especially in a new and uncertain situation, you may want to issue stock for $0.01 or $0.001 per share. Upon issuing 100,000 shares at $0.01 (or a million shares at $0.001) you will have a taxable receipt of $1,000, instead of valuing the same amount of shares at $1.00 each and paying taxes on $100,000. You can also exchange shares for money, equipment or other assets. Assign a value to your computers, office furniture, etc. and transfer these items into the company in exchange for shares of equivalent value.

To fully appreciate entity ownership, the differences in ownership terms must be comprehended. Each entity has owners. But in a corporation, the shareholders are the owners. The owner of a limited liability company is a member. And the owner of a limited partnership is a general or limited partner. This concept is worthy of greater discussion since we want to reap the benefits of ownership.

Corporations issue shares. Shares come in two basic flavors, common and preferred. With the definitions of common and preferred, shares can be broken down again into specific classes of stock, which may hold varying rights. The rights for each type of stock and each sub-class of stock are defined by the corporation, usually in its bylaws. These rights can be changed, or new classes of stock can be added or deleted through shareholder meetings. And note, S Corporations can only have one class of common shares.

Common shares are the most common method of ownership. In this case, the word "common" means equal – each common share is equal to every other common share. Equality means voting power. Each common share translates into one vote.

The more common shares you hold, the more votes you have. Votes denote your voice in how the corporation operates. Among other things, as a shareholder, you have the right to elect the directors of the corporation who oversee its operation.

Common shares can be sold for any price, subject to the securities laws. Even though common shares are equal with respect to voting rights, the price each shareholder pays for their common shares can be different. For example, it is standard practice for the founding shareholders to receive their stock at a very low price – one 100th of a cent is very common. The reason for this is two-fold. First of all, the founding shareholders are the people taking the highest risk of losing all of their money. Remember, at the beginning, a corporation is just an idea. It takes time to establish a business and make a profit, so the first people in are the ones who will be waiting the longest to see something back – if they see anything at all. We rarely like to talk about it, but sometimes the best ideas and the biggest efforts do not succeed. So, the founding shareholders receive their shares at a low price to mitigate some of that risk.

The second reason is control. The more shares you hold, the bigger your voice in the corporation's business. While this isn't as much of an issue in a small, family-owned company, it becomes crucial if you are envisioning your company attracting outside shareholders and eventually going public. As new shareholders come in and more shares are issued, your percentage of ownership is going to decrease proportionately (the technical term for this is dilution). Because this is your company, your idea and your efforts, it would be a shame to dilute your ownership interest to such a point where other shareholders can band together and possibly remove you from the corporation's management.

So, while the founders may have received shares in the corporation at a very low rate, as the company grows, develops and becomes more profitable, the price at which it can offer its shares to other people can change. However, the voting rights do not change – whether you paid one 100th of a cent, or $1 per common share. At the meeting table it is still one vote per share.

Preferred shares received their name because in some instances they have preference over common shares. For example, preferred shareholders may have the right to receive profit distributions ahead of common shareholders, or they might receive a higher ratio of profit distributions. Preferred shares oftentimes have preferential liquidation rights when the company goes out of business. If your corporation is being dissolved or liquidated, then after the creditors are through, the preferred shareholders will receive a portion of whatever assets remain, before anything is divided among the common shareholders.

The trade-off for this preferential treatment is normally voting rights. Preferred shares do not, as a rule, have any voting rights, whereas common shares do vote.

If it helps, think about this in terms of active and passive. Common shares are active – their holders actively participate in company business by voting on the management and certain business decisions. With the right to vote comes the responsibility of paying for it – a bad business decision may reduce profits. Preferred shares, on the other hand, are usually passive. Preferred shareholders have given up their rights to vote on management and business affairs. In exchange for having no control over how the corporation is run and how their money is spent, preferred shareholders receive a higher portion of the profits, and if the corporation fails, a higher portion of the leftover assets.

Just like common shares, again subject to the securities laws, preferred shares can be sold for any price. Likewise, in the early development stages of a corporation, the risks are higher, and the share prices will likely be correspondingly lower to try and offset some of that risk. And note that S corporations cannot have preferred shares. Only one class of common shares is allowed.

Preferred shares can also have features such as a conversion right, which allows preferred shares to be converted into common shares. The conversion feature can be any ratio, from a straight one for one swap to several preferred shares for one common share. The right to convert can be left to the preferred shareholder, the corporation, or a combination of both. For example, if you are designing a class of preferred shares and are also considering taking your company public at some point in the future, you may want to design your preferred shares so that they will automatically be converted into common shares just before your corporation files its public offering documents. While public companies can have preferred shares, keeping everything straight when you're dealing with hundreds or thousands of shareholders can get tricky. Also, it may not make sense to have one class of shareholders receiving higher profits than the other shareholders at that point in time. It certainly won't make you popular with the new public common shareholders.

The most important thing to remember about shares is that you decide how much they are sold for, the types of shares, the various voting and preferential treatment rights. You can design a share structure to fit your needs, from a simple and straightforward single class of common shares, to a complex mix of several classes of common and preferred shares.

In this vein, have you ever heard the terms "par value" and "no par value," and wondered what they meant? And have you ever looked at a stock certificate that says the par value of a share is one 100th of a cent and wondered why you paid $1 per share?

Par value is a number given to a class or classes of shares, primarily to establish a base value of the corporation. Par value also acts as the absolute minimum price that those shares can be sold for.

"No par value" means exactly that. There is no minimum price established for those shares. That can be a good thing, or a bad thing, depending on the laws of the state where you incorporate.

One reason to go with a very low par value is that the par value you select is the absolute minimum for which you can sell those shares. So, if you did choose to incorporate a company with 75,000 shares at a par value of $1 per share, that means you could not ever sell shares for less than $1 per share – including the shares you received as a founder.

Wyoming and Nevada are some of only a few states that allow you to issue shares to people for services provided, including your own. Instead of ponying up $25,000 in cash at the beginning of operations to receive shares in your own corporation, you can count the work you are going to do for your corporation as your investment, and receive shares that way. So, if you put a value on your first year's service to the corporation of $5,000, that could get you 5,000 shares if your par value is set at $1 per share. Or, if your corporation's par value is set at one 100th of a cent, that same $5,000 valuation could net you 5 million shares, and that 5 million shares could take care of any control issues for the foreseeable future. And remember that receiving stock for services can amount to taxable income. So be sure to check with your CPA or other advisor when using this strategy.

So when designing your corporation's share structure, keep in mind not only the types of shares that you want (common or preferred), but also think in terms of future growth by planning to have enough shares to keep your corporation going for as long as possible. If you wind up needing more shares than you have authorized, you can get them by paying extra money for filing fees to amend your corporation's Articles of Incorporation. It will also require a shareholders vote ahead of time. One of Wyoming's many benefits is its allowance of the authorization of an unlimited amount of shares. If you authorize an unlimited amount of shares, you will not have to worry about running out!

Instead of a corporation, what if you are setting up an LLC or a Limited Partnership?

The term for a slice of ownership in an LLC is a "membership interest." Likewise, in a limited partnership, it's a "limited partnership interest."

There are some similarities between interests and shares – they both denote ownership. Like common shares, both membership and limited partnership interests have voting rights, usually on a 1:1 basis. However, depending on how an LLC or an LP is structured, the events that members or limited partners are allowed to vote upon may be quite restricted. For example, in an LLC designated as manager-managed, members may vote on little else other than the election of managers and the right to admit new members. Limited partners are often even more restricted in voting than members – a limited partner is, by definition, a passive position.

Interests are also more amorphous than shares because there is no set amount reserved when you organize an LLC or a limited partnership. With a corporation, you authorize a flat amount of shares that can be issued – for example, 75 million common shares, with a par value of one 100th of a cent. With either form of LLC or LP interest, you just have interests, and ownership is calculated on a percentage basis – 50%, 100%, 2%, and so on. The value paid for a percentage of interests may differ from one member or partner to another. Founders may receive an interest based on a very different valuation as opposed to other members or partners who buy in later. Please note that if you are going to charge different prices for the same interest, you will have to follow the securities laws. A discussion of all of these laws and related securities issues is found in SuccessDNA's *How Your Company Can Raise Money to Grow and Go Public*.

Chapter 8: Managing Your Wyoming Entity

So you've hired a competent attorney or full-service company to set up your entity. Your articles are filed, your bylaws, shareholders agreement or operating agreement is in place, you have your organizational minutes drawn up and any notice requirements met or waivers signed. Your stock has been issued, you just received your Federal ID or EIN number from the IRS and opened up a business account. Now what?

Use Your Proper Name

Running your corporation, LLC or LP is not difficult. The most important thing is to respect your business as its own creature. It is not you and you are not it. Whenever you sign a document for your business, it is not you signing as yourself, rather it is you signing on behalf of your entity. Thus, when acting on behalf of your entity, do not sign your name naked. You are John Doe, President or Jane Roe, Manager or Sue Slate, Member. Your signature block should look something like the following:

AMCO, Inc.
a Wyoming Corporation

By:______________________
Donald Jones, President [or Vice-President or Secretary or Treasurer or Director]

OR

AMCO, LLC
a Wyoming Limited Liability Company

By:______________________
Donald Jones, Manager [or Member, or Co-Operating Manager]

No matter your position in the company, if you are called to sign any document, be it a formal agreement or a personal letter, be sure to sign as a representative of your business and not as an individual.

As a limited partner you will rarely, if ever, be signing anything on behalf of your Limited Partnership. The general partner will be responsible for all decisions and thus have signatory authority for the LP. Because a general partner should be another limited liability entity, signing on behalf of the limited partnership can get confusing. Your signature block should look something like this:

AMCO, LP
a Wyoming Limited Partnership

By: ____
Donald Jones, President, XYZ, Inc., Corporate General Partner of AMCO, LP

Not only do you need to refer to yourself as your company's representative, it is equally important to refer to your company as a limited liability entity. This is accomplished simply by using the proper label -- "Inc." or "Corp." or "LLC" or "LP" should always follow your business name. This label is part of your business name and your business will be naked, literally exposed, without it.

No Commingling

Another big no-no is commingling funds. If your personal bank account is a little low one month and you need to write a check or can't wait for funds to clear, do not ever, no matter what, write a check or withdraw funds from your business account to cover personal obligations. Your business account is not yours -- it is that of your business. If you start treating that account as your own, a court may someday treat everything that is yours as that of your business. Commingling of personal and business assets is a sure way to have your entity veil pierced and personal liability imposed.

Have Meetings

Wyoming law (as well as most other states' laws) requires that a corporation hold one annual meeting per year. A Wyoming corporation may hold meetings anywhere in the world and in any setting. Directors and Officers may hold annual or special meetings. Shareholders must meet annually and must hold special meetings as occasion demands. Corporate bylaws should specify when and where shareholders meetings will take place.

If you are the sole shareholder and/or director of your corporation, you are not required to oddly and awkwardly speak aloud to yourself or formally vote. But you must hold regular meetings and keep track of your thoughts and decisions through the use of minutes. Document your thoughts in a minutes form and keep these thoughts and decisions in the corporate records. Special meetings should be called whenever significant decisions need to be made. Regular (or annual) meetings and records of those meetings are evidence that your corporation acted like a corporation in making important decisions. Minute forms can be obtained from your attorney or can be found in *Bulletproof Your Corporation, Limited Liability Company or Limited Partnership* by Garrett Sutton (Corporate Direct, 2005).

The law is unclear as to whether LLC/LP members or managers or partners need to hold annual meetings. However, more than a handful of courts have pierced through an LLC because the court found that proper formalities were not recognized. In other words, required or not, you should hold annual meetings for the members of your LLC just as you would for shareholders in a corporation. In the absence of precedent regarding LLCs, courts will look to corporate law for guidance. The more formalities you use, the more protection you have against potential liability.

Role Play

To understand the decision-making process in an entity, let's look at the various parts people traditionally play in an LLC or corporation: member, manager, shareholder, director and officer. As we consider these roles, keep in mind that in Wyoming, one person can play all of them.

Shareholders

Shareholders are the "owners" of the corporation. Their ownership is represented through stock (called shares, or ownership interests) in the corporation. A shareholder can hold any amount of stock from a fraction of one share to 100% of the authorized stock of a corporation. Shareholders' rights and duties are defined by state law, the articles of incorporation, the bylaws, and a shareholder's agreement, if any. Except in the case of a close corporation, shareholders do not actively participate in the management of a corporation but delegate it to the directors. Shareholders have the exclusive right to make the following decisions:

- Amend the articles of incorporation and bylaws
- Elect and remove directors
- Approve the sale of all or substantially all of the corporate assets
- Approve mergers and reorganizations, and
- Dissolve the corporation.

State laws typically require the shareholders to hold an annual meeting, but in many states, including Wyoming, shareholders can use a "consent action" or "consent resolution" -- a document signed by all of the shareholders in place of a face-to-face meeting.

Directors

The board of directors is responsible for the management and policy decisions of the corporation. Directors enjoy broad powers, but typically delegate day-to-day responsibilities to the officers. Of course, the same person may serve as both director and officer. Some of the actions that directors are generally responsible for include:

- The authorization and issuance of corporate stock
- Determining value and adequate consideration for stock
- Approving stock option plans
- Electing officers
- Setting officer and key employee salary amounts
- Approving large purchases, and
- Approving loans to or from the corporation.

Officers

Officers are appointed by the directors to operate the corporation on a daily basis. Corporations typically have a president, a secretary and a treasurer. Some elect to also have a vice-president. There is nothing wrong with being the sole shareholder, sole director and president or CEO of your own corporation. However, you may want to have another individual serve as the secretary because this officer may be required to witness the president's signature. This may not be an issue in all settings. The secretary is also charged with keeping the corporate records. The president is the chief officer and is responsible for the corporation's management; the treasurer is the corporation's financial officer.

Tasks typically delegated to an officer include:

- Hiring and firing employees
- Negotiating and signing contracts
- Dealing with vendors and customers
- Keeping records
- General daily management activities

Compensation of officers is separate from any compensation they may receive for their role as directors (if your corporation has directors that are also officers). If you are a shareholder as well, your decision as to how to compensate yourself will be largely dependent upon your status as a "C" or "S" corporation. The IRS allows corporations to claim a "reasonable allowance" as compensation for services rendered. Compensation can include salary, stock options, health and other insurance, and accessories such as cars and computers. A reasonable allowance of compensation will be determined by certain circumstances, such as the size of the business, the corporation's earnings history, local economic conditions and industry standards.

The organizational structure of corporations separates the powers and duties of shareholders, directors, and officers. However, this separation usually is not an issue for small or closely held corporations in Wyoming, where most shareholders also serve as directors and officers. You may even choose to operate without a board of directors if that is permissible in your state, as it is in Wyoming. It is important to keep in mind, however, that even if you are both a shareholder and director of your corporation, you must still observe the formalities required by law. This means you will be wearing different hats at different times. For example, sometimes you will have to sign a document in your capacity as director or officer, while at other times you will have to sign as a shareholder.

Corporate Records and Reports

A large part of following proper corporate formalities is about creating and maintaining good records. A Wyoming corporation must keep a copy of the following records at its principal office, which may be located outside the State of Wyoming:

- Its articles or restated articles of incorporation and all amendments to them currently in effect;

- Its bylaws or restated bylaws and all amendments to them currently in effect;
- Resolutions adopted by its board of directors creating one (1) or more classes or series of shares, and fixing their relative rights, preferences and limitations, if shares issued pursuant to those resolutions are outstanding;
- The minutes of all shareholders meetings and records of all actions taken by shareholders without a meeting for the past three (3) years;
- All written communications to shareholders generally within the past three (3) years, including any financial statements;
- A list of the names and business addresses of its current directors and officers;
- Its most recent annual report as delivered to the Wyoming Secretary of State; and
- Accounting records of the past three (3) years for tax purposes.

Although it is only required that a Wyoming corporation keep minutes of the last three years at its principal office, you cannot discard minutes from previous years. They should all be kept, usually in your corporate book or a special book maintained just for minutes.

Wyoming corporations are also required to maintain a list of shareholders' names and addresses. The list of shareholders must be made available to shareholders or their agents within two (2) days after notice of a meeting and must remain available up until the meeting is held.

Hopefully all this information doesn't have your head spinning. If it does, break it down into what it is -- paperwork. If you do not like paperwork, there are many companies and individuals out there who will be happy to do it for you. Just make sure someone keeps on top of it.

Conclusion

Hopefully this book has helped you to better understand the world of entity formation and management. Choosing the type of entity that is best suited to your business or investment is a very important step. Intrinsic to that step is where you want to domesticate that entity. Wyoming's laws are very business friendly, but its advantages may not be relevant to every endeavor. Assess your needs with a competent attorney and CPA.

Because insurance is still your first line of defense, please maintain adequate insurance coverage. It is strongly advised that you enhance any insurance you presently have with an umbrella policy. Umbrella policies are relatively inexpensive in relation to the additional coverage they provide. They are a necessity for anyone with rental properties, young drivers, swimming pools, recreational equipment and any other high-risk classification. Talk to your insurance agent about how you can boost your liability protection.

In an effort to keep this book simple, non-profit formation specifics were not included. The Wyoming Non-Profit Corporation Act can be found in Title 17, Chapter 19 of the Wyoming Statutes. Please consult an attorney who specializes in this area if you are interested in setting up a not for profit organization.

The Appendix contains excerpts from Title 17 of the Wyoming Statutes, "Corporations, Partnerships and Associations." I included those sections that are relevant to matters discussed in this book. Because of the length and complexity of Title 17, Chapter 4, Securities, it was not included in the Appendix. For securities related questions it is critical that you speak with a securities attorney. The State of Wyoming maintains a website at http://legisweb.state.wy.us/titles/statutes.htm with the current text of this and the other Titles of the Wyoming Statutes if you are interested in reading Title 17 in its entirety. Also, because laws are organic, the attached statutes are subject to change. Check with your attorney to be sure that the laws you are relying upon are up to date. Good luck with all your business, real estate and asset protection endeavors.

Appendix

Title 17
Chapters: 3, 14, 15, 16, 17, 21, 24, 25 & 26

TITLE 17
CORPORATIONS, PARTNERSHIPS AND ASSOCIATIONS

CHAPTER 3 : PRACTICE OF PROFESSIONS BY CORPORATIONS

17-3-101. Practice of profession through licensed stockholder or employee authorized.

A corporation organized under the Wyoming Business Corporation Act or the Wyoming Statutory Close Corporation Supplement [chapter 17 of this title], whose capital stock is owned exclusively by a person or persons licensed to practice a profession by the state of Wyoming or by an agency, office or instrumentality authorized by the laws of Wyoming to license individuals for the practice of such profession, may, by and through the person or persons of such licensed stockholder or stockholders, or licensed employees, practice and offer professional services in such profession.

17-3-102. Licensed stockholder or employee subject to certain requirements.

No corporation may offer professional services or practice a profession except by and through the person or persons of its licensed stockholder or stockholders, or licensed employees, each of whom shall retain his professional license in good standing, and shall remain as fully liable and responsible for his professional activities, and subject to all rules, regulations, standards and requirements pertaining thereto, as though practicing individually rather than in a corporation.

17-3-103. Words or initials to be contained in corporate name.

The corporate name of every professional corporation shall contain either the words "A Professional Corporation" or the capital initials "P.C.". These words or initials shall be the last word of the name of the professional corporation.

17-3-104. Language to be contained in articles of incorporation; location.

The articles of incorporation of a professional practice corporation incorporated after the date of this act shall contain the following language: "All shareholders of the corporation are, and will continually be, licensed in the profession for which the corporation is formed, and no professional service will be offered by the corporation except by or under the supervision of licensed stockholders or licensed employees." This language shall be inserted in the articles immediately after the provisions pertaining to the aggregate number of shares which the corporation is authorized to issue.

CHAPTER 14 : LIMITED PARTNERSHIPS

ARTICLE 2
GENERAL PROVISIONS

17-14-201. Short title.

This act may be cited as the "Uniform Limited Partnership Act".

17-14-202. Definitions.

(a) As used in this act, unless the context otherwise requires:

(i) "Certificate of limited partnership" means the certificate referred to in W.S. 17-14-301, and the certificate as amended or restated;

(ii) "Contribution" means any cash, property, services rendered, or a promissory note or other binding obligation to contribute cash or property or to perform services, which a partner contributes to a limited partnership in his capacity as a partner;

(iii) "Event of withdrawal of a general partner" means an event that causes a person to cease to be a general partner as provided in W.S. 17-14-502;

(iv) "Foreign limited partnership" means a partnership formed under the laws of any state other than this state and having as partners one (1) or more general partners and one (1) or more limited partners;

(v) "General partner" means a person who has been admitted to a limited partnership as a general partner in accordance with the partnership agreement and named in the certificate of limited partnership as a general partner;

(vi) "Limited partner" means a person who has been admitted to a limited partnership as a limited partner in accordance with the partnership agreement;

(vii) "Limited partnership" and "domestic limited partnership" mean a partnership formed by two (2) or more persons under the laws of this state and having one (1) or more general partners and one (1) or more limited partners;

(viii) "Partner" means a limited or general partner;

(ix) "Partnership agreement" means any valid agreement, written or oral, of the partners as to the affairs of a limited partnership and the conduct of its business;

(x) "Partnership interest" means a partner's share of the profits and losses of a limited partnership and the right to receive distributions of partnership assets;

(xi) "Person" means a natural person, partnership, limited partnership (domestic or foreign), limited liability company, trust, estate, association or corporation;

(xii) "State" means a state, territory or possession of the United States, the District of Columbia, or the Commonwealth of Puerto Rico;

(xiii) "Certificate of continuance" means the certificate issued under the provisions of this act to continue a foreign limited partnership in this state;

(xiv) "This act" means W.S. 17-14-201 through 17-14-1104.

17-14-203. Name.

(a) The name of each limited partnership as set forth in its certificate of limited partnership:

(i) Shall contain without abbreviation the words "limited partnership";

(ii) Shall not contain the name of a limited partner unless:

(A) It is also the name of a general partner or the corporate name of a corporate general partner; or

(B) The business of the limited partnership had been carried on under that name before the admission of that limited partner.

(iii) Repealed by Laws 1995, ch. 45, § 2.

(iv) Shall not be the same as, or deceptively similar to, any trademark or service mark registered in this state and shall be distinguishable upon the records of the secretary of state from other business names as provided in W.S. 17-16-401.

17-14-204. Reservation of name.

(a) The exclusive right to the use of a name may be reserved by:

(i) Any person intending to organize a limited partnership under this act and to adopt that name;

(ii) Any domestic limited partnership or any foreign limited partnership registered in this state which, in either case, intends to adopt that name;

(iii) Any foreign limited partnership intending to register in this state and adopt that name; and

(iv) Any person intending to organize a foreign limited partnership and intending to have it registered in this state and adopt that name.

(b) The reservation shall be made by filing with the secretary of state an application, executed by the applicant, to reserve a specified name. If the secretary of state finds that the name is available for use by a domestic or foreign limited partnership, he shall reserve the name for the exclusive use of the applicant for a period of one hundred twenty (120) days. The reservation of a name is not renewable. The right to the exclusive use of a reserved name may be transferred to any other person by filing in the office of the secretary of state a notice of the transfer, executed by the applicant for whom the name was reserved and specifying the name and address of the transferee.

17-14-205. Specified office and agent.

(a) Each limited partnership shall continuously maintain in this state:

(i) An office, which may but need not be a place of its business in this state, at which shall be kept the records required by W.S. 17-14-206 to be maintained; and

(ii) An agent for service of process on the limited partnership, which agent shall be an individual resident of this state, a domestic corporation, or a foreign corporation authorized to do business in this state.

17-14-206. Records to be kept.

(a) Each limited partnership shall keep at the office referred to in W.S. 17-14-205 the following:

(i) A current list of the full name and last known business address of each partner separately identifying in alphabetical order the general partners and the limited partners;

(ii) A copy of the certificate of limited partnership and all certificates of amendment thereto, and any application for and certificate of continuance, together with executed copies of any powers of attorney pursuant to which any certificate or application has been executed;

(iii) Copies of the limited partnership's federal, state and local income tax returns and reports, if any, for the three (3) most recent years;

(iv) Copies of any then effective written partnership agreements and of any financial statements of the limited partnership for the three (3) most recent years; and

(v) Unless contained in a written partnership agreement, a writing setting out:

(A) The amount of cash and a description and statement of the agreed value of the other property or services contributed by each partner and which each partner has agreed to contribute;

(B) The times at which or events on the happening of which any additional contributions agreed to be made by each partner are to be made;

(C) Any right of a partner to receive, or of a general partner to make, distributions to a partner which include a return of all or any part of the partner's contribution; and

(D) Any events upon the happening of which the limited partnership is to be dissolved and its affairs wound up.

(b) Records kept under this section are subject to inspection and copying at the reasonable request, and at the expense, of any partner during ordinary business hours.

17-14-207. Nature of business.

A limited partnership may carry on any business that a partnership without limited partners may carry on except banking or acting as an insurer as defined in W.S. 26-1-102(a)(xvi).

17-14-208. Business transactions of partner with partnership.

Except as provided in the partnership agreement, a partner may lend money to and transact other business with the limited partnership and, subject to other applicable law, has the same rights and obligations with respect thereto as a person who is not a partner.

17-14-209. Fees.

(a) The secretary of state shall charge and collect the following fees:

(i) For filing a certificate of limited partnership, for an application for a certificate of continuance or for registering a foreign limited partnership, a fee of one hundred dollars ($100.00);

(ii) For filing a certificate of amendment or cancellation, or for filing a reservation of name, fifty dollars ($50.00).

(iii) Repealed By Laws 2000, Ch. 35, § 2.

(iv) Repealed By Laws 2000, Ch. 35, § 2.

(b) In addition to the fees provided under subsection (a) of this section, each limited partnership or foreign limited partnership shall comply with and pay the fees provided by W.S. 17-16-1630(a) through (e) as if it were a corporation.

(c) Any limited partnership or foreign limited partnership failing to comply with subsection (b) of this section may be dissolved or its franchise revoked by the secretary of state as if it were a corporation.

ARTICLE 3
FORMATION; CERTIFICATE OF LIMITED PARTNERSHIP

17-14-301. Certificate of limited partnership.

(a) In order to form a limited partnership a certificate of limited partnership shall be executed and filed in the office of the secretary of state. The certificate shall set forth:

(i) The name of the limited partnership;

(ii) Repealed by Laws 1995, ch. 45, § 2.

(iii) The address of the office and the name and address of the agent for service of process required to be maintained by W.S. 17-14-205;

(iv) The name and the business address of each general partner;

(v) The amount of cash and a description and statement of the agreed value of the other property or services contributed or to be contributed in the future;

(vi) Repealed by Laws 1995, ch. 45, § 2.

(vii) Repealed by Laws 1995, ch. 45, § 2.

(viii) Repealed by Laws 1995, ch. 45, § 2.

(ix) Repealed by Laws 1995, ch. 45, § 2.

(x) Repealed by Laws 1995, ch. 45, § 2.

(xi) Repealed by Laws 1995, ch. 45, § 2.

(xii) Repealed by Laws 1995, ch. 45, § 2.

(xiii) The latest date upon which the limited partnership is to dissolve; and

(xiv) Any other matters the partners determine to include therein.

(b) A limited partnership is formed at the time of the filing of the certificate of limited partnership in the office of the secretary of state or at any later time specified in the certificate of limited partnership if, in either case, there has been substantial compliance with the requirements of this section.

17-14-302. Amendment of certificate.

(a) A certificate of limited partnership is amended by filing a certificate of amendment thereto in the office of the secretary of state. The certificate shall set forth:

(i) The name of the limited partnership;

(ii) The date of filing the certificate; and

(iii) The amendment to the certificate.

(b) Within thirty (30) days after the occurrence of any of the following events and except as provided by subsection (f) of this section, an amendment to a certificate of limited partnership reflecting the occurrence of the event shall be filed:

(i) Repealed by Laws 1995, ch. 45, § 2.

(ii) The admission of a new general partner; or

(iii) The withdrawal of a general partner.

(iv) Repealed By Laws 1999, ch. 145, § 2.

(c) A general partner who becomes aware that any statement in a certificate of limited partnership was false when made or that any arrangements or other facts described have changed, making the certificate inaccurate in any respect, shall promptly amend the certificate.

(d) A certificate of limited partnership may be amended at any time for any other proper purpose the general partners determine.

(e) A person is not liable because an amendment to a certificate of limited partnership has not been filed to reflect the occurrence of any event referred to in subsection (b) of this section if the amendment is filed within the periods [period] specified in subsection (b) or (f) of this section, whichever applies.

(f) An amendment to a certificate of limited partnership reflecting the occurrence of any event specified by subsection (b) of this section for a partnership comprised of ten (10) partners or less, who are natural persons, may be filed annually instead of within the thirty (30) day period prescribed by subsection (b) of this section. The amendment certificate shall reflect all events specified by subsection (b) of this section which occurred during the calendar year and shall be filed in the office of the secretary of state no later than January 31 of the year following the year for which the amendment certificate applies.

(g) A restated certificate of limited partnership may be executed and filed in the same manner as a certificate of amendment.

17-14-303. Cancellation of certificate.

(a) A certificate of limited partnership shall be cancelled upon the dissolution and the commencement of winding up of the partnership or at any other time there are no limited partners. A certificate of cancellation shall be filed in the office of the secretary of state and set forth:

(i) The name of the limited partnership;

(ii) The date of filing of its certificate of limited partnership;

(iii) The reason for filing the certificate of cancellation;

(iv) The effective date (which shall be a date certain) of cancellation if it is not to be effective upon the filing of the certificate; and

(v) Any other information the general partners filing the certificate determine.

17-14-304. Execution of certificates.

(a) Each certificate required by this article to be filed in the office of the secretary of state shall be executed in the following manner:

(i) An original certificate of limited partnership shall be signed by all general partners;

(ii) A certificate of amendment shall be signed by at least one (1) general partner and by each other general partner designated in the certificate as a new general partner; and

(iii) A certificate of cancellation shall be signed by all general partners.

(b) Any person may sign a certificate by an attorney-in-fact, but a power of attorney to sign a certificate relating to the admission of a general partner shall specifically describe the admission.

(c) The execution of a certificate by a general partner constitutes an affirmation under the penalties of perjury that the facts stated therein are true.

17-14-305. Execution by judicial act.

If a person required by W.S. 17-14-304 to execute any certificate fails or refuses to do so, any other person who is adversely affected by the failure or refusal, may petition the district court to direct the execution of the certificate. If the court finds that it is proper for the certificate to be executed and that any person so designated has failed or refused to execute the certificate, it shall order the secretary of state to record an appropriate certificate.

17-14-306. Filing in office of secretary of state.

(a) Two (2) signed copies of the certificate of limited partnership and of any certifrcates of amendment or cancellation (or of any judicial decree of amendment or cancellation) shall be delivered to the secretary of state. A person who executes a certificate as an agent or fiduciary need not exhibit evidence of his authority as a prerequisite to filing. Unless the secretary of state finds that any certificate does not conform to law, upon receipt of all filing fees required by law he shall:

(i) Endorse on each duplicate original the word "Filed" and the day, month and year of the filing thereof;

(ii) File one (1) duplicate original in his office; and

(iii) Return the other duplicate original to the person who filed it or his representative.

(b) Upon the filing of a certificate of amendment (or judicial decree of amendment) in the office of the secretary of state, the certificate of limited partnership shall be amended as set forth therein, and upon the effective date of a certificate of cancellation (or a judicial decree thereof), the certificate of limited partnership is cancelled.

17-14-307. Liability for false statement in certificate.

(a) If any certificate of limited partnership or certificate of amendment or cancellation contains a false statement, one who suffers loss by reliance on the statement may recover damages for the loss from:

(i) Any person who executes the certificate, or causes another to execute it on his behalf, and knew, and any general partner who knew or should have known, the statement to be false at the time the certificate was executed; and

(ii) Any general partner who thereafter knows or should have known that any arrangement or other fact described in the certificate has changed, making the statement inaccurate in any respect within a sufficient time before the statement was relied upon reasonably to have enabled that general partner to cancel or amend the certificate, or to file a petition for its cancellation or amendment under W.S. 17-14-305.

17-14-308. Scope of notice.

The fact that a certificate of limited partnership is on file in the office of the secretary of state is notice that the partnership is a limited partnership and the persons designated therein as general partners are general partners, but it is not notice of any other fact.

17-14-309. Delivery of certificates to limited partners.

Upon the return by the secretary of state pursuant to W.S. 17-14-306 of a certificate marked "Filed", the general partners shall promptly deliver or mail a copy of the certificate of limited partnership and each certificate to each limited partner unless the partnership agreement provides otherwise.

ARTICLE 4
LIMITED PARTNERS

17-14-401. Admission of limited partners.

(a) A person becomes a limited partner:

(i) At the time the limited partnership is formed; or

(ii) At any later time specified in the records of the limited partnership for becoming a limited partner.

(b) Repealed by Laws 1995, ch. 45, § 2.

(c) After the limited partnership is formed, a person may be admitted as an additional limited partner:

(i) In the case of a person acquiring a partnership interest directly from the limited partnership, upon the compliance with the partnership agreement or, if the partnership agreement does not so provide, upon the written consent of all partners; and

(ii) In the case of an assignee of a partnership interest of a partner who has the power, as provided in W.S. 17-14-804, to grant the assignee the right to become a limited partner, upon the exercise of that power and compliance with any conditions limiting the grant or exercise of the power.

17-14-402. Voting.

Subject to W.S. 17-14-403, the partnership agreement may grant to all or a specified group of the limited partners the right to vote (on a per capita or other basis) upon any matter.

17-14-403. Liability to third parties.

(a) Except as provided in subsection (d) of this section, a limited partner is not liable for the obligations of a limited partnership unless he is also a general partner or, in addition to the exercise of his rights and powers as a limited partner, he participates in the control of the business. However, if the limited partner participates in the control of the business, he is liable only to persons who transact business with the limited partnership with actual knowledge of his participation in control.

(b) A limited partner does not participate in the control of the business within the meaning of subsection (a) of this section solely by doing one (1) or more of the following:

(i) Being a contractor for or an agent or employee of the limited partnership or of a general partner or being an officer, director or shareholder of a general partner that is a corporation;

(ii) Consulting with and advising a general partner with respect to the business of the limited partnership;

(iii) Acting as surety for the limited partnership or guaranteeing or assuming one (1) or more specific obligations of the limited partnership;

(iv) Taking any action required or permitted by law to bring or pursue a derivative action in the right of the limited partnership;

(v) Requesting or attending a meeting of partners;

(vi) Proposing, approving or disapproving, by voting or otherwise, one (1) or more of the following matters:

(A) The dissolution and winding up of the limited partnership;

(B) The sale, exchange, lease, mortgage, pledge or other transfer of all or substantially all of the assets of the limited partnership;

(C) The incurrence of indebtedness by the limited partnership other than in the ordinary course of its business;

(D) A change in the nature of the business;

(E) The admission or removal of a general partner;

(F) The admission or removal of a limited partner;

(G) A transaction involving an actual or potential conflict of interest between a general partner and the limited partners;

(H) An amendment to the partnership agreement or certificate of limited partnership; or

(J) Matters related to the business of the limited partnership not otherwise enumerated in this subsection which the partnership agreement states in writing may be subject to the approval or disapproval of limited partners.

(vii) Winding up the limited partnership pursuant to W.S. 17-14-903; or

(viii) Exercising any right or power permitted to limited partners under this act and not specifically enumerated in this subsection.

(c) The enumeration in subsection (b) of this section does not mean that the possession or exercise of any other powers by a limited partner constitutes participation by him in the business of the limited partnership.

(d) A limited partner who knowingly permits his name to be used in the name of the limited partnership, except under circumstances permitted by W.S. 17-14-203(a)(ii)(A), is liable to creditors who extend credit to the limited partnership without actual knowledge that the limited partner is not a general partner.

17-14-404. Person erroneously believing himself limited partner.

(a) Except as provided in subsection (b) of this section, a person who makes a contribution to a business enterprise and erroneously but in good faith believes that he has become a limited partner in the enterprise is not a general partner in the enterprise and is not bound by its obligations by reason of making the contribution, receiving distributions from the enterprise, or exercising any rights of a limited partner, if, on ascertaining the mistake, he:

(i) Causes an appropriate certificate of limited partnership or a certificate of amendment to be executed and filed; or

(ii) Withdraws from future equity participation in the enterprise.

(b) A person who makes a contribution of the kind described in subsection (a) of this section is liable as a general partner to any third party who transacts business with the enterprise:

(i) Before the person withdraws and an appropriate certificate is filed to show withdrawal; or

(ii) Before an appropriate certificate is filed to show that he is not a general partner, but in either case only if the third party actually believed in good faith that the person was a general partner at the time of the transaction.

17-14-405. Information.

(a) Each limited partner has the right to:

(i) Inspect and copy any of the partnership records required to be maintained by W.S. 17-14-206; and

(ii) Obtain from the general partners from time to time upon reasonable demand:

(A) True and full information regarding the state of the business and financial condition of the limited partnership;

(B) Promptly after becoming available, a copy of the limited partnership's federal, state and local income tax returns for each year; and

(C) Other information regarding the affairs of the limited partnership as is just and reasonable.

ARTICLE 5
GENERAL PARTNERS

17-14-501. Admission of additional general partners.

After the filing of a limited partnership's original certificate of limited partnership, additional general partners may be admitted as provided in writing in the partnership agreement or, if the partnership agreement does not provide in writing for the admission of additional general partners, with the written consent of all partners.

17-14-502. Events of withdrawal.

(a) Except as approved by the specific written consent of all partners at the time, a person ceases to be a general partner of a limited partnership upon the happening of any of the following events:

(i) The general partner withdraws from the limited partnership as provided in W.S. 17-14-702;

(ii) The general partner ceases to be a member of the limited partnership as provided in W.S. 17-14-802;

(iii) The general partner is removed as a general partner in accordance with the partnership agreement;

(iv) Unless otherwise provided in writing in the partnership agreement, the general partner:

(A) Makes an assignment for the benefit of creditors;

(B) Files a voluntary petition in bankruptcy;

(C) Is adjudicated as bankrupt or insolvent;

(D) Files a petition or answer seeking for himself any reorganization, arrangement, composition, readjustment, liquidation, dissolution or similar relief under any statute, law or regulation;

(E) Files an answer or other pleading admitting or failing to contest the material allegations of a petition filed against him in any proceeding of this nature; or

(F) Seeks, consents to or acquiesces in the appointment of a trustee, receiver or liquidator of the general partner or of all or any substantial part of his properties.

(v) Unless otherwise provided in writing in the partnership agreement, one hundred twenty (120) days after the commencement of any proceeding against the general partner seeking reorganization, arrangement, composition, readjustment, liquidation, dissolution or similar relief under any statute, law or regulation, the proceeding has not been dismissed, or if within ninety (90) days after the appointment without his consent or acquiescence of a trustee, receiver or liquidator of the general partner or of all or any substantial part of his properties, the appointment is not vacated or stayed or within ninety (90) days after the expiration of any such stay, the appointment is not vacated;

(vi) In the case of a general partner who is a natural person:

(A) His death; or

(B) The entry by a court of competent jurisdiction adjudicating him incompetent to manage his person or his estate.

(vii) In the case of a general partner who is acting as a general partner by virtue of being a trustee of a trust, the termination of the trust (but not merely the substitution of a new trustee);

(viii) In the case of a general partner that is a separate partnership, the dissolution and commencement of winding up of the separate partnership;

(ix) In the case of a general partner that is a corporation, the filing of a certificate of dissolution, or its equivalent, for the corporation or the revocation of its charter; or

(x) In the case of an estate, the distribution by the fiduciary of the estate's entire interest in the partnership.

17-14-503. General powers and liabilities.

Except as provided in this act or in the partnership agreement, a general partner of a limited partnership has the rights and powers and is subject to the restrictions and liabilities of a partner in a partnership without limited partners.

17-14-504. Contributions by, and distributions to, general partner.

A general partner of a limited partnership may make contributions to the partnership and share in the profits and losses of, and in the distributions from, the limited partnership as a general partner. A general partner also may make contributions to and share in profits, losses and distributions as a limited partner. A person who is both a general partner and a limited partner has the rights and powers, and is subject to the restrictions and liabilities, of a general partner and, except as provided in the partnership agreement, also has the powers, and is subject to the restrictions, of a limited partner to the extent of his participation in the partnership as a limited partner.

17-14-505. Voting.

The partnership agreement may grant to all or certain identified general partners the right to vote (on a per capita or any other basis), separately or with all or any class of the limited partners, on any matter.

ARTICLE 6
FINANCE

17-14-601. Form of contribution.

The contribution of a partner may be in cash, property or services rendered, or a promissory note or other obligation to contribute cash or property or to perform services.

17-14-602. Liability for contribution.

(a) A promise by a limited partner to contribute to the limited partnership is not enforceable unless set out in a writing signed by the limited partner.

(b) Except as provided in the partnership agreement, a partner is obligated to the limited partnership to perform any enforceable promise to contribute cash or property or to perform services, even if he is unable to perform because of death, disability or any other reason. If a partner does not make the required contribution of property or services, he is obligated at the option of the limited partnership to contribute cash equal to that portion of the value (as stated in the partnership records required to be kept pursuant to W.S. 17-14-206) of the stated contribution that has not been made.

(c) Unless otherwise provided in the partnership agreement, the obligation of a partner to make a contribution or return money or other property paid or distributed in violation of this act may be compromised only by consent of all the partners. Notwithstanding the compromise, a creditor of a limited partnership who extends credit, or otherwise acts in reliance on that obligation after the partner signs a writing which reflects the obligation, and before the amendment or cancellation thereof to reflect the compromise, may enforce the original obligation.

17-14-603. Sharing of profits and losses.

The profits and losses of a limited partnership shall be allocated among the partners, and among classes of partners, in the manner provided in writing in the partnership agreement. If the partnership agreement does not so provide in writing, profits and losses shall be allocated on the basis of the value (as stated in the partnership records required to be kept pursuant to W.S. 17-14-206) of the contributions made by each partner to the extent they have been received by the partnership and have not been returned.

17-14-604. Sharing of distributions.

Distributions of cash or other assets of a limited partnership shall be allocated among the partners, and among classes of partners, in the manner provided in writing in the partnership agreement. If the partnership agreement does not so provide in writing, distributions shall be made on the basis of the value (as stated in the partnership records required to be kept pursuant to W.S. 17-14-206) of the contributions made by each partner to the extent they have been received by the partnership and have not been returned.

ARTICLE 7
DISTRIBUTIONS AND WITHDRAWAL

17-14-701. Interim distributions.

(a) Except as provided in this article, a partner is entitled to receive distributions from a limited partnership before his withdrawal from the limited partnership and before the dissolution and winding up thereof to the extent and at the times or upon the happening of the events specified in the partnership agreement.

(i) Amended into (a) by Laws 1995, ch. 45, § 1.

(ii) Repealed by Laws 1995, ch. 45, § 2.

17-14-702. Withdrawal of general partner.

A general partner may withdraw from a limited partnership at any time by giving written notice to the other partners, but if the withdrawal violates the partnership agreement, the limited partnership may recover from the withdrawing general partner damages for breach of the partnership agreement and offset the damages against the amount otherwise distributable to him.

17-14-703. Withdrawal of limited partner.

(a) A limited partner may withdraw from a limited partnership at the time or upon the happening of events specified in writing in the partnership agreement. If the agreement does not specify in writing the time or the events upon the happening of which a limited partner may withdraw or a definite time for the dissolution and winding up of the limited partnership, a limited partner may withdraw upon not less than six (6) months prior written notice to each general partner at his address on the books of the limited partnership at its office in this state. The provisions of this subsection shall apply to limited partnerships formed under this act prior to July 1, 1999, unless the limited partnership properly adopts the provisions of subsection (b) of this section.

(b) A limited partner may only withdraw from a limited partnership at the time or upon the happening of events specified in writing in the partnership agreement. This subsection applies to limited partnerships formed under this act on or after July 1, 1999. A limited partnership formed under this act prior to July 1, 1999, may adopt the provisions of this subsection by filing a certificate of amendment with the secretary of state after July 1, 1999 that expressly refers to and adopts this subsection.

17-14-704. Distribution upon withdrawal.

Except as provided in this article, upon withdrawal any withdrawing partner is entitled to receive any distribution to which he is entitled under the partnership agreement and, if not otherwise provided in the agreement, he is entitled to receive, within a reasonable time after withdrawal, the fair value of his interest in the limited partnership as of the date of withdrawal based upon his right to share in distributions from the limited partnership.

17-14-705. Distribution in kind.

Except as provided in writing in the partnership agreement, a partner, regardless of the nature of his contribution, has no right to demand and receive any distribution from a limited partnership in any form other than cash. Except as provided in writing in the partnership agreement, a partner may not be compelled to accept a distribution of any asset in kind from a limited partnership to the extent that the percentage of the asset distributed to him exceeds a percentage of that asset which is equal to the percentage in which he shares in distributions from the limited partnership.

17-14-706. Right to distribution.

At the time a partner becomes entitled to receive a distribution, he has the status of, and is entitled to all remedies available to, a creditor of the limited partnership with respect to the distribution.

17-14-707. Limitations on distribution.

A partner may not receive a distribution from a limited partnership to the extent that, after giving effect to the distribution, all liabilities of the limited partnership, other than liabilities to partners on account of their partnership interests, exceed the fair value of the partnership assets.

17-14-708. Liability upon return of contribution.

(a) If a partner has received the return of any part of his contribution without violation of the partnership agreement or this act, he is liable to the limited partnership for a period of one (1) year thereafter for the amount of the returned contribution, but only to the extent necessary to discharge the limited partnership's liabilities to creditors who extended credit to the limited partnership during the period the contribution was held by the partnership.

(b) If a partner has received the return of any part of his contribution in violation of the partnership agreement or this act, he is liable to the limited partnership for a period of six (6) years thereafter for the amount of the contribution wrongfully returned.

(c) A partner receives a return of his contribution to the extent that a distribution to him reduces his share of the fair value of the net assets of the limited partnership below the value (as set forth in the partnership records required to be kept pursuant to W.S. 17-14-206) of his contribution which has not been distributed to him.

ARTICLE 8
ASSIGNMENT OF PARTNERSHIP INTERESTS

17-14-801. Nature of partnership interest.

A partnership interest is personal property.

17-14-802. Assignment of partnership interest.

Except as provided in the partnership agreement, a partnership interest is assignable in whole or in part. An assignment of a partnership interest does not dissolve a limited partnership or entitle the assignee to become or to exercise any rights of a partner. An assignment entitles the assignee to receive, to the extent assigned, only the distribution to which the assignor would be entitled. Except as provided in the partnership agreement, a partner ceases to be a partner upon assignment of all his partnership interest.

17-14-803. Rights of creditor.

On application to a court of competent jurisdiction by any judgment creditor of a partner, the court may charge the partnership interest of the partner with payment of the unsatisfied amount of the judgment with interest. To the extent so charged, the judgment creditor has only the rights of an assignee of the partnership interest. This act does not deprive any partner of the benefit of any exemption laws applicable to his partnership interest.

17-14-804. Right of assignee to become limited partner.

(a) An assignee of a partnership interest, including an assignee of a general partner, may become a limited partner if and to the extent that:

(i) The assignor gives the assignee that right in accordance with authority described in the partnership agreement; or

(ii) All other partners consent.

(b) An assignee who has become a limited partner has, to the extent assigned, the rights and powers, and is subject to the restrictions and liabilities, of a limited partner under the partnership agreement and this act. An assignee who becomes a limited partner also is liable for the obligations of his assignor to make and return contributions as provided in articles 6 and 7. However, the assignee is not obligated for liabilities unknown to the assignee at the time he became a limited partner.

(c) If an assignee of a partnership interest becomes a limited partner, the assignor is not released from his liability to the limited partnership under W.S. 17-14-307 and 17-14-602.

17-14-805. Deceased or incompetent partner; dissolved or terminated partner.

If a partner who is an individual dies or a court of competent jurisdiction adjudges him to be incompetent to manage his person or his property, the partner's executor, administrator, guardian, conservator or other legal representative may exercise all the partner's rights for the purpose of settling his estate or administering his property, including any power the partner had to give an assignee the right to become a limited partner. If a partner is a corporation, trust or other entity and is dissolved or terminated, the powers of that partner may be exercised by its legal representative or successor.

ARTICLE 9
DISSOLUTION

17-14-901. Nonjudicial dissolution.

(a) A limited partnership is dissolved and its affairs shall be wound up upon the happening of the first to occur of the following:

(i) At the time specified in the certificate of limited partnership;

(ii) Upon the happening of events specified in writing in the partnership agreement;

(iii) Written consent of all partners;

(iv) Repealed By Laws 1999, ch. 145, § 2.

(v) Entry of a decree of judicial dissolution under W.S. 17-14-902;

(vi) A vote to dissolve by all of the limited partners, or a number or percentage of limited partners specified in the partnership agreement, within ninety (90) days after an event of withdrawal of the last remaining general partner; or

(vii) The failure of the limited partners to admit or appoint another general partner within ninety (90) days after an event of withdrawal of the last remaining general partner.

17-14-902. Judicial dissolution.

On application by or for a partner the district court may decree dissolution of a limited partnership whenever it is not reasonably practicable to carry on the business in conformity with the partnership agreement.

17-14-903. Winding up.

Except as provided in the partnership agreement, the general partners who have not wrongfully dissolved a limited partnership or, if none, the limited partners, may wind up the limited partnership's affairs; but the district court may wind up the limited partnership's affairs upon application of any partner, his legal representative, or assignee.

17-14-904. Distribution of assets.

(a) Upon the winding up of a limited partnership, the assets shall be distributed as follows:

(i) To creditors, including partners who are creditors, to the extent permitted by law, in satisfaction of liabilities of the limited partnership other than liabilities for distributions to partners under W.S. 17-14-701 or 17-14-704;

(ii) Except as provided in the partnership agreement, to partners and former partners in satisfaction of liabilities for distributions under W.S. 17-14-701 or 17-14-704; and

(iii) Except as provided in the partnership agreement, to partners first for the return of their contributions and secondly respecting their partnership interests, in the proportions in which the partners share in distributions.

ARTICLE 10
FOREIGN LIMITED PARTNERSHIPS

17-14-1001. Law governing.

(a) Subject to the constitution of this state:

(i) The laws of the state under which a foreign limited partnership is organized govern its organization and internal affairs and the liability of its limited partners, unless the partnership has been issued a certificate of continuance pursuant to this article; and

(ii) A foreign limited partnership shall not be denied registration by reason of any difference between the laws of the state under which it was organized and the laws of this state.

17-14-1002. Registration.

(a) Before transacting business in this state, a foreign limited partnership shall register with the secretary of state. In order to register, a foreign limited partnership shall submit to the secretary of state, in duplicate, an application for registration as a foreign limited partnership, signed by a general partner and setting forth:

(i) The name of the foreign limited partnership and, if different, the name under which it proposes to register and transact business in this state;

(ii) The state and date of its formation;

(iii) Repealed by Laws 1995, ch. 45, § 2.

(iv) The name and address of any agent for service of process on the foreign limited partnership whom the foreign limited partnership elects to appoint; the agent shall be an individual resident of this state, a domestic corporation or a foreign corporation having a place of business in, and authorized to do business in, this state;

(v) A statement that the secretary of state is appointed the agent of the foreign limited partnership for service of process if no agent has been appointed under paragraph (a)(iv) of this section or, if appointed, the agent's authority has been revoked or if the agent cannot be found or served with the exercise of reasonable diligence;

(vi) The address of the office required to be maintained in the state of its organization by the laws of that state or, if not so required, of the principal office of the foreign limited partnership;

(vii) Repealed by Laws 1995, ch. 45, § 2.

(viii) The name and business address of each general partner; and

(ix) The address of the office at which is kept a list of the names and addresses of the limited partners and their capital contributions, together with an undertaking by the foreign limited partnership to keep those records until the foreign limited partnership's registration in this state is cancelled or withdrawn.

(b) The foreign limited partnership shall deliver with the completed application a certificate of existence, duly authenticated by the secretary of state or other official having custody of limited partnership records in the state or country under whose laws it is formed, which verifies the active existence of the foreign limited partnership.

17-14-1003. Issuance of registration.

(a) If the secretary of state finds that an application for registration conforms to law and all requisite fees have been paid, he shall:

(i) Endorse on the application the word "Filed", and the month, day and year of the filing thereof;

(ii) File in his office a duplicate original of the application; and

(iii) Issue a certificate of registration to transact business in this state.

(b) The certificate of registration, together with a duplicate original of the application, shall be returned to the person who filed the application or his representative.

17-14-1004. Name.

A foreign limited partnership may register with the secretary of state under any name (whether or not it is the name under which it is registered in its state of organization) that includes without abbreviation the words "limited partnership" and that could be registered by a domestic limited partnership.

17-14-1005. Changes and amendments.

If any statement in the application for registration of a foreign limited partnership was false when made or any arrangements or other facts described have changed, making the application inaccurate in any respect, the foreign limited partnership shall promptly file in the office of the secretary of state a certificate, signed and sworn to by a general partner, correcting such statement.

17-14-1006. Cancellation of registration.

A foreign limited partnership may cancel its registration by filing with the secretary of state a certificate of cancellation signed and sworn to by a general partner. A cancellation does not terminate the authority of the secretary of state to accept service of process on the foreign limited partnership with respect to causes of action arising out of the transactions of business in this state.

17-14-1007. Transaction of business without registration.

(a) A foreign limited partnership transacting business in this state may not maintain any action, suit or proceeding in any court of this state until it has registered in this state.

(b) The failure of a foreign limited partnership to register in this state does not impair the validity of any contract or act of the foreign limited partnership or prevent the foreign limited partnership from defending any action, suit or proceeding in any court of this state.

(c) A limited partner of a foreign limited partnership is not liable as a general partner of the foreign limited partnership solely by reason of having transacted business in this state without registration.

(d) A foreign limited partnership, by transacting business in this state without registration, appoints the secretary of state as its agent for service of process with respect to causes of actions arising out of the transaction of business in this state.

(e) Any foreign limited partnership transacting business in this state without registering is subject to the penalties provided by W.S. 17-16-1502(d).

17-14-1008. Action by secretary of state.

The secretary of state may bring an action to restrain a foreign limited partnership from transacting business in this state in violation of this article.

17-14-1009. Applicability of other provisions.

(a) In any case not provided for in this act, the provisions of the Uniform Partnership Act [§§ 17-21-101 through 17-21-1105] apply.

(b) In cases concerning service of process on the secretary of state as agent for a foreign limited partnership, provisions of the Wyoming Business Corporations Act concerning service of process, the manner of service and fees charged apply.

17-14-1010. Continuance of a foreign limited partnership.

Any foreign limited partnership, except partnerships acting as an insurer as defined in W.S. 26-1-102(a)(xvi) or acting as a financial institution as defined in W.S. 13-1-101(a)(ix), may apply to the secretary of state for a certificate of continuance to permit the foreign limited partnership to continue in Wyoming as if the partnership had been formed under the laws of this state.

17-14-1011. Application for certificate of continuance; requirements.

(a) To continue in this state, a foreign limited partnership shall submit to the secretary of state, in duplicate, an application for a certificate of continuance setting forth:

(i) Written confirmation from the state in which the partnership was formed that the partnership's domicile in that state is terminated or will be terminated upon continuance in this state;

(ii) A certified copy of the limited partnership's original certificate of limited partnership, or equivalent authorization, including any amendments;

(iii) The name of the limited partnership;

(iv) The duration of the limited partnership from date of formation to present;

(v) The address of the office and the name and address of the agent for service of process required to be maintained by W.S. 17-14-205;

(vi) The name and business address of each general partner;

(vii) A statement that the limited partnership will abide by the constitution and laws of this state;

(viii) The latest date upon which the limited partnership is to dissolve;

(ix) Any other matters the partners determine to include in the application;

(x) Any additional information necessary to enable the secretary of state to determine whether the foreign limited partnership is entitled to a certificate of continuance.

(b) The application may vary from the original certificate that formed the foreign limited partnership provided that the change would be permissible as an amendment for a limited partnership organized in this state.

17-14-1012. Execution of application.

(a) The application for a certificate of continuance filed in the office of the secretary of state shall be signed by all general partners.

(b) Any person may sign an application by an attorney-in-fact, but a power of attorney to sign a certificate relating to the admission of a general partner shall specifically describe the admission.

(c) The execution of an application by a general partner constitutes an affirmation under the penalties of perjury that the facts stated therein are true.

17-14-1013. Issuance of certificate of continuance.

(a) If the secretary of state finds that an application for continuance substantially conforms to law and all requisite fees have been paid, he shall:

(i) Endorse on each duplicate original application the word "filed," and the month, day and year of the filing;

(ii) File one (1) duplicate original in his office;

(iii) Issue a certificate of continuance to continue in this state;

(iv) Notify the secretary of state or appropriate official in the state of terminated domicile that a certificate of continuance has been issued in this state.

(b) The certificate of continuance, together with a duplicate original of the application, shall be returned to the person who filed the application or his representative.

(c) The certificate of continuance may incorporate by reference the original certificate of limited partnership. The original certificate is deemed amended to the extent necessary to conform to the laws of Wyoming and the provisions of the certificate of continuance.

17-14-1014. Effect of certification.

(a) Upon issuance of a certificate of continuance by the secretary of state, the certificate of continuance shall be deemed to be a certificate of limited partnership and the limited partnership shall be subject to the provisions of this act as though formed under the laws of this state.

(b) Except for the purpose of W.S. 16-6-101 through 16-6-121, the existence of any limited partnership issued a certificate of continuance shall be deemed to have commenced on the date the limited partnership was originally formed under the laws of another state.

(c) The laws of Wyoming shall apply to a limited partnership continuing under this act from the date a certificate of continuance is issued by the secretary of state.

(d) The continuance shall not affect the ownership of partnership property, liability for any existing obligation, cause of action, claim, pending or threatened prosecution, civil or administrative action, conviction, ruling, order or judgment. The continuance does not deprive a partner of any right or privilege, nor relieve a partner of any liability.

ARTICLE 11
DERIVATIVE ACTIONS

17-14-1101. Right of action.

A limited partner may bring an action in the right of a limited partnership to recover a judgment in its favor if general partners with authority to do so have refused to bring the action or if an effort to cause those general partners to bring the action is not likely to succeed.

17-14-1102. Proper plaintiff.

(a) In a derivative action, the plaintiff shall be a partner at the time of bringing the action and:

(i) At the time of the transaction of which he complains; or

(ii) His status as a partner had devolved upon him by operation of law or pursuant to the terms of the partnership agreement from a person who was a partner at the time of the transaction.

17-14-1103. Pleading.

In a derivative action, the complaint shall set forth with particularity the effort of the plaintiff to secure initiation of the action by a general partner or the reasons for not making the effort.

17-14-1104. Expenses.

If a derivative action is successful, in whole or in part, or if anything is received by the plaintiff as a result of a judgment, compromise or settlement of an action or claim, the court may award the plaintiff reasonable expenses, including reasonable attorney's fees, and shall direct him to remit to the limited partnership the remainder of those proceeds received by him.

CHAPTER 15
LIMITED LIABILITY COMPANIES

17-15-101. Short title.

This act shall be known and may be cited as the "Wyoming Limited Liability Company Act".

17-15-102. Definitions.

(a) As used in this act:

(i) "Bankrupt" means bankrupt under the federal Bankruptcy Act;

(ii) "Court" includes every court and judge having jurisdiction in the case;

(iii) "Limited liability company" or "company" means a limited liability company organized and existing under this act;

(iv) "Person" includes individuals, general partnerships, limited partnerships, limited liability companies, corporations, trusts, business trusts, real estate investment trusts, estates and other associations;

(v) "Real property" includes land, any interest, leasehold or estate in land and any improvements on it;

(vi) "This act" means W.S. 17-15-101 through 17-15-144;

(vii) "Flexible limited liability company" means a limited liability company organized and existing under this act which shall have elected, by affirmative statement in its articles of organization expressly referring to W.S. 17-15-107(a)(x), to be authorized to adopt provisions within its operating agreement as authorized by W.S. 17-15-144.

17-15-103. Purpose.

(a) Limited liability companies may be organized under this act for any lawful purpose, except for the purpose of banking or acting as an insurer as defined in W.S. 26-1-102(a)(xvi).

(b) Nothing in this act shall be interpreted as precluding an individual whose occupation requires licensure under Wyoming law from forming a limited liability company if the applicable licensing statutes do not prohibit it and the licensing body does not prohibit it by rule or regulation adopted consistent with the appropriate licensing statute. No limited liability company may offer professional services or practice a profession except by and through its licensed members or licensed employees, each of whom shall retain his professional license in good standing and shall remain as fully liable and responsible for his professional activities, and subject to all rules, regulations, standards and requirements pertaining thereto, as though practicing individually rather than in a limited liability company.

17-15-104. Powers.

(a) Each limited liability company organized and existing under this act may:

(i) Sue and be sued, complain and defend, in its name;

(ii) Purchase, take, receive, lease or otherwise acquire, own, hold, improve, use and otherwise deal in and with real or personal property, or an interest in it, wherever situated;

(iii) Sell, convey, mortgage, pledge, lease, exchange, transfer and otherwise dispose of all or any part of its property and assets;

(iv) Lend money to and otherwise assist its members, managers and employees;

(v) Purchase, take, receive, subscribe for or otherwise acquire, own, hold, vote, use, employ, sell, mortgage, lend, pledge or otherwise dispose of, and otherwise use and deal in and with shares or other interests in or obligations of other limited liability companies, domestic or foreign corporations, associations, general or limited partnerships or individuals, or direct or indirect obligations of the United States or of any government, state, territory, governmental district or municipality or of any instrumentality of it;

(vi) Make contracts and guarantees and incur liabilities, borrow money at such rates of interest as the limited liability company may determine, issue its notes, bonds and other obligations and secure any of its obligations by mortgage or pledge of all or any part of its property, franchises and income;

(vii) Lend money for its proper purposes, invest and reinvest its funds and take and hold real property and personal property for the payment of funds so loaned or invested;

(viii) Conduct its business, carry on its operations and have and exercise the powers granted by this act in any state, territory, district or possession of the United States, or in any foreign country;

(ix) Elect or appoint managers, officers, employees and agents of the limited liability company, and define their duties and authority, which may include authority also delegated to the members or managers under W.S. 17-15-117 and 17-15-118, and fix their compensation;

(x) Make and alter operating agreements, not inconsistent with its articles of organization or with the laws of this state, for the administration and regulation of the affairs of the limited liability company;

(xi) Indemnify a member or manager or former member or manager of the limited liability company against expenses actually and reasonably incurred by him or it in connection with the defense of an action, suit or proceeding, civil or criminal, in which he or it is made a party by reason of being or having been such member or manager, except in relation to matters as to which he or it shall be adjudged in the action, suit or proceeding to be liable to the company for negligence or misconduct in the performance of duty or to have received improper personal benefit on account thereof; and to make any other indemnification that is authorized by the articles of organization or by an article of the operating agreement or resolution adopted by the members after notice;

(xii) Cease its activities and surrender its certificate of organization;

(xiii) Have and exercise all powers necessary or convenient to effect any or all of the purposes for which the limited liability company is organized;

(xiv) Become a member of a general partnership, limited partnership, joint venture or similar association, or any other limited liability company;

(xv) Pay pensions and establish pension plans, pension trusts, profit-sharing plans, ownership interest bonus plans and option plans, and benefit or incentive plans for any or all of its current or former managers, officers, employees and agents;

(xvi) Make donations for the public welfare or for charitable, scientific or educational purposes.

17-15-105. Name.

(a) The words "limited liability company," or its abbreviations "LLC" or "L.L.C.," "limited company," or its abbreviations "LC" or "L.C.," "Ltd. liability company," "Ltd. liability co." or "limited liability co." shall be included in the name of every limited liability company formed under the provisions of this act and, in addition, the limited liability company name may not:

(i) Contain a word or phrase which indicates or implies that it is organized for a purpose other than one (1) or more of the purposes contained in its articles of organization;

(ii) Be the same as, or deceptively similar to, any trademark or service mark registered in this state and shall be distinguishable upon the records of the secretary of state from other business names as provided in W.S. 17-16-401;

(iii) Contain a word or phrase which indicates or implies that it is organized under the Wyoming Business Corporation Act, the Wyoming Statutory Close Corporation Supplement, or the Nonprofit Corporation Act.

(b) Omission of the words "limited liability company," or its abbreviations "LLC" or "L.L.C.," "limited company," or its abbreviations "LC" or "L.C.," "Ltd. liability company," "Ltd. liability co." or "limited liability co." in the use of the name of the limited liability company shall render any person who participates in the omission, or knowingly acquiesces in it, liable for indebtedness, damage or liability occasioned by the omission.

(c) Repealed by Laws 1993, ch. 196, § 5.

(d) A limited liability company may reserve a name in accordance with rules promulgated under this act.

17-15-106. Formation.

Any person may form a limited liability company which shall have two (2) or more members by signing and delivering one (1) original and one (1) exact or conformed copy of the articles of organization to the secretary of state for filing. The person forming the company need not be a member of the limited liability company.

17-15-107. Articles of organization.

(a) The articles of organization shall set forth:

(i) The name of the limited liability company;

(ii) The period of its duration, which shall be thirty (30) years from the date of filing with the secretary of state if no period of duration is specifically set forth in the articles of organization;

(iii) The purpose for which the limited liability company is organized;

(iv) The name and address of its registered agent in the state;

(v) The total amount of cash and a description and agreed value of property other than cash contributed;

(vi) The total additional contributions, if any, agreed to be made by all members and the times at which or events upon the happening of which they shall be made;

(vii) The right, if given, of the members to admit additional members, and the terms and conditions of the admission;

(viii) The right, if given, of the remaining members of the limited liability company to continue the business on the death, retirement, resignation, expulsion, bankruptcy or dissolution of a member or occurrence of any other event which terminates the continued membership of a member in the limited liability company;

(ix) If the limited liability company is to be managed by a manager or managers, the articles of organization shall so state and shall set out the names and addresses of such manager or managers who are to serve as managers until the first annual meeting of members or until their successors are elected and qualify. If the management of a limited liability company is reserved to the members, the names and addresses of the members shall be set out in the articles of organization;

(x) If the limited liability company is to elect status as a flexible limited liability company, the articles of organization shall so state by express reference to this paragraph, and the limited liability company thereby shall be authorized to adopt provisions within its operating agreement as authorized by W.S. 17-15-144;

(xi) Any other provision, not inconsistent with law, which the members elect to set out in the articles of organization for the regulation of the internal affairs of the limited liability company, including any provisions which under this act are required or permitted to be set out in the operating agreement of the limited liability company.

(b) It is not necessary to set out in the articles of organization any of the powers enumerated in this act.

(c) The articles of organization shall be accompanied by a written consent to appointment manually signed by the registered agent.

17-15-108. Filing of articles of organization.

(a) One (1) original and one (1) exact or conformed copy of the articles of organization shall be delivered to the secretary of state. If the secretary of state finds that the articles of organization conform to law, he shall, when all fees have been paid, as in this act prescribed:

(i) Endorse on the original and conformed copy the word "Filed" and the month, day and year of the filing thereof;

(ii) File the original in his office;

(iii) Issue a certificate of organization to which he shall affix the conformed copy.

(b) The certificate of organization, together with the conformed copy of the articles of organization affixed to it by the secretary of state, shall be returned to the representative of the limited liability company.

17-15-109. Effect of issuance of certificate of organization.

(a) Upon the issuance of the certificate of organization, the limited liability company shall be considered organized, and such certificate of organization shall be conclusive evidence that all conditions precedent required to be performed by the members have been complied with and that the limited liability company has been legally organized under this act, except as against this state in a proceeding to cancel or revoke the certificate of organization or for involuntary dissolution of the limited liability company.

(b) A limited liability company shall not transact business or incur indebtedness, except that which is incidental to its organization or to obtaining subscriptions for or payment of contributions, until the secretary of state has issued a certificate of organization.

17-15-110. Registered office and registered agent to be maintained.

(a) Each limited liability company shall have and continuously maintain in this state:

(i) A registered office which may be, but need not be, the same as its place of business;

(ii) A registered agent, which agent may be either an individual resident in this state whose business office is identical with such registered office, or a domestic corporation, or a foreign corporation authorized to transact business in this state, having a business office identical with such registered office.

17-15-111. Change of registered office or registered agent.

(a) A limited liability company may change its registered office or agent, or both, upon filing in the office of the secretary of state a statement setting forth:

(i) The name of the limited liability company;

(ii) The address of its then registered office;

(iii) If the address of its registered office be changed, the address to which the registered office is to be changed;

(iv) The name of its then registered agent;

(v) If its registered agent be changed, the name of its successor registered agent;

(vi) That the address of its registered office and the address of the business office of its registered agent, as changed, will be identical;

(vii) That the change was authorized by affirmative vote of a majority of the members of the limited liability company.

(b) The statement shall be signed and delivered to the secretary of state. If the secretary of state finds that the statement conforms to the provisions of this act, he shall file the statement in his office, and upon filing the change of address of the registered office or the appointment of a new registered agent or both, as the case may be is effective.

c) Any registered agent of a limited liability company may resign as agent upon filing a written notice thereof, signed with one (1) original and one (1) exact or conformed copy, with the secretary of state, who shall forthwith mail a copy thereof to the limited liability company at its principal mailing address as defined and prescribed by the secretary of state. The appointment of the agent shall terminate upon the expiration of thirty (30) days after receipt of notice by the secretary of state.

17-15-112. Failure to maintain registered agent or registered office or pay annual fee.

(a) If any limited liability company has failed for thirty (30) days to appoint and maintain a registered agent in this state, or has failed for thirty (30) days after change of its registered office or registered agent to file in the office of the secretary of state a statement of the change it shall be deemed to be transacting business within this state without authority and to have forfeited any franchises, rights or privileges acquired under the laws thereof and the forfeiture shall be made effective in the following manner. The secretary of state shall mail by certified mail a notice of its failure to comply with aforesaid provisions. Unless compliance is made within thirty (30) days of the delivery of notice, the limited liability company shall be deemed defunct and to have forfeited its certificate of organization acquired under the laws of this state. Provided, that any defunct limited liability company may at any time within two (2) years after the forfeiture of its certificate, in the manner herein provided, be revived and reinstated, by filing the necessary statement under this act and paying a reinstatement fee established by the secretary of state by rule, together with a penalty of one hundred dollars ($100.00). The reinstatement fee shall not exceed the costs of providing the reinstatement service. The limited liability company shall retain its registered name during the two (2) year reinstatement period under this section.

(b) If any limited liability company has failed to pay the tax required by W.S. 17-15-132(a)(vi) it shall be deemed to be transacting business within this state without authority and to have forfeited any franchises, rights or privileges acquired under the laws thereof. The forfeiture shall be made effective in the following manner. The secretary of state shall provide notice to the limited liability company at its last known mailing address by first class mail and publish once a week for two (2) consecutive weeks in a newspaper of general circulation in the county in which the registered office of the company is located, notice that the company failed to comply with W.S. 17-15-132(a)(vi). Unless compliance is made within sixty (60) days of the date of the first publication, the limited liability company shall be deemed defunct and to have forfeited its certificate of organization acquired under the laws of this state. Provided, that any defunct limited liability company may at any time within two (2) years after the forfeiture of its certificate, be revived and reinstated by paying double the amount of the delinquent taxes.

17-15-113. Liability of members and managers.

Neither the members of a limited liability company nor the managers of a limited liability company managed by a manager or managers are liable under a judgment, decree or order of a court, or in any other manner, for a debt, obligation or liability of the limited liability company.

17-15-114. Service of process.

(a) The registered agent so appointed by a limited liability company shall be an agent of the company upon whom any process, notice or demand required or permitted by law to be served upon the company may be served.

(b) Whenever a limited liability company shall fail to appoint or maintain a registered agent in this state, or whenever its registered agent cannot with reasonable diligence be found at the registered office, then the secretary of state shall be an agent of the company upon whom any process, notice or demand may be served. Service on the secretary of state of any process, notice or demand shall be made by delivering to and leaving with him, or with any clerk of his office, duplicate copies of such process, notice or demand. In the event any such process, notice or demand is served on the secretary of state, he shall immediately cause one (1) of the copies thereof to be forwarded by registered mail addressed to the limited liability company at its principal mailing address as defined and prescribed by the secretary of state. Any service so had on the secretary of state shall be returnable in not less than thirty (30) days.

(c) The secretary of state shall keep a record of all processes, notices and demands served upon him under this section and shall record therein the time of such service and his action with reference thereto.

(d) Nothing herein contained shall limit or affect the right to serve any process, notice or demand required or permitted by law to be served upon a limited liability company in any other manner now or hereafter permitted by law.

17-15-115. Contributions to capital.

The contributions to capital of a member to the limited liability company may consist of cash or other property, promissory notes or services rendered or to be rendered.

17-15-116. Management.

Management of the limited liability company shall be vested in its members, which unless otherwise provided in the operating agreement shall be in proportion to their contribution to the capital of the limited liability company, as adjusted from time to time to properly reflect any additional contributions or withdrawals by the members; however, if provision is made for it in the articles of organization, management of the limited liability company may be vested in a manager or managers who shall be elected by the members in the manner prescribed by the operating agreement of the limited liability company. If the articles of organization provide for the management of the limited liability company by a manager or managers, unless the operating agreement expressly dispenses with or substitutes for the requirement of annual elections, the manager or managers shall be elected annually by the members in a manner provided in the operating agreement. The manager or managers, or persons appointed by the manager or managers, shall also hold the offices and have the responsibilities accorded to them by the members and set out in the operating agreement of the limited liability company.

17-15-117. Contracting debts.

Except as otherwise provided in this act, no debt shall be contracted or liability incurred by or on behalf of a limited liability company, except by one (1) or more of its managers if management of the limited liability company has been vested by the members in a manager or managers or, if management of the limited liability company is retained by the members, then by any member.

17-15-118. Property.

Real and personal property owned or purchased by a limited liability company shall be held and owned, and conveyance made, in the limited liability company name. Instruments and documents providing for the acquisition, mortgage or disposition of property of the limited liability company shall be valid and binding upon the limited liability company if executed by one (1) or more managers of a limited liability company having a manager or managers or one (1) or more members of a limited liability company in which management has been retained in the members.

17-15-119. Division of profits; impairment of capital.

The limited liability company may, from time to time, divide and allocate the profits and losses of its business among the members and among classes of members of the limited liability company upon the basis stipulated in the operating agreement; provided, that after distribution is made, the assets of the limited liability company are in excess of all liabilities of the limited liability company except liabilities to members on account of their contributions. If the operating agreement does not so provide, profits and losses shall be allocated on the basis of the value of the contributions made by each member to the extent they have been received by the limited liability company and have not been returned. Distributions of cash or other assets of a limited liability company shall be allocated among the members and among classes of members in the manner provided in the operating agreement. If the operating agreement does not so provide, distributions shall be made on the basis of the value of the contributions made by each member to the extent they have been received by the limited liability company and have not been returned. The provisions of this section regarding the allocation of losses shall not affect the limitation on liability of members and managers set forth in W.S. 17-15-113.

17-15-120. Withdrawal or reduction of members' contributions to capital.

(a) A member shall not receive out of limited liability company property any part of his or its contribution to capital until:

(i) All liabilities of the limited liability company, except liabilities to members on account of their contributions to capital, have been paid or there remains property of the limited liability company sufficient to pay them;

(ii) The consent of all members is had, unless the return of the contribution to capital may be rightfully demanded as provided in this act;

(iii) The articles of organization are cancelled or so amended as to set out the withdrawal or reduction.

(b) Subject to the provisions of subsection (a) of this section, a member may rightfully demand the return of his or its contribution:

(i) On the dissolution of the limited liability company; or

(ii) Unless otherwise prohibited or restricted in the operating agreement, after the member has given all other members of the limited liability company prior notice in writing in conformity with the operating agreement. If the operating agreement does not prohibit or restrict the right to demand the return of capital and no notice period is specified, a member making the demand must give six (6) months prior notice in writing.

(c) In the absence of a statement in the articles of organization to the contrary or the consent of all members of the limited liability company, a member, irrespective of the nature of his or its contribution, has only the right to demand and receive cash in return for his or its contribution to capital.

(d) A member of a limited liability company may have the limited liability company dissolved and its affairs wound up when:

(i) The member rightfully but unsuccessfully has demanded the return of his or its contribution; or

(ii) The other liabilities of the limited liability company have not been paid, or the limited liability company property is insufficient for their payment and the member would otherwise be entitled to the return of his or its contribution.

17-15-121. Liability of member to company.

(a) A member is liable to the limited liability company:

(i) For the difference between his or its contributions to capital as actually made and that stated in the articles of organization, operating agreement, subscription for contribution or other document executed by the member as having been made by the member; and

(ii) For any unpaid contribution to capital which he or it agreed in the articles of organization, operating agreement or other document executed by the member to make in the future at the time and on the conditions stated in the articles of organization, operating agreement or other document evidencing such agreement.

(b) A member holds as trustee for the limited liability company:

(i) Specific property stated in the articles of organization, operating agreement or other document executed by the member as contributed by such member, but which was not contributed or which has been wrongfully or erroneously returned; and

(ii) Money or other property wrongfully paid or conveyed to such member on account of his or its contribution.

(c) The liabilities of a member as set out in this section can be waived or compromised only by the consent of all members; but a waiver or compromise shall not affect the right of a creditor of the limited liability company who extended credit or whose claim arose after the filing and before a cancellation or amendment of the articles of organization, to enforce the liabilities.

(d) When a contributor has rightfully received the return in whole or in part of the capital of his or its contribution, the contributor is nevertheless liable to the limited liability company, for a period of six (6) years after return of the capital contribution, for any sum, not in excess of the return without interest, necessary to discharge its liability to all creditors of the limited liability company who extended credit during the period the capital contribution was held by the limited liability company or whose claims arose before the return.

17-15-122. Interest in company; transferability of interest.

The interest of all members in a limited liability company constitutes the personal estate of the member, and may be transferred or assigned as provided in the operating agreement. However, if all of the other members of the limited liability company other than the member proposing to dispose of his or its interest do not approve of the proposed transfer or assignment by unanimous written consent, the transferee of the member's interest shall have no right to participate in the management of the business and affairs of the limited liability company or to become a member. The transferee shall only be entitled to receive the share of profits or other compensation by way of income and the return of contributions, to which that member would otherwise be entitled.

17-15-123. Dissolution.

(a) A limited liability company organized under this chapter shall be dissolved upon the occurrence of any of the following events:

(i) When the period fixed for the duration of the limited liability company shall expire;

(ii) By the unanimous written agreement of all members; or

(iii) Upon the death, retirement, resignation, expulsion, bankruptcy, dissolution of a member or occurrence of any other event which terminates the continued membership of a member in the limited liability company, unless the business of the limited liability company is continued by the consent of all the remaining members under a right to do so stated in the articles of organization of the limited liability company.

(b) As soon as possible following the occurrence of any of the events specified in this section effecting the dissolution of the limited liability company, the limited liability company shall execute a statement of intent to dissolve in such form as shall be prescribed by the secretary of state.

17-15-124. Filing of statement of intent to dissolve.

(a) One (1) original and one (1) exact or conformed copy of the statement of intent to dissolve shall be delivered to the secretary of state. If the secretary of state finds that such statement conforms to law, he shall, when all fees and license taxes have been paid as are by law prescribed:

(i) Endorse on each original and exact or conformed copy the word "Filed" and the month, day and year of the filing thereof;

(ii) File the original in his office;

(iii) Return the exact or conformed copy to the limited liability company or its representative.

17-15-125. Effect of filing of dissolving statement.

Upon the filing by the secretary of state of a statement of intent to dissolve, the limited liability company shall cease to carry on its business, except insofar as may be necessary for the winding up of its business, but its separate existence shall continue until a certificate of dissolution has been issued by the secretary of state or until a decree dissolving the limited liability company has been entered by a court of competent jurisdiction.

17-15-126. Distribution of assets upon dissolution.

(a) In settling accounts after dissolution, the liabilities of the limited liability company shall be entitled to payment in the following order:

(i) Those to creditors, in the order of priority as provided by law, except those to members of the limited liability company on account of their contributions;

(ii) Those to members of the limited liability company in respect of their share of the profits and other compensation by way of income on their contributions; and

(iii) Those to members of the limited liability company in respect of their contributions to capital.

(b) Subject to any statement in the operating agreement, members share in the limited liability company assets in respect to their claims for capital and in respect to their claims for profits or for compensation by way of income on their contributions, respectively, in proportion to the respective amounts of the claims.

17-15-127. Articles of dissolution.

(a) When all debts, liabilities and obligations have been paid and discharged or adequate provision has been made therefor and all of the remaining property and assets have been distributed to the members, articles of dissolution shall be delivered to the secretary of state. The statement shall set forth:

(i) The name of the limited liability company;

(ii) That the secretary of state has theretofore filed a statement of intent to dissolve the company and the date on which such statement was filed;

(iii) That all debts, obligations and liabilities have been paid and discharged or that adequate provision has been made therefor;

(iv) That all the remaining property and assets have been distributed among its members in accordance with their respective rights and interests;

(v) That there are no suits pending against the company in any court or that adequate provision has been made for the satisfaction of any judgment, order or decree which may be entered against it in any pending suit.

17-15-128. Filing of articles of dissolution.

(a) One (1) original and one (1) exact or conformed copy of such articles of dissolution shall be delivered to the secretary of state. If the secretary of state finds that such articles of dissolution conform to law, he shall when all fees and license taxes have been paid as are by law prescribed:

(i) Endorse on each original and exact or conformed copy the word "Filed" and the month, day and year of the filing thereof;

(ii) File the original in his office;

(iii) Issue a certificate of dissolution to which he shall affix the exact or conformed copy.

(b) The certificate of dissolution, together with the exact or conformed copy of the articles of dissolution affixed thereto by the secretary of state, shall be returned to the representative of the dissolved limited liability company. Upon the issuance of such certificate of dissolution the existence of the company shall cease, except for the purpose of suits, other proceedings and appropriate action as provided in this act. The manager or managers in office at the time of dissolution, or the survivors of them, shall thereafter be trustees for the members and creditors of the dissolved limited liability company and as such shall have authority to distribute any company property discovered after dissolution, convey real estate and take such other action as may be necessary on behalf of and in the name of such dissolved limited liability company.

17-15-129. Cancellation of certificate of organization; amendment of articles of organization.

(a) The certificate of organization shall be cancelled by the secretary of state upon issuance of the certificate of dissolution.

(b) The articles of organization shall be amended when:

(i) There is a change in the name of the limited liability company or in the amount or the character of the contributions to capital;

(ii) There is a change in the stated purpose of the business of the limited liability company;

(iii) There is a false or erroneous statement in the articles of organization;

(iv) There is a change in the time as stated in the articles of organization for the dissolution of the limited liability company;

(v) A time is fixed for the dissolution of the limited liability company if no time is specified in the articles of organization; or

(vi) The members desire to make a change in any other statement in the articles of organization in order that it shall accurately represent the agreement between them.

(c) The form and time for evidencing an amendment to the articles of organization of a limited liability company shall be promulgated by the secretary of state and shall contain such terms and provisions, consistent with this chapter as shall be determined by the secretary of state, provided that amendments evidencing a change in the amount or the character of the contributions to capital of the limited liability company need be made not more frequently than one (1) time per year. One (1) original and one (1) exact or conformed copy of the amendment shall be forwarded to the secretary of state for filing, accompanied by the requisite filing fee.

(d) Any amendment to the articles of organization shall be adopted in accordance with the operating agreement or with the consent of all members.

17-15-130. Parties to actions.

A member of a limited liability company is not a proper party to proceedings by or against a limited liability company, except where the object is to enforce a member's right against or liability to the limited liability company.

17-15-131. Waiver of notice.

When, under the provisions of this act or under the provisions of the articles of organization or operating agreement of a limited liability company, notice is required to be given to a member or to a manager of a limited liability company having a manager or managers, a waiver in writing signed by the person or persons entitled to the notice, whether before or after the time stated in it, is equivalent to the giving of notice.

17-15-132. Fees; annual tax.

(a) The secretary of state shall charge and collect fees from limited liability companies and foreign limited liability companies for:

(i) Filing the original articles of organization and issuing certificates of organization, or issuing a certificate of authority for a foreign limited liability company, one hundred dollars ($100.00);

(ii) For amending the articles of organization, a filing fee of fifty dollars ($50.00);

(iii) Repealed by Laws 1993, ch. 196, § 5.

(iv) Repealed by Laws 1993, ch. 196, § 5.

(v) Repealed by Laws 1993, ch. 196, § 5.

(vi) An annual fee provided by W.S. 17-16-1630(a) as if the company were a corporation, due and payable on or before the first day of the month of registration from every limited liability company organized under the laws of this state and from every foreign limited liability company which obtains the right to transact business in this state;

(vii) Filing, service and copying fees for those services provided by his office for which a fee is not otherwise established. A fee shall not exceed the cost of providing the service.

(b) Except for articles of organization, any document to be filed with the secretary of state shall be signed by the member, members, manager, managers or other authorized individual as set forth in the operating agreement. A person signing a document, including the articles of organization, he knows is false in any material respect with intent that the document be delivered to the secretary of state for filing under this act is guilty of a misdemeanor punishable by a fine of not more than one thousand dollars ($1,000.00), by imprisonment for not more than six (6) months, or both.

(c) Any foreign limited liability company transacting business in this state without qualifying is subject to the penalties provided by W.S. 17-16-1502(d).

17-15-133. Unauthorized assumption of powers.

All persons who assume to act as a limited liability company without authority to do so shall be jointly and severally liable for all debts and liabilities.

17-15-134. Charge for service of process.

The secretary of state shall charge and collect a fee at the time of any service of process on him as resident agent of a limited liability company, which may be recovered as taxable costs by the party to the suit or action causing the service to be made if the party prevails in the suit or action.

17-15-135. Applicability of provisions to foreign and interstate commerce.

The provisions of this act shall apply to commerce with foreign nations and among the several states only as permitted by law.

17-15-136. Repealed by Laws 1993, ch. 196, § 5.

17-15-137. Secretary of state powers.

The secretary of state has the power reasonably necessary to perform the duties required of him by this act. The secretary of state shall promulgate reasonable rules and regulations necessary to carry out the purposes of this act.

17-15-138. Correcting filed document.

(a) A company or foreign company may correct a document filed by the secretary of state if the document:

(i) Contains an incorrect statement; or

(ii) Was defectively executed, attested, sealed, verified or acknowledged.

(b) A document is corrected:

(i) By preparing articles of correction that:

(A) Describe the document, including its filing date, or attach a copy of the document to the articles of correction;

(B) Specify the incorrect statement and the reason it is incorrect or the manner in which the execution was defective; and

(C) Correct the incorrect statement or defective execution.

(ii) By delivering the articles of correction to the secretary of state for filing.

17-15-139. Merger.

(a) Pursuant to a written plan of merger, a domestic limited liability company may merge with one (1) or more domestic or foreign limited liability companies, limited partnerships or corporations if:

(i) The merger is not prohibited by the articles of organization or operating agreement of any domestic limited liability company that is a party to the merger, and each domestic limited liability company party to the merger approves the plan of merger in accordance with W.S. 17-15-140 and complies with the terms of its articles of organization and operating agreement;

(ii) Each domestic limited partnership that is a party to the merger complies with any provisions of law applicable to merger of domestic limited partnership;

(iii) Each domestic corporation that is a party to the merger complies with any provisions of law applicable to merger of domestic corporations;

(iv) The merger is permitted by the laws under which each foreign limited liability company, foreign limited partnership and foreign corporation party to the merger is organized, formed or incorporated, and each such foreign limited liability company, limited partnership or corporation complies with those laws in effecting the merger;

(v) No member of a domestic limited liability company that is a party to the merger will, as a result of the merger, become personally liable for the liabilities or obligations of any other person or entity unless that member approves the plan of merger and otherwise consents to becoming personally liable;

(vi) In the case of a merger of a limited liability company to which one (1) or more domestic or foreign corporations are parties, a domestic or foreign corporation or limited liability company party to the merger is the surviving entity of the merger.

(b) The plan of merger shall set forth:

(i) The name of each domestic or foreign limited liability company, limited partnership or corporation planning to merge and the name of the surviving domestic or foreign limited liability company, limited partnership or corporation into which each other domestic or foreign limited liability company, limited partnership or corporation plans to merge;

(ii) The name of the state or country under whose law each domestic or foreign limited liability company, limited partnership or corporation planning to merge is organized, formed or incorporated and the name of the state or country or organization, formation or incorporation of the surviving domestic or foreign limited liability company, limited partnership or corporation;

(iii) The terms and conditions of the merger; and

(iv) The manner and basis of converting the membership interests of each domestic limited liability company, the partnership interests of each domestic limited partnership and the shares of each domestic corporation party to the merger into membership interests, partnership interests, shares, obligations or other securities of the surviving or any other domestic or foreign limited liability company, limited partnership or corporation or into cash or other property in whole or in part, and the manner and basis of converting rights to acquire the membership interests of each domestic limited liability company, the partnership interests of each domestic limited partnership and the shares of each domestic corporation party to the merger into rights to acquire membership interests, partnership interests, shares, obligations or other securities of the surviving or any other domestic or foreign limited liability company, limited partnership or corporation or into cash or other property in whole or in part.

(c) The plan of merger may set forth:

(i) If a domestic limited liability company is to be the surviving entity, amendments to the articles of organization or the operating agreement of that limited liability company;

(ii) If the merger is not to be effective upon the issuance of the certificate of merger described in W.S. 17-15-141(c) by the secretary of state, the future effective date or time of the merger; or

(iii) Other provisions relating to the merger.

17-15-140. Approval of merger by domestic limited liability company.

(a) Each domestic limited liability company that is to be a party to a proposed merger shall approve the proposed merger, unless the articles of organization or the operating agreement of that limited liability company provide otherwise, by the unanimous vote of the members of the limited liability company. However, a provision of a limited liability company's operating agreement purporting to authorize the limited liability company to approve a merger by a less than unanimous vote of the members shall be effective to permit approval of a merger by a less than unanimous vote only if either:

(i) The operating agreement included that provision at the time each member who does not vote in favor of the merger became bound by the operating agreement; or

(ii) The provision was added to the operating agreement through an amendment to which each member who does not vote in favor of the merger specifically consented.

(b) Any plan of merger may provide for the manner, if any, in which the plan may be amended by a domestic limited liability company party to the merger at any time before the effective date of the certificate of merger issued by the secretary of state for the merger.

(c) If an amendment to a plan of merger is made in accordance with subsection (b) of this section, and articles of merger already have been filed with the secretary of state, amended articles of merger shall be filed with the secretary of state before the effective date of any certificate of merger issued by the secretary of state for the articles of merger which the amended articles are to supersede.

(d) Unless the domestic limited liability company's articles of organization or operating agreement or the plan of merger provides otherwise, after the merger has been authorized and at any time before the effective date of the certificate of merger issued by the secretary of state for the merger, the merger may be abandoned by majority vote of the members of the domestic limited liability company. If articles of merger already have been filed with the secretary of state, written notice of abandonment shall be filed with the secretary of state before the effective date of the certificate of merger.

17-15-141. Articles of merger.

(a) After a plan of merger is approved by each domestic or foreign limited liability company, limited partnership or corporation party to the merger, the surviving domestic or foreign limited liability company, limited partnership or corporation shall file with the secretary of state articles of merger setting forth:

(i) The plan of merger;

(ii) The address including street and number, if any, of its principal office under the laws of the jurisdiction in which it was organized, formed or incorporated, if the surviving entity of the merger is a foreign limited liability company not registered with the secretary of state under W.S. 17-16-1533, a foreign limited partnership not registered with the secretary of state under W.S. 17-14-1001 et seq., or a foreign corporation without a certificate of authority issued by the secretary of state under W.S. 17-16-1501 et seq.;

(iii) A statement that the plan of merger was adopted by each domestic limited liability company party to the merger in accordance with W.S. 17-15-140 and by each domestic limited partnership party to the merger in accordance with any applicable provisions of Wyoming law; and

(iv) Any additional information required by W.S. 17-16-1105, if a domestic corporation is a party to the merger.

(b) If a foreign limited liability company, limited partnership or corporation is a party to the merger, the articles of merger shall contain a statement that the merger is permitted by the state or country under whose law that limited liability company is organized, that limited partnership is formed or that corporation is incorporated and that the foreign limited liability company, limited partnership or corporation has complied with that law in effecting the merger.

(c) If the secretary of state finds that the articles of merger comply with the requirements of law and that all required fees have been paid, he shall issue a certificate of merger. The certificate of merger shall become effective when issued unless the plan of merger specifies a future effective date, in which case the certificate of merger shall be effective on the earlier of:

(i) That date; or

(ii) The date that is fifteen (15) days after the date on which the secretary of state issues the certificate of merger.

17-15-142. Effect of merger.

(a) When a merger takes effect:

(i) The separate existence of every domestic limited liability company that is a party to the merger except the surviving domestic limited liability company, if any, ceases;

(ii) The title to all real estate and other property owned by each domestic limited liability company party to the merger is vested in the surviving domestic or foreign limited liability company, limited partnership or corporation without reversion of impairment;

(iii) The surviving domestic or foreign limited liability company, limited partnership or corporation obtains all liabilities of each domestic limited liability company party to the merger;

(iv) A proceeding pending by or against any domestic limited liability company party to the merger may be continued as if the merger had not occurred, or the surviving domestic or foreign limited liability company, limited partnership or corporation may be substituted in the proceeding for the domestic limited liability company whose existence ceased;

(v) The articles of organization and operating agreement of that limited liability company are amended to the extent provided in the plan of merger, if a domestic limited liability company is the surviving entity of the merger; and

(vi) The former holders of membership interests of every domestic limited liability company party to the merger are entitled only to the rights provided in the plan of merger.

17-15-143. Continuance.

(a) Subject to subsection (b) of this section, any limited liability company organized for any purpose except acting as an insurer as defined in W.S. 26-1-102(a)(xvi), or acting as a financial institution as described by W.S. 13-1-101(a)(ix) under the laws of any foreign jurisdiction may, if the foreign jurisdiction confirms in writing that the limited liability company's domicile has terminated in the foreign jurisdiction, apply to the secretary of state for registration under this act. The secretary of state may issue a certificate of registration upon receipt of an application supported by articles of continuance as provided by this act together with the statements, information and documents set out in subsection (c) of this section. The certificate of registration may then be issued continuing the foreign limited liability company in Wyoming as if it had been organized in this state. The certificate of registration may be subject to any limitations and conditions as may appear proper to the secretary of state.

(b) The secretary of state shall cause notice of issuance of a certificate of registration to be given forthwith to the proper officer of the foreign jurisdiction in which the limited liability company was previously organized.

(c) The articles of continuance filed by a foreign limited liability company with the secretary of state shall contain:

(i) A certified copy of its original articles of organization and all amendments thereto or its equivalent basic charter;

(ii) The names of the limited liability company and the foreign jurisdiction in which it has previously been lawfully organized;

(iii) The date of organization and the period of duration;

(iv) The address of its principal mailing address;

(v) The name and address of the proposed registered agent in this state;

(vi) The business purposes which it proposes to pursue in this state;

(vii) The names and respective business addresses of its members or, if the limited liability company has a manager or managers, the names and respective business addresses of the manager or managers;

(viii) Repealed By Laws 2000, Ch. 35, § 2.

(ix) A statement that the limited liability company will abide by the constitution and laws of this state;

(x) Any additional information necessary or appropriate to enable the secretary of state to determine whether the limited liability company is entitled to a certificate of registration evidencing its authority to transact business in the state and to determine and assess any fees and taxes under the laws of this state;

(xi) Any additional information permitted in articles of organization under W.S. 17-15-107(a)(xi).

(d) The application shall be executed by the manager or managers if any or by any member who is authorized to execute the application on behalf of the limited liability company and shall be verified by the officer signing the application.

(e) The provisions of the articles of continuance may, without expressly so stating, vary from the provisions of the limited liability company's articles of organization or equivalent basic charter or other authorization, if the variation is one which a company organized under the Wyoming Limited Liability Company Act could effect by way of amendment to its articles of organization. Upon issuance of a certificate of continuance by the secretary of state, the articles of continuance shall be deemed to be the articles of organization of the continued limited liability company. The limited liability company may elect to incorporate by reference in the articles of continuance its basic charter or other authorization which has been adopted by it in the foreign jurisdiction, in order to permit the same to continue to act as the articles of organization, provided, however, that the basic charter or other authorization shall be deemed amended to the extent necessary to make the same conform to the laws of Wyoming and to the provisions of the articles of continuance.

(f) Except for the purpose of W.S. 16-6-101 through 16-6-118, the existence of any limited liability company heretofore or hereafter issued a certificate of continuation under this act shall be deemed to have commenced on the date the limited liability company commenced its existence in the jurisdiction in which it was first formed, organized or otherwise came into being. The laws of Wyoming shall apply to a limited liability company continuing under this act to the same extent as if it had been organized under the laws of Wyoming from and after the issuance of a certificate of continuation under this act by the secretary of state. When a foreign limited liability company is continued under this act, the continuance shall not affect the ownership of its property, or its liability for any existing obligations, causes of action, claims, pending or threatened prosecution or civil or administration actions, convictions, rulings, orders or judgments.

(g) Continuance under this act does not deprive a member of any right or privilege that he claims under, or relieve any member of any liability in respect of, his membership.

17-15-144. Flexible limited liability company.

(a) The provisions of this section shall apply only to those limited liability companies which have elected to be flexible limited liability companies by an affirmative statement in their articles of organization expressly referring to W.S. 17-15-107(a)(x). All provisions of the Wyoming Limited Liability Company Act shall be applicable to a flexible limited liability company except to the extent expressly replaced or superseded by the provisions of this section.

(b) Notwithstanding any other provision contained in this act, the interest of a member of a flexible limited liability company is assignable in whole or in part except as provided in the operating agreement. The assignee of a member's interest in a flexible limited liability company shall have no rights other than those permitted to assignees under W.S. 17-15-122 except as provided in the operating agreement or as permitted by the unanimous consent of the members of the flexible limited liability company other than the member assigning his interest in the flexible limited liability company.

(c) Notwithstanding any other provision in this act, a flexible limited liability company is dissolved and its affairs shall be wound up upon the occurrence of any event described in W.S. 17-15-123(a) or upon the happening of any other event or events specified in the operating agreement, unless the business of the flexible limited liability company is continued either by the consent of all of the remaining members following the occurrence of any such event or pursuant to a right to continue stated in the operating agreement.

(d) Notwithstanding any other provision in this act, a flexible limited liability company may have fewer than two (2) members.

(e) Notwithstanding any other provision in this act, a flexible limited liability company may elect to set forth in its articles of organization a provision which allows for the personal liability of its officers, agents, managers or members. If the articles of organization of a flexible limited liability company do not expressly set forth such election and specifically refer to this subsection, it shall be presumed that the flexible limited liability company has not made the election authorized under this subsection.

17-15-145. Rights of creditor.

On application to a court of competent jurisdiction by a judgment creditor of a member of a limited liability company or a member's transferee, the court may charge the member's distributional interest in the limited liability company with payment of the unsatisfied amount of the judgment with interest. To the extent so charged, the judgment creditor has only the rights of a transferee of the member's interest as provided in W.S. 17-15-122. The charging order is the exclusive remedy by which a judgment creditor of the member or transferee may satisfy a judgment against the member's interest in a limited liability company. This section does not deprive any member of a limited liability company of the benefit of any exemption laws applicable to the member's interest.

17-15-146. Conversion of limited liability company to corporation.

(a) A domestic limited liability company may be converted to a domestic corporation pursuant to this section.

(b) A foreign limited liability company may be converted to a domestic corporation pursuant to this section.

(c) The terms and conditions of a conversion of a limited liability company to a corporation shall be approved by all the members or by a number or percentage specified in the articles of organization or the operating agreement, provided that any member who will be liable to a greater extent after conversion, solely by reason of being an owner, shall approve the terms and conditions of the conversion.

(d) After the conversion is approved by the members, the limited liability company shall file articles of incorporation which satisfy the requirements of W.S. 17-16-202 and include:

(i) A statement that the limited liability company was converted to a corporation;

(ii) Its former name;

(iii) The state of formation and the date of organization; and

(iv) A statement of the number of votes cast by the members for and against conversion and if the vote is less than unanimous, the number or percentage required to approve the conversion under the articles of organization or the operating agreement.

(e) The conversion takes effect when the articles of incorporation are filed or at any later date specified in the articles.

17-15-147. Effect of conversion.

(a) Upon conversion:

(i) All property owned by the limited liability company remains in the corporation;

(ii) All obligations of the converting limited liability company continue as obligations of the resulting corporation; and

(iii) An action or proceeding pending against the converting limited liability company may be continued as if the conversion had not occurred.

CHAPTER 16 : WYOMING BUSINESS CORPORATION ACT

ARTICLE 1
GENERAL PROVISIONS

17-16-101. Short title.

This act shall be known and may be cited as the "Wyoming Business Corporation Act."

17-16-102. Reservation of power to amend or repeal.

The legislature has power to amend or repeal all or part of this act at any time and all domestic and foreign corporations subject to this act are governed by the amendment or repeal.

Subarticle B. Filing Documents

17-16-120. Filing requirements.

(a) A document shall satisfy the requirements of this section, and of any other section that adds to or varies from these requirements, to be entitled to filing by the secretary of state.

(b) This act shall require or permit filing the document in the office of the secretary of state.

(c) The document shall contain the information required by this act. It may contain other information as well.

(d) The document shall be typewritten or printed.

(e) The document shall be in the English language. A corporate name need not be in English if written in English letters or Arabic or Roman numerals, and the certificate of existence required of foreign corporations need not be in English if accompanied by an English translation acceptable to the secretary of state.

(f) The document shall be executed:

(i) By the chairman of the board of directors of a domestic or foreign corporation, by its president, or by another of its officers;

(ii) If directors have not been selected or the corporation has not been formed, by an incorporator; or

(iii) If the corporation is in the hands of a receiver, trustee, or other court-appointed fiduciary, by that fiduciary.

(g) The person executing the document shall sign it manually and shall state beneath or opposite his signature his name and the capacity in which he signs. The document may but need not contain:

(i) The corporate seal;

(ii) An attestation by the secretary or an assistant secretary;

(iii) An acknowledgment, verification or proof.

(h) If the secretary of state has prescribed a mandatory form for the document under W.S. 17-16-121, the document shall be in or on the prescribed form.

(j) The document shall be delivered to the office of the secretary of state for filing and shall be accompanied by:

(i) One (1) exact or conformed copy except as provided in W.S. 17-16-503 and 17-16-1509;

(ii) The correct filing fee; and

(iii) Any franchise tax, license fee, or penalty required by this act or other law.

17-16-121. Forms.

(a) If the secretary of state so requires, use of forms provided by the secretary of state pursuant to this subsection is mandatory. The secretary of state may prescribe and furnish on request forms for:

(i) An application for a certificate of existence;

(ii) A foreign corporation's application for a certificate of authority to transact business in this state;

(iii) A foreign corporation's application for a certificate of withdrawal;

(iv) The annual report;

(v) A foreign corporation's application for a certificate of continuance;

(vi) An application for a certificate of transfer;

(vii) A foreign corporation's application for certificate of domestication; and

(viii) A consent of registered agent to appointment.

(b) The secretary of state may prescribe and furnish on request forms for other documents required or permitted to be filed by this act but their use is not mandatory.

17-16-122. Filing, service and copying fees.

The secretary of state shall set and collect filing, service and copying fees to recover his costs to administer this act. Fees shall not exceed the costs of providing these services.

17-16-123. Effective time and date of document.

(a) Except as provided in subsection (b) of this section and W.S. 17-16-124(c), a document accepted for filing is effective:

(i) At the time of filing on the date it is filed, as evidenced by the secretary of state's date and time endorsement on the original document; or

(ii) At the time specified in the document as its effective time on the date it is filed.

(b) A document may specify a delayed effective time and date, and if it does so the document becomes effective at the time and date specified. If a delayed effective date but no time is specified, the document is effective at the close of business on that date. A delayed effective date for a document may not be later than the ninetieth (90th) day after the date it is filed.

17-16-124. Correcting filed document.

(a) A domestic or foreign corporation may correct a document filed by the secretary of state if the document:

(i) Contains an incorrect statement; or

(ii) Was defectively executed, attested, sealed, verified, or acknowledged.

(b) A document is corrected:

(i) By preparing articles of correction that:

(A) Describe the document, including its filing date, or attach a copy of the document to the articles of correction;

(B) Specify the incorrect statement and the reason it is incorrect or the manner in which the execution was defective; and

(C) Correct the incorrect statement or defective execution.

(ii) By delivering the articles of correction to the secretary of state for filing.

(c) Articles of correction are effective on the effective date of the document they correct except as to persons relying on the uncorrected document and adversely affected by the correction. As to those persons, articles of correction are effective when filed.

17-16-125. Filing duty of secretary of state.

(a) If a document delivered to the office of the secretary of state for filing satisfies the requirements of W.S. 17-16-120, the secretary of state shall file the document.

(b) The secretary of state files a document by stamping or otherwise endorsing "Filed," together with his official title and the date and time of filing, on both the original and the document copy and on the receipt for the filing fee. After filing a document, except as provided in W.S. 17-16-503 and 17-16-1510, the secretary of state shall deliver the document copy, with the filing fee receipt (or acknowledgement of receipt if no fee is required) attached, to the domestic or foreign corporation or its representative. The secretary of state, in his discretion, may issue a certificate evidencing the filing of a document upon the payment of the requisite fee.

(c) If the secretary of state refuses to file a document, he shall return it to the domestic or foreign corporation or its representative within five (5) days after the document was delivered, together with a brief, written explanation of the reason for his refusal.

(d) The secretary of state's duty to file documents under this section is ministerial. His filing or refusing to file a document does not:

(i) Affect the validity or invalidity of the document in whole or part;

(ii) Relate to the correctness or incorrectness of information contained in the document; or

(iii) Create a presumption that the document is valid or invalid or that information contained in the document is correct or incorrect.

17-16-126. Appeal from secretary of state's refusal to file document.

(a) If the secretary of state refuses to file a document delivered to his office for filing, the domestic or foreign corporation may, within thirty (30) days after the return of the document, appeal the refusal to the district court of the county where the corporation's principal office is located in the state or, if the corporation does not have a principal office in the state, the district court of the county where its registered office is or will be located, or the district court of the county of residence of an incorporator for a domestic corporation, or in the district court of Laramie county. The appeal is commenced by petitioning the court to compel filing the document and by attaching to the petition the document and the secretary of state's explanation of his refusal to file.

(b) The court may summarily order the secretary of state to file the document or take other action the court considers appropriate.

(c) The court's final decision may be appealed as in other civil proceedings.

17-16-127. Evidentiary effect of copy of filed document.

A certificate attached to a copy of a document filed by the secretary of state, bearing his signature (which may be in facsimile) and the seal of this state, is conclusive evidence that the original document is on file with the secretary of state.

17-16-128. Certificate of existence.

(a) Anyone may apply to the secretary of state to furnish a certificate of existence for a domestic corporation or a certificate of authorization for a foreign corporation.

(b) A certificate of existence or authorization sets forth:

(i) The domestic corporation's corporate name or the foreign corporation's corporate name used in this state;

(ii) That:

(A) The domestic corporation is duly incorporated under the law of this state, the date of its incorporation, and the period of its duration if less than perpetual; or

(B) The foreign corporation is authorized to transact business in this state.

(iii) That all fees, taxes, and penalties owed to this state have been paid, if:

(A) Payment is reflected in the records of the secretary of state; and

(B) Nonpayment affects the existence or authorization of the domestic or foreign corporation.

(iv) That its most recent annual report required by W.S. 17-16-1630 has been filed by the secretary of state;

(v) That articles of dissolution have not been filed; and

(vi) Other facts of record in the office of the secretary of state that may be requested by the applicant.

(c) Subject to any qualification stated in the certificate, a certificate of existence or authorization issued by the secretary of state may be relied upon as conclusive evidence that the domestic or foreign corporation is in existence or is authorized to transact business in this state.

17-16-129. Penalty for signing false document.

(a) A person commits an offense if he signs a document he knows is false in any material respect with intent that the document be delivered to the secretary of state for filing.

(b) An offense under this section is a misdemeanor and shall be punished by a fine not exceeding one thousand dollars ($1,000.00), or by imprisonment not exceeding six (6) months, or both.

17-16-130. Powers.

The secretary of state has the power reasonably necessary to perform the duties required of him by this act. The secretary of state shall promulgate reasonable forms, rules and regulations necessary to carry out the purposes of this act.

17-16-140. Definitions.

(a) In this act:

(i) "Articles of incorporation" include amended and restated articles of incorporation and articles of merger;

(ii) "Authorized shares" means the shares of all classes a domestic or foreign corporation is authorized to issue;

(iii) "Conspicuous" means so written that a reasonable person against whom the writing is to operate should have noticed it. For example, printing in italics or boldface or contrasting color, or typing in capitals or underlined, is conspicuous;

(iv) "Corporation" or "domestic corporation" means a corporation for profit, which is not a foreign corporation, incorporated under or subject to the provisions of this act;

(v) "Deliver" includes mail;

(vi) "Distribution" means a direct or indirect transfer of money or other property, except the corporation's own shares, or incurrence of indebtedness by a corporation to or for the benefit of its shareholders in respect of any of its shares. A distribution may be in the form of a declaration or payment of a dividend, a purchase, redemption, or other acquisition of shares, a distribution of indebtedness, or otherwise;

(vii) "Effective date of notice" is defined in W.S. 17-16-141;

(viii) "Employee" includes an officer but not a director. A director may accept duties that make him also an employee;

(ix) "Entity" includes corporation and foreign corporation, not-for-profit corporation, profit and not-for-profit unincorporated association, business trust, estate, partnership, trust, or two (2) or more persons having a joint or common economic interest, and state, United States or foreign government;

(x) "Foreign corporation" means a corporation for profit incorporated under a law other than the law of this state;

(xi) "Governmental subdivision" includes authority, county, district, municipality, and any other political subdivision;

(xii) "Includes" denotes a partial definition;

(xiii) "Individual" includes the estate of an incompetent or deceased individual;

(xiv) "Means" denotes an exhaustive definition;

(xv) "Net assets" means the amount by which the total assets of a corporation exceed the total debts of the corporation;

(xvi) "Notice" is defined in W.S. 17-16-141;

(xvii) "Person" includes an individual, partnership, joint venture, corporation, joint stock company, limited liability company or any other association or entity, public or private;

(xviii) "Principal office" means the office within or outside of this state, so designated in the annual report;

(xix) "Proceeding" includes civil suit and criminal, administrative, and investigatory action;

(xx) "Record date" means the date established under article 6 or 7 on which a corporation determines the identity of its shareholders and their shareholdings for purposes of this act. The determinations shall be made as of the close of business on the record date unless another time for doing so is specified when the record date is fixed;

(xxi) "Secretary" means the corporate officer to whom the board of directors has delegated responsibility under W.S. 17-16-840(c) for custody of the minutes of the meetings of the board of directors and of the shareholders and for authenticating records of the corporation;

(xxii) "Shareholder" means the person in whose name shares are registered in the records of a corporation or the beneficial owner of shares to the extent of the rights granted by a nominee certificate on file with a corporation;

(xxiii) "Shares" means the units into which the proprietary interests in a corporation are divided;

(xxiv) "State," when referring to a part of the United States, includes a state and commonwealth, and their agencies and governmental subdivisions, and a territory and insular possession, and their agencies and governmental subdivisions, of the United States;

(xxv) "Subscriber" means a person who subscribes for shares in a corporation, whether before or after incorporation;

(xxvi) "United States" includes district, authority, bureau, commission, department, and any other agency of the United States;

(xxvii) "Voting group" means all shares of one (1) or more classes or series that under the articles of incorporation or this act are entitled to vote and be counted together collectively on a matter at a meeting of shareholders. All shares entitled by the articles of incorporation or this act to vote generally on the matter are for that purpose a single voting group;

(xxviii) "Electronic transmission" or "transmitted electronically" means any process of communication not directly involving the physical transfer of paper that is suitable for the retention, retrieval and reproduction of information by the recipient;

(xxix) "This act" means W.S. 17-16-101 through 17-16-1803.

17-16-141. Notice.

(a) Notice under this act shall be in writing unless oral notice is reasonable under the circumstances.

(b) Notice may be communicated in person; by telephone, telegraph, teletype, or other form of wire or wireless communication; or by mail or private carrier. If these forms of personal notice are impracticable, notice may be communicated by a newspaper of general circulation in the area where published; or by radio, television, or other form of public broadcast communication.

(c) Written notice by a domestic or foreign corporation to its shareholder, if in a comprehensible form, is effective when mailed, if mailed postpaid and correctly addressed to the shareholder's address shown in the corporation's current record of shareholders.

(d) Written notice to a domestic or foreign corporation authorized to transact business in this state may be addressed to its registered agent at its registered office or to the corporation or its secretary at its principal office shown in its most recent annual report or, in the case of a foreign corporation that has not yet delivered an annual report, in its application for a certificate of authority.

(e) Except as provided in subsection (c) of this section, written notice, if in a comprehensible form, is effective at the earliest of the following:

(i) When received;

(ii) Five (5) days after its deposit in the United States mail, as evidenced by the postmark, if mailed postpaid and correctly addressed; or

(iii) On the date shown on the return receipt, if sent by registered or certified mail, or comparable private carrier, return receipt requested, and the receipt is signed, either manually or in facsimile, by or on behalf of the addressee.

(f) Oral notice is effective when communicated if communicated in a comprehensible manner.

(g) If this act prescribes notice requirements for particular circumstances, those requirements govern. If articles of incorporation or bylaws prescribe notice requirements, not inconsistent with this section or other provisions of this act, those requirements govern.

17-16-142. Number of shareholders.

(a) For purposes of this act, the following identified as a shareholder in a corporation's current record of shareholders constitutes one (1) shareholder:

(i) Three (3) or fewer coowners;

(ii) A corporation, partnership, trust, estate, or other entity; or

(iii) The trustees, guardians, custodians, or other fiduciaries of a single trust, estate, or account.

(b) For purposes of this act, shareholdings registered in substantially similar names constitute one (1) shareholder if it is reasonable to believe that the names represent the same person.

ARTICLE 2
INCORPORATION

17-16-201. Incorporators.

One (1) or more persons may act as the incorporator or incorporators of a corporation by delivering articles of incorporation to the secretary of state for filing.

17-16-202. Articles of incorporation.

(a) The articles of incorporation shall set forth:

(i) A corporate name for the corporation that satisfies the requirements of W.S. 17-16-401;

(ii) The number of shares the corporation is authorized to issue, which may be unlimited if so stated;

(iii) The street address of the corporation's initial registered office and the name of its initial registered agent at that office; and

(iv) The name and address of each incorporator.

(b) The articles of incorporation may set forth:

(i) The names and addresses of the individuals who are to serve as the initial directors;

(ii) Provisions not inconsistent with law including:

(A) The purpose or purposes for which the corporation is organized;

(B) Managing the business and regulating the affairs of the corporation;

(C) Defining, limiting, and regulating the powers of the corporation, its board of directors, and shareholders;

(D) A par value for authorized shares or classes of shares;

(E) The imposition of personal liability on shareholders for the debts of the corporation to a specified extent and upon specified conditions.

(iii) Any provision that under this act is required or permitted to be set forth in the bylaws;

(iv) A provision eliminating or limiting the liability of a director to the corporation or its shareholders for money damages for any action taken, or any failure to take any action, as a director, except liability for:

(A) The amount of financial benefit received by a director to which he is not entitled;

(B) An intentional infliction of harm on the corporation or shareholders;

(C) A violation of W.S. 17-16-833; or

(D) An intentional violation of criminal law; and

(v) A provision permitting or making obligatory indemnification of a director for liability (as defined in W.S. 17-16-850(a)(v)) to any person for any action taken, or failure to take any action, as a director, except liability for:

(A) Receipt of a financial benefit to which he is not entitled;

(B) An intentional infliction of harm on the corporation or its shareholders;

(C) A violation of W.S. 17-16-833; or

(D) An intentional violation of criminal law.

(c) The articles of incorporation need not set forth any of the corporate powers enumerated in this act.

(d) The articles of incorporation shall be accompanied by a written consent to appointment manually signed by the registered agent.

17-16-203. Incorporation.

(a) Unless a delayed effective date is specified, the corporate existence begins when the articles of incorporation are filed.

(b) The secretary of state's filing of the articles of incorporation is conclusive proof that the incorporators satisfied all conditions precedent to incorporation except in a proceeding by the state to cancel or revoke the incorporation or involuntarily dissolve the corporation.

17-16-204. Liability for preincorporation transactions.

All persons purporting to act as or on behalf of a corporation, knowing there was no incorporation under this act, are jointly and severally liable for all liabilities created while so acting.

17-16-205. Organization of corporation.

(a) After incorporation:

(i) If initial directors are named in the articles of incorporation, the initial directors shall hold an organizational meeting, at the call of a majority of the directors, to complete the organization of the corporation by appointing officers, adopting bylaws, and carrying on any other business brought before the meeting;

(ii) If initial directors are not named in the articles, the incorporator or incorporators shall hold an organizational meeting at the call of a majority of the incorporators to:

(A) Elect directors and complete the organization of the corporation; or

(B) Elect a board of directors who shall complete the organization of the corporation.

(b) Action required or permitted by this act to be taken by incorporators at an organizational meeting may be taken without a meeting if the action taken is evidenced by one (1) or more written consents describing the action taken and signed, either manually or in facsimile, by each incorporator.

(c) An organizational meeting may be held within or outside of this state.

(d) Within sixty (60) days after filing articles of incorporation, a corporation which maintains a registered agent required to register by W.S. 17-16-505, shall provide information to the registered agent as required by W.S. 17-16-507.

17-16-206. Bylaws.

(a) The incorporators or board of directors of a corporation shall adopt initial bylaws for the corporation.

(b) The bylaws of a corporation may contain any provision for managing the business and regulating the affairs of the corporation that is not inconsistent with law or the articles of incorporation.

(c) If bylaws are not adopted:

(i) An annual meeting shall be held within three (3) months after the close of the corporation's fiscal year;

(ii) The required officers shall be the president, the secretary and the treasurer; and

(iii) Bylaws may be adopted at any director or shareholder meeting.

17-16-207. Emergency bylaws.

(a) Unless the articles of incorporation provide otherwise, the board of directors of a corporation may adopt bylaws to be effective only in an emergency defined in subsection (d) of this section. The emergency bylaws, which are subject to amendment or repeal by the shareholders, may make all provisions necessary for managing the corporation during the emergency, including:

(i) Procedures for calling a meeting of the board of directors;

(ii) Quorum requirements for the meeting; and

(iii) Designation of additional or substitute directors.

(b) All provisions of the regular bylaws consistent with the emergency bylaws remain effective during the emergency. The emergency bylaws are not effective after the emergency ends.

(c) Corporate action taken in good faith in accordance with the emergency bylaws:

(i) Binds the corporation; and

(ii) May not be used to impose liability on a corporate director, officer, employee, or agent.

(d) An emergency exists for purposes of this section if a quorum of the corporation's directors cannot readily be assembled because of some extraordinary event.

ARTICLE 3
PURPOSES AND POWERS

17-16-301. Purposes.

(a) Every corporation incorporated under this act has the purpose of engaging in any lawful business unless a more limited purpose is set forth in the articles of incorporation.

(b) A corporation engaging in a business that is subject to regulation under another statute of this state may incorporate under this act only if permitted by, and subject to all limitations of, the other statute.

17-16-302. General powers.

(a) Unless its articles of incorporation provide otherwise, every corporation has perpetual duration and succession in its corporate name and has the same powers as an individual to do all things necessary or convenient to carry out its business and affairs, including without limitation power to:

(i) Sue and be sued, complain and defend in its corporate name;

(ii) Have a corporate seal, which may be altered at will, and to use it, or a facsimile of it, by impressing or affixing it or in any other manner reproducing it;

(iii) Make and amend bylaws, not inconsistent with its articles of incorporation or with the laws of this state, for managing the business and regulating the affairs of the corporation;

(iv) Purchase, receive, lease, or otherwise acquire, and own, hold, improve, use, and otherwise deal with, real or personal property, or any legal or equitable interest in property, wherever located;

(v) Sell, convey, mortgage, pledge, lease, exchange, and otherwise dispose of all or any part of its property;

(vi) Purchase, receive, subscribe for, or otherwise acquire; own, hold, vote, use, sell, mortgage, lend, pledge, or otherwise dispose of; and deal in and with shares or other interests in, or obligations of, any other entity;

(vii) Make contracts and guarantees, incur liabilities, borrow money, issue its notes, bonds, and other obligations which may be convertible into or include the option to purchase other securities of the corporation, and secure any of its obligations by mortgage or pledge of any of its property, franchises, or income;

(viii) Lend money, invest and reinvest its funds, and receive and hold real and personal property as security for repayment;

(ix) Be a promoter, partner, member, associate, or manager of any partnership, joint venture, trust, or other entity;

(x) Conduct its business, locate offices, and exercise the powers granted by this act within or without this state;

(xi) Elect directors and appoint officers, employees, and agents of the corporation, define their duties, fix their compensation, and lend them money and credit;

(xii) Pay pensions and establish pension plans, pension trusts, profit sharing plans, share bonus plans, share option plans, and benefit or incentive plans for any or all of its current or former directors, officers, employees, and agents;

(xiii) Make donations for the public welfare or for charitable, scientific, or educational purposes;

(xiv) Transact any lawful business; and

(xv) Make payments or donations, or do any other act, not inconsistent with law, that furthers the business and affairs of the corporation.

17-16-303. Emergency powers.

(a) In anticipation of or during an emergency defined in subsection (d) of this section, the board of directors of a corporation may:

(i) Modify lines of succession to accommodate the incapacity of any director, officer, employee, or agent; and

(ii) Relocate the principal office, designate alternative principal offices or regional offices, or authorize the officers to do so.

(b) During an emergency defined in subsection (d) of this section, unless emergency bylaws provide otherwise:

(i) Notice of a meeting of the board of directors need be given only to those directors whom it is practicable to reach and may be given in any practicable manner, including by publication and radio; and

(ii) One (1) or more officers of the corporation present at a meeting of the board of directors may be deemed to be directors for the meeting, in order of rank and within the same rank in order of seniority, as necessary to achieve a quorum.

(c) Corporate action taken in good faith during an emergency under this section to further the ordinary business affairs of the corporation:

(i) Binds the corporation; and

(ii) May not be used to impose liability on a corporate director, officer, employee, or agent.

(d) An emergency exists for the purposes of this section if a quorum of the corporation's directors cannot readily be assembled because of some extraordinary event.

17-16-304. Ultra vires.

(a) Except as provided in subsection (b) of this section, the validity of corporate action may not be challenged on the ground that the corporation lacks or lacked power to act.

(b) A corporation's power to act may be challenged in a proceeding by:

(i) A shareholder against the corporation to enjoin the act;

(ii) The corporation, directly, derivatively, or through a receiver, trustee, or other legal representative, against an incumbent or former director, officer, employee, or agent of the corporation; or

(iii) The attorney general under W.S. 17-16-1430.

(c) In a shareholder's proceeding under paragraph (b)(i) of this section to enjoin an unauthorized corporate act the court may enjoin or set aside the act, if equitable and if all affected persons are parties to the proceeding, and may award damages for loss, other than anticipated profits, suffered by the corporation or another party because of enjoining the unauthorized act.

ARTICLE 4
NAME

17-16-401. Corporate name.

(a) A corporate name may not contain language stating or implying that the corporation is organized for a purpose other than that permitted by W.S. 17-16-301 and its articles of incorporation.

(b) Except as authorized by subsections (c) and (d) of this section, a corporate name shall not be the same as, or deceptively similar to any trademark or service mark registered in this state and shall be distinguishable upon the records of the secretary of state from the name of any profit or nonprofit corporation, trade name, limited liability company, statutory trust company, limited partnership or other business entity organized, continued or domesticated under the laws of this state or licensed or registered as a foreign profit or nonprofit corporation, foreign limited partnership, foreign joint stock company, foreign statutory trust company, foreign limited liability company or other foreign business entity in this state or any fictitious or reserved name.

(c) A corporation may apply to the secretary of state for authorization to use a name that is not distinguishable from one (1) or more of the names described in subsection (b) of this section. The secretary of state shall authorize use of the name applied for if:

(i) The other person whose name is not distinguishable from the name which the applicant desires to register or reserve, irrevocably consents to the use in writing and submits an undertaking in a form satisfactory to the secretary of state to change its name to a name that is distinguishable from the name of the applicant; or

(ii) The applicant delivers to the secretary of state a certified copy of the final judgment of a court of competent jurisdiction establishing the applicant's right to use the name applied for in this state.

(d) A corporation may use the name, including the fictitious name, of another domestic or foreign corporation that is used in this state if the other corporation is incorporated or authorized to transact business in this state and the proposed user corporation:

(i) Has merged with the other corporation; or

(ii) Has been formed by reorganization of the other corporation; or

(iii) Has acquired all or substantially all of the assets, including the corporate name, of the other corporation.

(iv) Repealed By Laws 1996, ch. 80, § 3.

(e) This act does not control the use of fictitious names.

(f) A name is distinguishable from other names, on the records of the secretary of state, if it contains one (1) or more different letters or numerals, or if it has a different sequence of letters or numerals from the other names on the secretary of state's records. Differences which are not distinguishable are:

(i) The words or abbreviations of the words "corporation," "company," "incorporated," "limited partnership," "L.P.," "limited," "ltd.," "limited liability company," "limited company," "L.C." or "L.L.C.";

(ii) The presence or absence of the words or symbols of the words "the," "and" or "a";

(iii) Differences in punctuation and special characters;

(iv) Differences in capitalization; or

(v) Differences between singular and plural forms of words.

(g) The secretary of state has the power and authority reasonably necessary to interpret and efficiently administer this section and to perform the duties imposed by this section.

17-16-402. Reserved name.

(a) A person may apply to reserve the exclusive use of a corporate name, including a fictitious name for a foreign corporation whose corporate name is not available, by delivering an application to the secretary of state for filing. The application shall set forth the name and address of the applicant and the name proposed to be reserved. If the secretary of state finds that the corporate name applied for is available, he shall file the application pursuant to W.S. 17-16-125 and reserve the name for the applicant's exclusive use for a nonrenewable one hundred twenty (120) day period.

(b) The owner of a reserved corporate name may transfer the reservation to another person by delivering to the secretary of state a manually signed notice of the transfer that states the name and address of the transferee.

ARTICLE 5
OFFICE AND AGENT

17-16-501. Registered office and registered agent.

(a) Each corporation shall continuously maintain in this state:

(i) A registered office that may be the same as any of its places of business; and

(ii) A registered agent, who may be:

(A) An individual who resides in this state and whose business office is identical with the registered office;

(B) A domestic corporation or not-for-profit domestic corporation whose business office is identical with the registered office; or

(C) A foreign corporation or not-for-profit foreign corporation authorized to transact business in this state whose business office is identical with the registered office.

17-16-502. Change of registered office or registered agent.

(a) A corporation may change its registered office or registered agent by delivering to the secretary of state for filing a statement of change that sets forth:

(i) The name of the corporation;

(ii) The street address of its current registered office;

(iii) If the current registered office is to be changed, the street address of the new registered office;

(iv) The name of its current registered agent;

(v) If the current registered agent is to be changed, the name of the new registered agent and the new agent's written consent to the appointment executed by the registered agent, either on the statement or attached to it; and

(vi) That after the change or changes are made, the street addresses of its registered office and the business office of its registered agent will be identical.

(b) If a registered agent changes the street address of his business office, he may change the street address of the registered office of any corporation for which he is the registered agent by notifying the corporation in writing of the change and signing, either manually or in facsimile, and delivering to the secretary of state for filing a statement that complies with the requirements of subsection (a) of this section and recites that the corporation has been notified of the change.

17-16-503. Resignation of registered agent.

(a) A registered agent may resign his agency appointment by signing and delivering to the secretary of state for filing the manually signed original and two (2) exact or conformed copies of a statement of resignation. The statement may include a statement that the registered office is also discontinued.

(b) After filing the statement the secretary of state shall mail one (1) copy to the registered office, if it is not discontinued, and the other copy to the corporation at its principal office.

(c) The agency appointment is terminated, and the registered office discontinued if so provided, on the thirty-first (31st) day after the date on which the statement was filed.

17-16-504. Service on corporation.

(a) A corporation's registered agent is the corporation's agent for service of process, notice, or demand required or permitted by law to be served on the corporation.

(b) If a corporation has no registered agent, or the agent cannot with reasonable diligence be served, the corporation may be served by registered or certified mail, return receipt requested, addressed to the secretary of the corporation at its principal office. Service is perfected under this subsection at the earliest of:

(i) The date the corporation receives the mail;

(ii) The date shown on the return receipt, if signed, either manually or in facsimile, on behalf of the corporation; or

(iii) Five (5) days after its deposit in the United States mail, as evidenced by the postmark, if mailed postpaid and correctly addressed.

(c) This section does not prescribe the only means, or necessarily the required means, of serving a corporation.

17-16-505. Registered agent registration required.

(a) Except as provided in subsection (b) of this section, no person shall transact business in this state as a registered agent unless the person is registered with the secretary of state in accordance with the provisions of this article.

(b) The registration requirements of this section and W.S. 17-16-506 shall not apply to a person who serves as registered agent for five (5) or fewer corporations.

(c) Any person claiming to be exempt from registration requirements based upon the provisions of subsection (b) of this section shall have the burden of proving the exemption in any administrative or other civil action.

17-16-506. Registration requirements.

(a) A registered agent shall obtain an initial or renewal registration by filing an application with the secretary of state. The application shall contain information the secretary of state requires by rule including:

(i) The legal name of the applicant;

(ii) The applicant's physical address where service may be made during regular business hours;

(iii) Whether the applicant, or in the case of a corporation or other business entity its officers or directors, members, partners or persons serving in a similar capacity, has ever been convicted of a felony; and

(iv) Other information the secretary of state deems appropriate in the registration and identification of registered agents.

(b) Every applicant for initial or renewal registration shall pay a filing fee as set by rule adopted pursuant to this act. The fee shall be designed to recover the cost of administering the provisions of this act relating to registered agents. If an application is withdrawn or denied, the secretary of state shall retain the entire fee.

(c) Initial registration of a registered agent shall be valid for the calendar year of registration and thereafter shall be renewed annually by January 31 of each year. A registered agent who does not renew by January 31 of each year shall no longer have registered agent status.

(d) The secretary of state may publish or cause a listing of registrants to be disseminated to interested persons under such rules as the secretary of state prescribes.

17-16-507. Duties of the registered agent.

(a) The registered agent shall:

(i) Maintain a physical address in accordance with W.S. 17-16-502(a)(ii) and as defined by the secretary of state by rule;

(ii) Accept service of process in accordance with W.S. 17-16-504(a);

(iii) Maintain the address of record to which all service of process is to be delivered for each corporate entity represented; and

(iv) Maintain at the registered office, the following information which shall be current within sixty (60) days of any change until the corporation's first annual report is accepted for filing with the secretary of state:

(A) Names and addresses of the corporation's directors; and

(B) Names and addresses of the corporation's officers.

17-16-508. Production of records.

(a) All records maintained pursuant to W.S. 17-16-507 are subject to periodic, special or other examination by the secretary of state or his representatives as deemed necessary or appropriate in investigations.

(b) The secretary of state may compel production of records required to be maintained pursuant to W.S. 17-16-507 in accordance with the provisions of the Wyoming Administrative Procedure Act.

(c) The secretary of state shall hold any records obtained pursuant to this section confidential except for information required to be in the annual report required by W.S. 17-16-1630(a). The secretary of state may release any such confidential information only pursuant to court subpoena or to a bona fide law enforcement agency for use in a criminal investigation.

17-16-509. Actions against registered agents.

(a) The secretary of state may impose a civil penalty not to exceed five hundred dollars ($500.00) for each violation of this section for which no other specific penalty is provided, and may deny or revoke any registration, require enhanced record keeping or refuse to accept filings for corporations served by a registered agent if the registered agent:

(i) Has failed to make payment for the application or renewal fee on or before fifteen (15) days following receipt of notice of the deficiency;

(ii) Has failed to maintain records as required by W.S. 17-16-507;

(iii) Cannot be served during regular business hours at the address of the registered office;

(iv) Has willfully violated or willfully failed to comply with any provision of this article; or

(v) Cannot be located at the address on the application provided to the secretary of state.

(b) A registered agent is presumed to have complied with W.S. 17-16-507 if he has timely requested the required information from the corporation by certified letter. It shall be a defense to an action under paragraph (a)(ii) of this section if the registered agent notifies the secretary of state of the corporation's failure to provide the required information and resigns as registered agent within sixty (60) days after the date current documents were to be filed. No fee shall be assessed a registered agent resigning pursuant to this subsection.

(c) The secretary of state may revoke the registration of a registered agent who has been convicted of any felony regarding securities laws, tax evasion or for other fraudulent acts concerning financial activities or in the case of a corporation or other business entity, its officers, directors, members, partners or persons serving in a similar capacity have been convicted of any such felony in violation of the laws of any state, country or province.

ARTICLE 6
SHARES AND DISTRIBUTIONS

17-16-601. Authorized shares.

(a) The articles of incorporation shall prescribe the classes of shares and the number, which may be unlimited, of shares of each class that the corporation is authorized to issue. If more than one (1) class of shares is authorized, the articles of incorporation shall prescribe a distinguishing designation for each class, and, prior to the issuance of shares of a class, the preferences, limitations, and relative rights of that class shall be described in the articles of incorporation. All shares of a class shall have preferences, limitations, and relative rights identical with those of other shares of the same class except to the extent otherwise permitted by W.S. 17-16-602.

(b) The articles of incorporation shall authorize:

(i) One (1) or more classes of shares that together have unlimited voting rights; and

(ii) One (1) or more classes of shares, which may be the same class or classes as those with voting rights, that together are entitled to receive the net assets of the corporation upon dissolution.

(c) The articles of incorporation may authorize one (1) or more classes of shares that:

(i) Have special, conditional, or limited voting rights, or no right to vote, except to the extent prohibited by this act;

(ii) Are redeemable or convertible as specified in the articles of incorporation as follows:

(A) At the option of the corporation, the shareholder, or another person or upon the occurrence of a designated event;

(B) For cash, indebtedness, securities, or other property;

(C) In a designated amount or in an amount determined in accordance with a designated formula or by reference to extrinsic data or events.

(iii) Entitle the holders to distributions calculated in any manner, including dividends that may be cumulative, noncumulative, or partially cumulative; or

(iv) Have preference over any other class of shares with respect to distributions, including dividends and distributions upon the dissolution of the corporation.

(d) The description of the designations, preferences, limitations, and relative rights of share classes in subsection (c) of this section is not exhaustive.

17-16-602. Terms of class or series determined by board of directors.

(a) If the articles of incorporation so provide, the board of directors may determine, in whole or part, the preferences, limitations, and relative rights, within the limits set forth in W.S. 17-16-601, of:

(i) Any class of shares before the issuance of any shares of that class; or

(ii) One (1) or more series within a class before the issuance of any shares of that series.

(b) Each series of a class shall be given a distinguishing designation.

(c) All shares of a series shall have preferences, limitations, and relative rights identical with those of other shares of the same series and, except to the extent otherwise provided in the description of the series, with those of other series of the same class.

(d) Before issuing any shares of a class or series created under this section, the corporation shall deliver to the secretary of state for filing articles of amendment, which are effective without shareholder action, that set forth:

(i) The name of the corporation;

(ii) The text of the amendment determining the terms of the class or series of shares;

(iii) The date the amendment was adopted; and

(iv) A statement that the amendment was duly adopted by the board of directors.

17-16-603. Issued and outstanding shares.

(a) A corporation may issue the number of shares of each class or series authorized by the articles of incorporation. Shares that are issued are outstanding shares until they are reacquired, redeemed, converted, or cancelled.

(b) The reacquisition, redemption, or conversion of outstanding shares is subject to the limitations of subsection (c) of this section and to W.S. 17-16-640.

(c) At all times that shares of the corporation are outstanding, one (1) or more shares that together have unlimited voting rights and one (1) or more shares that together are entitled to receive the net assets of the corporation upon dissolution shall be outstanding.

17-16-604. Fractional shares.

(a) A corporation may:

(i) Issue fractions of a share or pay in money the value of fractions of a share;

(ii) Arrange for disposition of fractional shares by the shareholders; or

(iii) Issue scrip in registered or bearer form entitling the holder to receive a full share upon surrendering enough scrip to equal a full share.

(b) Each certificate representing scrip shall be conspicuously labeled "scrip" and shall contain the information required by W.S. 17-16-625(b).

(c) The holder of a fractional share is entitled to exercise the rights of a shareholder, including the right to vote, to receive dividends, and to participate in the assets of the corporation upon liquidation. The holder of scrip is not entitled to any of these rights unless the scrip provides for them.

(d) The board of directors may authorize the issuance of scrip subject to any condition considered desirable, including:

(i) That the scrip will become void if not exchanged for full shares before a specified date; and

(ii) That the shares for which the scrip is exchangeable may be sold and the proceeds paid to the scripholders.

17-16-620. Subscription for shares before incorporation.

(a) A subscription for shares entered into before incorporation is irrevocable for six (6) months unless the subscription agreement provides a longer or shorter period or all the subscribers agree to revocation.

(b) The board of directors may determine the payment terms of subscriptions for shares that were entered into before incorporation, unless the subscription agreement specifies them. A call for payment by the board of directors shall be uniform so far as practicable as to all shares of the same class or series, unless the subscription agreement specifies otherwise.

(c) Shares issued pursuant to subscriptions entered into before incorporation are fully paid and nonassessable when the corporation receives the consideration specified in the subscription agreement.

(d) If a subscriber defaults in payment of money or property under a subscription agreement entered into before incorporation, the corporation may collect the amount owed as any other debt. Alternatively, unless the subscription agreement provides otherwise, the corporation may rescind the agreement and may sell the shares if the debt remains unpaid more than twenty (20) days after the corporation sends written demand for payment to the subscriber.

(e) A subscription agreement entered into after incorporation is a contract between the subscriber and the corporation subject to W.S. 17-16-621.

17-16-621. Issuance of shares.

(a) The powers granted in this section to the board of directors may be reserved to the shareholders by the articles of incorporation.

(b) The board of directors may authorize shares to be issued for consideration consisting of any tangible or intangible property or benefit to the corporation, including cash, promissory notes, services performed, contracts for services to be performed, or other securities of the corporation.

(c) Before the corporation issues shares, the board of directors shall determine that the consideration received or to be received for shares to be issued is adequate. That determination by the board of directors is conclusive insofar as the adequacy of consideration for the issuance of shares relates to whether the shares are validly issued, fully paid, and nonassessable.

(d) When the corporation receives the consideration for which the board of directors authorized the issuance of shares, the shares issued therefor are fully paid and nonassessable.

(e) The corporation may place in escrow shares issued for a contract for future services or benefits or a promissory note, or make other arrangements to restrict the transfer of the shares, and may credit distributions in respect of the shares against their purchase price, until the services are performed, the note is paid, or the benefits received. If the services are not performed, the note is not paid, or the benefits are not received, the shares escrowed or restricted and the distributions credited may be cancelled in whole or part.

17-16-622. Liability of shareholders.

(a) A purchaser from a corporation of its own shares is not liable to the corporation or its creditors with respect to the shares except to pay the consideration for which the shares were authorized to be issued pursuant to W.S. 17-16-621 or specified in the subscription agreement pursuant to W.S. 17-16-620.

(b) Unless otherwise provided in the articles of incorporation, a shareholder of a corporation is not personally liable for the acts or debts of the corporation except that he may become personally liable by reason of his own acts or conduct.

17-16-623. Share dividends.

(a) Unless the articles of incorporation provide otherwise, shares may be issued pro rata and without consideration to the corporation's shareholders or to the shareholders of one (1) or more classes or series. An issuance of shares under this subsection is a share dividend.

(b) Shares of one (1) class or series may not be issued as a share dividend in respect of shares of another class or series unless:

(i) The articles of incorporation so authorize;

(ii) A majority of the votes entitled to be cast by the class or series to be issued approve the issue; or

(iii) There are no outstanding shares of the class or series to be issued.

(c) If the board of directors does not fix the record date for determining shareholders entitled to a share dividend, it is the date the board of directors authorizes the share dividend.

17-16-624. Share options.

A corporation may issue rights, options, or warrants for the purchase of shares of the corporation. The board of directors shall determine the terms upon which the rights, options, or warrants are issued, their form and content, and the consideration for which the shares are to be issued.

17-16-625. Form and content of certificates.

(a) Shares may but need not be represented by certificates. Unless this act or another statute expressly provides otherwise, the rights and obligations of shareholders are identical whether or not their shares are represented by certificates.

(b) At a minimum each share certificate shall state on its face:

(i) The name of the issuing corporation and that it is organized under the law of this state;

(ii) The name of the person to whom issued; and

(iii) The number and class of shares and the designation of the series, if any, the certificate represents.

(c) If the issuing corporation is authorized to issue different classes of shares or different series within a class, the designations, relative rights, preferences, and limitations applicable to each class and the variations in rights, preferences, and limitations determined for each series, and the authority of the board of directors to determine variations for future series, shall be summarized on the front or back of each certificate. Alternatively, each certificate may state conspicuously on its front or back that the corporation will furnish the shareholder this information on request in writing and without charge.

(d) Each share certificate:

(i) Shall be signed, either manually or in facsimile, by two (2) officers designated in the bylaws or by the board of directors; and

(ii) May bear the corporate seal or its facsimile.

(e) If the person who signed, either manually or in facsimile, a share certificate no longer holds office when the certificate is issued, the certificate is nevertheless valid.

17-16-626. Shares without certificates.

(a) Unless the articles of incorporation or bylaws provide otherwise, the board of directors of a corporation may authorize the issue of some or all of the shares of any or all of the classes or series without certificates. The authorization does not affect shares already represented by certificates until they are surrendered to the corporation.

(b) Within a reasonable time after the issue or transfer of shares without certificates, the corporation shall send the shareholder a written statement of the information required on certificates by W.S. 17-16-625(b) and (c), and, if applicable, W.S. 17-16-627.

17-16-627. Restriction on transfer of shares and other securities.

(a) The articles of incorporation, bylaws, an agreement among shareholders, or an agreement between shareholders and the corporation may impose restrictions on the transfer or registration of transfer of shares of the corporation. A restriction does not affect shares issued before the restriction was adopted unless the holders of the shares are parties to the restriction agreement or voted in favor of the restriction.

(b) A restriction on the transfer or registration of transfer of shares is valid and enforceable against the holder or a transferee of the holder if the restriction is authorized by this section and its existence is noted conspicuously on the front or back of the certificate or is contained in the information statement required by W.S. 17-16-626(b). Unless so noted, a restriction is not enforceable against a person without knowledge of the restriction.

(c) A restriction on the transfer or registration of transfer of shares is authorized:

(i) To maintain the corporation's status when it is dependent on the number or identity of its shareholders;

(ii) To preserve exemptions under federal or state securities law; or

(iii) For any other reasonable purpose.

(d) A restriction on the transfer or registration of transfer of shares may:

(i) Obligate the shareholder first to offer the corporation or other persons, separately, consecutively, or simultaneously, an opportunity to acquire the restricted shares;

(ii) Obligate the corporation or other persons, separately, consecutively, or simultaneously, to acquire the restricted shares;

(iii) Require the corporation, the holders of any class of its shares, or another person to approve the transfer of the restricted shares, if the requirement is not manifestly unreasonable; or

(iv) Prohibit the transfer of the restricted shares to designated persons or classes of persons, if the prohibition is not manifestly unreasonable.

(e) For purposes of this section, "shares" includes a security convertible into or carrying a right to subscribe for or acquire shares.

17-16-628. Expense of issue.

A corporation may pay the expenses of selling or underwriting its shares, and of organizing or reorganizing the corporation, from the consideration received for shares.

17-16-630. Shareholders' preemptive rights.

(a) The shareholders of a corporation do not have a preemptive right to acquire the corporation's unissued shares except to the extent the articles of incorporation so provide.

(b) A statement included in the articles of incorporation that "the corporation elects to have preemptive rights," or words of similar import, means that the following principles apply except to the extent the articles of incorporation expressly provide otherwise:

(i) The shareholders of the corporation have a preemptive right, granted on uniform terms and conditions prescribed by the board of directors to provide a fair and reasonable opportunity to exercise the right, to acquire proportional amounts of the corporation's unissued shares upon the decision of the board of directors to issue them;

(ii) A shareholder may waive his preemptive right. A waiver evidenced by a writing is irrevocable even though it is not supported by consideration;

(iii) There is no preemptive right with respect to:

(A) Shares issued as compensation to directors, officers, agents, or employees of the corporation, its subsidiaries or affiliates;

(B) Shares issued to satisfy conversion or option rights created to provide compensation to directors, officers, agents, or employees of the corporation, its subsidiaries or affiliates;

(C) Shares authorized in articles of incorporation that are issued within six (6) months from the effective date of incorporation; or

(D) Shares sold otherwise than for money.

(iv) Holders of shares of any class without general voting rights but with preferential rights to distributions or assets have no preemptive rights with respect to shares of any class;

(v) Holders of shares of any class with general voting rights but without preferential rights to distributions or assets have no preemptive rights with respect to shares of any class with preferential rights to distributions or assets unless the shares with preferential rights are convertible into or carry a right to subscribe for or acquire shares without preferential rights;

(vi) Shares subject to preemptive rights that are not acquired by shareholders may be issued to any person for a period of one (1) year after being offered to shareholders at a consideration set by the board of directors that is not lower than the consideration set for the exercise of preemptive rights. An offer at a lower consideration or after the expiration of one (1) year is subject to the shareholders' preemptive rights.

(c) For purposes of this section, "shares" includes a security convertible into or carrying a right to subscribe for or acquire shares.

17-16-631. Corporation's acquisition of its own shares.

(a) A corporation may acquire its own shares and shares so acquired constitute authorized but unissued shares.

(b) If the articles of incorporation prohibit the reissue of acquired shares, the number of authorized shares is reduced by the number of shares acquired, effective upon amendment of the articles of incorporation.

(c) The board of directors may adopt articles of amendment under this section without shareholder action and deliver them to the secretary of state for filing. The articles shall set forth:

(i) The name of the corporation;

(ii) The reduction in the number of authorized shares, itemized by class and series; and

(iii) The total number of authorized shares, itemized by class and series, remaining after reduction of the shares.

17-16-640. Distributions to shareholders.

(a) A board of directors may authorize and the corporation may make distributions to its shareholders subject to restrictions imposed by the articles of incorporation and the limitation in subsection (c) of this section.

(b) If the board of directors does not fix the record date for determining shareholders entitled to a distribution, other than one (1) involving a purchase, redemption, or other acquisition of the corporation's shares, it is the date the board of directors authorizes the distribution.

(c) No distribution may be made if, after giving it effect:

(i) The corporation would not be able to pay its debts as they become due in the usual course of business; or

(ii) The corporation's total assets would be less than the sum of its total liabilities plus (unless the articles of incorporation permit otherwise) the amount that would be needed, if the corporation were to be dissolved at the time of the distribution, to satisfy the preferential rights upon dissolution of shareholders whose preferential rights are superior to those receiving the distribution.

(d) The board of directors may base a determination that a distribution is not prohibited under subsection (c) of this section either on financial statements prepared on the basis of accounting practices and principles that are reasonable in the circumstances or on a fair valuation or other method that is reasonable in the circumstances.

(e) Except as provided in subsection (g) of this section, the effect of a distribution under subsection (c) of this section is measured:

(i) In the case of distribution by purchase, redemption, or other acquisition of the corporation's shares, as of the earlier of:

(A) The date money or other property is transferred or debt incurred by the corporation; or

(B) The date the shareholder ceases to be a shareholder with respect to the acquired shares.

(ii) In the case of any other distribution of indebtedness, as of the date the indebtedness is distributed; and

(iii) In all other cases, as of:

(A) The date the distribution is authorized if the payment occurs within one hundred twenty (120) days after the date of authorization; or

(B) The date the payment is made if it occurs more than one hundred twenty (120) days after the date of authorization.

(f) A corporation's indebtedness to a shareholder incurred by reason of a distribution made in accordance with this section is at parity with the corporation's indebtedness to its general, unsecured creditors except to the extent subordinated by agreement.

(g) Indebtedness of a corporation, including indebtedness issued as a distribution, is not considered a liability for purposes of determinations under subsection (c) of this section if its terms provide that payment of principal and interest are made only if and to the extent that payment of a distribution to shareholders could then be made under this section. If the indebtedness is issued as a distribution, each payment of principal or interest is treated as a distribution, the effect of which is measured on the date the payment is actually made.

ARTICLE 7
SHAREHOLDERS

17-16-701. Annual meeting.

(a) A corporation shall hold a meeting of shareholders annually at a time stated in or fixed in accordance with the bylaws.

(b) Annual shareholders' meetings may be held in or out of this state at the place stated in or fixed in accordance with the bylaws. If no place is stated in or fixed in accordance with the bylaws, annual meetings shall be held at the corporation's principal office.

(c) The failure to hold an annual meeting at the time stated in or fixed in accordance with a corporation's bylaws does not affect the validity of any corporate action.

17-16-702. Special meeting.

(a) A corporation shall hold a special meeting of shareholders:

(i) On call of its board of directors or the person or persons authorized to do so by the articles of incorporation or bylaws; or

(ii) If the holders of at least ten percent (10%) of all the votes entitled to be cast on any issue proposed to be considered at the proposed special meeting sign, either manually or in facsimile, date, and deliver to the corporation one (1) or more written demands for the meeting describing the purpose or purposes for which it is to be held, provided that the articles of incorporation may fix a lower percentage or a higher percentage not exceeding twenty-five percent (25%) of all the votes entitled to be cast on any issue proposed to be considered. Unless otherwise provided in the articles of incorporation, a written demand for a special meeting may be revoked by a writing to that effect received by the corporation prior to the receipt by the corporation of demands sufficient in number to require the holding of a special meeting.

(b) If not otherwise fixed under W.S. 17-16-703 or 17-16-707, the record date for determining shareholders entitled to demand a special meeting is the date the first shareholder signs the demand.

(c) Special shareholders' meetings may be held in or out of this state at the place stated in or fixed in accordance with the bylaws. If no place is stated or fixed in accordance with the bylaws, special meetings shall be held at the corporation's principal office.

(d) Only business within the purpose or purposes described in the meeting notice required by W.S. 17-16-705(c) may be conducted at a special shareholders' meeting.

17-16-703. Court-ordered meeting.

(a) The district court of the county where a corporation's principal office or, if none in this state, its registered office is located may summarily order a meeting to be held:

(i) On application of any shareholder of the corporation entitled to participate in an annual meeting if an annual meeting was not held within the earlier of six (6) months after the end of the corporation's fiscal year or fifteen (15) months after its last annual meeting; or

(ii) On application of a shareholder who signed a demand for a special meeting valid under W.S. 17-16-702, if:

(A) Notice of the special meeting was not given within sixty (60) days after the date the demand was delivered to the corporation's secretary; or

(B) The special meeting was not held in accordance with the notice.

(b) The court may fix the time and place of the meeting, determine the shares entitled to participate in the meeting, specify a record date for determining shareholders entitled to notice of and to vote at the meeting, prescribe the form and content of the meeting notice, fix the quorum required for specific matters to be considered at the meeting or direct that the votes represented at the meeting constitute a quorum for action on those matters, and enter other orders necessary to accomplish the purpose or purposes of the meeting.

17-16-704. Action without meeting.

(a) Action required or permitted by this act to be taken at a shareholders' meeting may be taken without a meeting if notice of the proposed action is given to all voting shareholders and the action is taken by the holders of all shares entitled to vote on the action. The action shall be evidenced by one (1) or more written consents bearing the date of signature and describing the action taken, signed, either manually or in facsimile, by the holders of the requisite number of shares entitled to vote on the action, and delivered to the corporation for inclusion in the minutes or filing with the corporate records.

(b) If not otherwise fixed under W.S. 17-16-703 or 17-16-707, the record date for determining shareholders entitled to take action without a meeting is the date the first shareholder signs the consent under subsection (a) of this section. No written consent shall be effective to take the corporate action referred to therein unless, within sixty (60) days of the earliest date appearing on a consent delivered to the corporation in the manner required by this section, written consents signed by all shareholders entitled to vote on the action are received by the corporation. A written consent may be revoked by a writing to that effect received by the corporation prior to the receipt by the corporation of unrevoked written consents sufficient in number to take corporate action.

(c) A consent signed under this section has the effect of a meeting vote and may be described as such in any document.

(d) If this act requires that notice of proposed action be given to nonvoting shareholders and the action is to be taken by consent of the voting shareholders, the corporation shall give its nonvoting shareholders written notice of the proposed action at least ten (10) days before the action is taken. The notice shall contain or be accompanied by the same material that, under this act, would have been required to be sent to nonvoting shareholders in a notice of meeting at which the proposed action would have been submitted to the shareholders for action.

17-16-705. Notice of meeting.

(a) A corporation shall notify shareholders of the date, time, and place of each annual and special shareholders' meeting no fewer than ten (10) nor more than sixty (60) days before the meeting date. Unless this act or the articles of incorporation require otherwise, the corporation is required to give notice only to shareholders entitled to vote at the meeting.

(b) Unless this act or the articles of incorporation require otherwise, notice of an annual meeting need not include a description of the purpose or purposes for which the meeting is called.

(c) Notice of a special meeting shall include a description of the purpose or purposes for which the meeting is called.

(d) If not otherwise fixed under W.S. 17-16-703 or 17-16-707, the record date for determining shareholders entitled to notice of and to vote at an annual or special shareholders' meeting is the day before the first notice is delivered to shareholders.

(e) Unless the bylaws require otherwise, if an annual or special shareholders' meeting is adjourned to a different date, time, or place, notice need not be given of the new date, time, or place if the new date, time or place is announced at the meeting before adjournment. If a new record date for the adjourned meeting is or shall be fixed under W.S. 17-16-707, however, notice of the adjourned meeting shall be given under this section to persons who are shareholders as of the new record date.

17-16-706. Waiver of notice.

(a) A shareholder may waive any notice required by this act, the articles of incorporation, or bylaws before or after the date and time stated in the notice. The waiver shall be in writing, be signed, either manually or in facsimile, by the shareholder entitled to the notice, and be delivered to the corporation for inclusion in the minutes or filing with the corporate records.

(b) A shareholder's attendance at a meeting:

(i) Waives objection to lack of notice or defective notice of the meeting, unless the shareholder at the beginning of the meeting objects to holding the meeting or transacting business at the meeting; and

(ii) Waives objection to consideration of a particular matter at the meeting that is not within the purpose or purposes described in the meeting notice, unless the shareholder objects to considering the matter when it is presented.

17-16-707. Record date.

(a) The bylaws may fix or provide the manner of fixing the record date for one (1) or more voting groups in order to determine the shareholders entitled to notice of a shareholders' meeting, to demand a special meeting, to vote, or to take any other action. If the bylaws do not fix or provide for fixing a record date, the board of directors of the corporation may fix a future date as the record date.

(b) A record date fixed under this section may not be more than seventy (70) days before the meeting or action requiring a determination of shareholders.

(c) A determination of shareholders entitled to notice of or to vote at a shareholders' meeting is effective for any adjournment of the meeting unless the board of directors fixes a new record date, which it shall do if the meeting is adjourned to a date more than one hundred twenty (120) days after the date fixed for the original meeting.

(d) If a court orders a meeting adjourned to a date more than one hundred twenty (120) days after the date fixed for the original meeting, it may provide that the original record date continues in effect or it may fix a new record date.

17-16-708. Conduct of the meeting.

(a) At each meeting of shareholders, a chair shall preside. The chair shall be appointed as provided in the bylaws or, in the absence of such provision, by the board.

(b) The chair, unless the articles of incorporation or bylaws provide otherwise, shall determine the order of business and shall establish rules for the conduct of the meeting.

(c) Any rules adopted for, and the conduct of, the meeting shall be fair to shareholders.

(d) The chair of the meeting shall announce at the meeting when the polls close for each matter voted upon. If no announcement is made, the polls shall be deemed to have closed upon the final adjournment of the meeting. After the polls close, no ballots, proxies or votes nor any revocations or changes thereto may be accepted.

17-16-720. Shareholders' list for meeting.

(a) After fixing a record date for a meeting, a corporation shall prepare an alphabetical list of the names of all its shareholders who are entitled to notice of a shareholders' meeting. The list shall be arranged by voting group, and within each voting group by class or series of shares, and show the address of and number of shares held by each shareholder.

(b) The shareholders' list shall be available for inspection by any shareholder, beginning two (2) business days after notice of the meeting is given for which the list was prepared and continuing through the meeting, at the corporation's principal office or at a place identified in the meeting notice in the city where the meeting will be held. A shareholder, his agent, or attorney is entitled on written demand to inspect and, subject to the requirements of W.S. 17-16-1602(c), to copy the list, during regular business hours and at his expense, during the period it is available for inspection.

(c) The corporation shall make the shareholders' list available at the meeting, and any shareholder, his agent, or attorney is entitled to inspect the list at any time during the meeting or any adjournment.

(d) If the corporation refuses to allow a shareholder, his agent, or attorney to inspect the shareholders' list before or at the meeting, or to copy the list as permitted by subsection (b) of this section, the district court of the county where a corporation's principal office or, if none in this state, its registered office, is located, on application of the shareholder, may summarily order the inspection or copying at the corporation's expense, order payment by the corporation of the shareholder's cost of suit including reasonable attorney fees and may postpone the meeting for which the list was prepared until the inspection or copying is complete.

(e) Refusal or failure to prepare or make available the shareholders' list does not affect the validity of action taken at the meeting.

17-16-721. Voting entitlement of shares.

(a) Except as provided in subsections (b) and (c) of this section or unless the articles of incorporation provide otherwise, each outstanding share, regardless of class, is entitled to one (1) vote on each matter voted on at a shareholders' meeting. Only shares are entitled to vote.

(b) The shares of a corporation are not entitled to vote if they are owned, directly or indirectly, by a second corporation, domestic or foreign, and the first corporation owns, directly or indirectly, a majority of the shares entitled to vote for directors of the second corporation.

(c) Subsection (b) of this section does not limit the power of a corporation to vote any shares, including its own shares, held by it in a fiduciary capacity.

(d) Redeemable shares are not entitled to vote after notice of redemption is mailed to the holders and a sum sufficient to redeem the shares has been deposited with a bank, trust company, or other financial institution under an irrevocable obligation to pay the holders the redemption price on surrender of the shares.

17-16-722. Proxies.

(a) A shareholder may vote his shares in person or by proxy.

(b) A shareholder or his agent or attorney-in-fact may appoint a proxy to vote or otherwise act for the shareholder by signing, either manually or in facsimile, an appointment form or by an electronic transmission. An electronic transmission must contain or be accompanied by information from which one can determine that the shareholder, the shareholder's agent, or the shareholder's attorney-in-fact authorized the electronic transmission.

(c) An appointment of a proxy is effective when a signed appointment form or an electronic transmission of the appointment is received by the inspector of election or the officer or agent of the corporation authorized to tabulate votes. An appointment is valid for eleven (11) months unless a longer period is expressly provided in the appointment.

(d) An appointment of a proxy is revocable unless the appointment form or electronic transmission states that it is irrevocable and the appointment is coupled with an interest. Appointments coupled with an interest include the appointment of:

(i) A pledgee;

(ii) A person who purchased or agreed to purchase the shares;

(iii) A creditor of the corporation who extended it credit under terms requiring the appointment;

(iv) An employee of the corporation whose employment contract requires the appointment; or

(v) A party to a voting agreement created under W.S. 17-16-731.

(e) The death or incapacity of the shareholder appointing a proxy does not affect the right of the corporation to accept the proxy's authority unless notice of the death or incapacity is received by the secretary or other officer or agent authorized to tabulate votes before the proxy exercises his authority under the appointment.

(f) An appointment made irrevocable under subsection (d) of this section is revoked when the interest with which it is coupled is extinguished.

(g) A transferee for value of shares subject to an irrevocable appointment may revoke the appointment if he did not know of its existence when he acquired the shares and the existence of the irrevocable appointment was not noted conspicuously on the certificate representing the shares or on the information statement for shares without certificates.

(h) Subject to W.S. 17-16-724 and to any express limitation on the proxy's authority stated in the appointment form or electronic transmission, a corporation is entitled to accept the proxy's vote or other action as that of the shareholder making the appointment.

17-16-723. Shares held by nominees.

(a) A corporation may establish a procedure by which the beneficial owner of shares that are registered in the name of a nominee is recognized by the corporation as the shareholder. The extent of this recognition may be determined in the procedure.

(b) The procedure may set forth:

(i) The types of nominees to which it applies;

(ii) The rights or privileges that the corporation recognizes in a beneficial owner;

(iii) The manner in which the procedure is selected by the nominee;

(iv) The information that shall be provided when the procedure is selected;

(v) The period for which selection of the procedure is effective; and

(vi) Other aspects of the rights and duties created.

17-16-724. Corporation's acceptance of votes.

(a) If the name signed on a vote, consent, waiver, or proxy appointment corresponds to the name of a shareholder, the corporation if acting in good faith is entitled to accept the vote, consent, waiver, or proxy appointment and give it effect as the act of the shareholder.

(b) If the name signed on a vote, consent, waiver, or proxy appointment does not correspond to the name of its shareholder, the corporation if acting in good faith is nevertheless entitled to accept the vote, consent, waiver, or proxy appointment and give it effect as the act of the shareholder if:

(i) The shareholder is an entity and the name signed purports to be that of an officer or agent of the entity;

(ii) The name signed purports to be that of an administrator, executor, guardian, or conservator representing the shareholder and, if the corporation requests, evidence of fiduciary status acceptable to the corporation has been presented with respect to the vote, consent, waiver, or proxy appointment;

(iii) The name signed purports to be that of a receiver or trustee in bankruptcy of the shareholder and, if the corporation requests, evidence of this status acceptable to the corporation has been presented with respect to the vote, consent, waiver, or proxy appointment;

(iv) The name signed purports to be that of a pledgee, beneficial owner, or attorney-in-fact of the shareholder and, if the corporation requests, evidence acceptable to the corporation of the signatory's authority to sign for the shareholder has been presented with respect to the vote, consent, waiver, or proxy appointment; or

(v) Two (2) or more persons are the shareholder as cotenants or fiduciaries and the name signed purports to be the name of at least one (1) of the coowners and the person signing appears to be acting on behalf of all the coowners.

(c) The corporation is entitled to reject a vote, consent, waiver, or proxy appointment if the secretary or other officer or agent authorized to tabulate votes, acting in good faith, has reasonable basis for doubt about the validity of the signature on it or about the signatory's authority to sign for the shareholder.

(d) The corporation and its officer or agent who accepts or rejects a vote, consent, waiver, or proxy appointment in good faith and in accordance with the standards of this section or W.S. 17-16-722(b) are not liable in damages to the shareholder for the consequences of the acceptance or rejection.

(e) Corporate action based on the acceptance or rejection of a vote, consent, waiver, or proxy appointment under this section or W.S. 17-16-722(b) is valid unless a court of competent jurisdiction determines otherwise.

17-16-725. Quorum and voting requirements for voting groups.

(a) Shares entitled to vote as a separate voting group may take action on a matter at a meeting only if a quorum of those shares exists with respect to that matter. Unless the articles of incorporation or this act provide otherwise, a majority of the votes entitled to be cast on the matter by the voting group constitutes a quorum of that voting group for action on that matter.

(b) Once a share is represented for any purpose at a meeting, it is deemed present for quorum purposes for the remainder of the meeting and for any adjournment of that meeting unless a new record date is or shall be set for that adjourned meeting.

(c) If a quorum exists, action on a matter other than the election of directors by a voting group is approved if the votes cast within the voting group favoring the action exceed the votes cast opposing the action, unless the articles of incorporation or this act require a greater number of affirmative votes.

(d) Reserved.

(e) The election of directors is governed by W.S. 17-16-728.

17-16-726. Action by single and multiple voting groups.

(a) If the articles of incorporation or this act provide for voting by a single voting group on a matter, action on that matter is taken when voted upon by that voting group as provided in W.S. 17-16-725.

(b) If the articles of incorporation or this act provide for voting by two (2) or more voting groups on a matter, action on that matter is taken only when voted upon by each of those voting groups counted separately as provided in W.S. 17-16-725. Action may be taken by one (1) voting group on a matter even though no action is taken by another voting group entitled to vote on the matter.

17-16-727. Reserved.

17-16-728. Voting for directors; cumulative voting.

(a) Unless otherwise provided in the articles of incorporation, directors are elected by a plurality of the votes cast by the shares entitled to vote in the election at a meeting at which a quorum is present.

(b) Shareholders do not have a right to cumulate their votes for directors unless the articles of incorporation so provide.

(c) A statement included in the articles of incorporation that "[all] [a designated voting group of] shareholders are entitled to cumulate their votes for directors," or words of similar import, means that the shareholders designated are entitled to multiply the number of votes they are entitled to cast by the number of directors for whom they are entitled to vote and cast the product for a single candidate or distribute the product among two (2) or more candidates.

(d) Shares otherwise entitled to vote cumulatively may not be voted cumulatively at a particular meeting unless:

(i) The meeting notice or proxy statement accompanying the notice states conspicuously that cumulative voting is authorized; or

(ii) A shareholder who has the right to cumulate his votes gives notice to the corporation not less than forty-eight (48) hours before the time set for the meeting of his intent to cumulate his votes during the meeting. If one (1) shareholder gives this notice all other shareholders in the same voting group participating in the election are entitled to cumulate their votes without giving further notice.

17-16-729. Inspectors of election.

(a) A corporation having any shares listed on a national securities exchange or regularly traded in a market maintained by one (1) or more members of a national or affiliated securities association shall, and any other corporation may, appoint one (1) or more inspectors to act at a meeting of shareholders and make a written report of the inspectors' determinations. Each inspector shall take and sign an oath faithfully to execute the duties of inspector with strict impartiality and according to the best of the inspector's ability.

(b) The inspectors shall:

(i) Ascertain the number of shares outstanding and the voting power of each;

(ii) Determine the shares represented at a meeting;

(iii) Determine the validity of proxies and ballots;

(iv) Count all votes; and

(v) Determine the result.

(c) An inspector may be an officer or employee of the corporation.

17-16-730. Voting trusts.

(a) One (1) or more shareholders may create a voting trust, conferring on a trustee the right to vote or otherwise act for them, by signing, either manually or in facsimile, an agreement setting out the provisions of the trust, which may include anything consistent with its purpose, and transferring their shares to the trustee. When a voting trust agreement is signed, the trustee shall prepare a list of the names and addresses of all owners of beneficial interests in the trust, together with the number and class of shares each transferred to the trust, and deliver copies of the list and agreement to the corporation's principal office.

(b) A voting trust becomes effective on the date the first shares subject to the trust are registered in the trustee's name. A voting trust is valid for not more than ten (10) years after its effective date unless extended under subsection (c) of this section.

(c) All or some of the parties to a voting trust may extend it for additional terms of not more than ten (10) years each by signing, either manually or in facsimile, an extension agreement and obtaining the voting trustee's written consent to the extension. An extension is valid for ten (10) years from the date the first shareholder signs the extension agreement. The voting trustee shall deliver copies of the extension agreement and list of beneficial owners to the corporation's principal office. An extension agreement binds only those parties signing it.

17-16-731. Voting agreements.

(a) Any shareholder may agree with one (1) or more other shareholders or the corporation to provide for the manner in which he will vote his shares by signing, either manually or in facsimile, an agreement for that purpose. A voting agreement created under this section is not subject to the provisions of W.S. 17-16-730.

(b) A voting agreement created under this section is specifically enforceable.

17-16-732. Shareholder agreements.

(a) An agreement among the shareholders of a corporation that complies with this section is effective among the shareholders and the corporation even though it is inconsistent with one (1) or more other provisions of this act in that it:

(i) Eliminates the board of directors or restricts the discretion or powers of the board of directors;

(ii) Governs the authorization or making of distributions whether or not in proportion to ownership of shares, subject to the limitations in W.S. 17-16-640;

(iii) Establishes who shall be directors or officers of the corporation, or their terms of office or manner of selection or removal;

(iv) Governs, in general or in regard to specific matters, the exercise or division of voting power by or between the shareholders and directors or by or among any of them, including use of weighted voting rights or director proxies;

(v) Establishes the terms and conditions of any agreement for the transfer or use of property or the provision of services between the corporation and any shareholder, director, officer or employee of the corporation or among any of them;

(vi) Transfers to one (1) or more shareholders or other persons all or part of the authority to exercise the corporate powers or to manage the business and affairs of the corporation, including the resolution of any issue about which there exists a deadlock among directors or shareholders;

(vii) Requires dissolution of the corporation at the request of one (1) or more of the shareholders or upon the occurrence of a specified event or contingency; or

(viii) Otherwise governs the exercise of the corporate powers or the management of the business and affairs of the corporation or the relationship among the shareholders, the directors and the corporation, or among any of them, and is not contrary to public policy.

(b) An agreement authorized by this section shall be:

(i) Set forth:

(A) In the articles of incorporation or bylaws and approved by all persons who are shareholders at the time of the agreement; or

(B) In a written agreement that is signed by all persons who are shareholders at the time of the agreement and is made known to the corporation.

(ii) Subject to amendment only by all persons who are shareholders at the time of the amendment, unless the agreement provides otherwise; and

(iii) Valid for ten (10) years, unless the agreement provides otherwise. Nothing herein affects agreements in force on July 1, 1997.

(c) The existence of an agreement authorized by this section shall be noted conspicuously on the front or back of each certificate for outstanding shares or on the information statement required by W.S. 17-16-626(b). If at the time of the agreement the corporation has shares outstanding represented by certificates, the corporation shall recall the outstanding certificates and issue substitute certificates that comply with this subsection. The failure to note the existence of the agreement on the certificate or information statement shall not affect the validity of the agreement or any action taken pursuant to it. Any purchaser of shares who, at the time of purchase, did not have knowledge of the existence of the agreement shall be entitled to rescission of the purchase. A purchaser shall be deemed to have knowledge of the existence of the agreement if its existence is noted on the certificate or information statement for the shares in compliance with this subsection and, if the shares are not represented by a certificate, the information statement is delivered to the purchaser at or prior to the time of purchase of the shares. An action to enforce the right of rescission authorized by this subsection must be commenced within the earlier of ninety (90) days after discovery of the existence of the agreement or two (2) years after the time of purchase of the shares.

(d) An agreement authorized by this section shall cease to be effective when shares of the corporation are listed on a national securities exchange or regularly traded in a market maintained by one (1) or more members of a national or affiliated securities association. If the agreement ceases to be effective for any reason, the board of directors may, if the agreement is contained or referred to in the corporation's articles of incorporation or bylaws, adopt an amendment to the articles of incorporation or bylaws, without shareholder action, to delete the agreement and any references to it.

(e) An agreement authorized by this section that limits the discretion or powers of the board of directors shall relieve the directors of, and impose upon the person or persons in whom such discretion or powers are vested, liability for acts or omissions imposed by law on directors to the extent that the discretion or powers of the directors are limited by the agreement.

(f) The existence or performance of an agreement authorized by this section shall not be a ground for imposing personal liability on any shareholder for the acts or debts of the corporation even if the agreement or its performance treats the corporation as if it were a partnership or results in failure to observe the corporate formalities otherwise applicable to the matters governed by the agreement.

(g) Incorporators or subscribers for shares may act as shareholders with respect to an agreement authorized by this section if no shares have been issued when the agreement is made.

17-16-740. Subarticle definitions.

(a) Repealed By Laws 1997, ch. 190, § 3.

(b) Repealed By Laws 1997, ch. 190, § 3.

(c) Repealed By Laws 1997, ch. 190, § 3.

(d) Repealed By Laws 1997, ch. 190, § 3.

(e) Repealed By Laws 1997, ch. 190, § 3.

(f) As used in this subarticle:

(i) "Derivative proceeding" means a civil suit in the right of a domestic corporation or, to the extent provided in W.S. 17-16-747, in the right of a foreign corporation;

(ii) "Shareholder" includes a beneficial owner whose shares are held in a voting trust or held by a nominee on the beneficial owner's behalf.

17-16-741. Standing.

(a) A shareholder may not commence or maintain a derivative proceeding unless the shareholder:

(i) Was a shareholder of the corporation at the time of the act or omission complained of, or became a shareholder through transfer by operation of law from one who was a shareholder at the time; and

(ii) Fairly and adequately represents the interests of the corporation in enforcing the right of the corporation.

17-16-742. Demand.

(a) No shareholder may commence a derivative proceeding until:

(i) A written demand has been made upon the corporation to take suitable action; and

(ii) Ninety (90) days have expired from the date the demand was made unless the shareholder has earlier been notified that the demand has been rejected by the corporation or unless irreparable injury to the corporation would result by waiting for the expiration of the ninety (90) day period.

17-16-743. Stay of proceedings.

If the corporation commences an inquiry into the allegations made in the demand or complaint, the court may stay any derivative proceeding for such period as the court deems appropriate.

17-16-744. Dismissal.

(a) A derivative proceeding shall be dismissed by the court on motion by the corporation if the panel specified in subsection (b) of this section has determined in good faith after conducting a reasonable inquiry upon which its conclusions are based that the maintenance of the derivative proceeding is not in the best interests of the corporation.

(b) The court may appoint a panel of one (1) or more independent persons upon motion by the corporation to make a determination whether the maintenance of the derivative proceeding is in the best interests of the corporation. In such case, the plaintiff shall have the burden of proving that the requirements of subsection (a) of this section have not been met.

17-16-745. Discontinuance or settlement.

A derivative proceeding may not be discontinued or settled without the court's approval. If the court determines that a proposed discontinuance or settlement will substantially affect the interests of the corporation's shareholders or a class of shareholders, the court shall direct that notice be given to the shareholders affected.

17-16-746. Payment of expenses.

(a) On termination of the derivative proceeding the court may:

(i) Order the corporation to pay the plaintiff's reasonable expenses, including counsel fees, incurred in the proceeding if it finds that the proceeding resulted in a substantial benefit to the corporation;

(ii) Order the plaintiff to pay any defendant's reasonable expenses, including counsel fees, incurred in defending the proceeding if it finds that the proceeding was commenced or maintained without reasonable cause or for an improper purpose; or

(iii) Order a party to pay an opposing party's reasonable expenses, including counsel fees, incurred because of the filing of a pleading, motion or other paper, if it finds that the pleading, motion or other paper was not well grounded in fact, after reasonable inquiry, or warranted by existing law or a good faith argument for the extension, modification or reversal of existing law and was interposed for an improper purpose, such as to harass or to cause unnecessary delay or needless increase in the cost of litigation.

17-16-747. Applicability to foreign corporations.

In any derivative proceeding in the right of a foreign corporation, the matters covered by this subarticle shall be governed by the laws of the jurisdiction of incorporation of the foreign corporation except for W.S. 17-16-743, 17-16-745 and 17-16-746.

ARTICLE 8
DIRECTORS AND OFFICERS

17-16-801. Requirement for and duties of board of directors.

(a) Except as provided in W.S. 17-16-732, each corporation shall have a board of directors.

(b) All corporate powers shall be exercised by or under the authority of, and the business and affairs of the corporation managed under the direction of, its board of directors, subject to any limitation set forth in the articles of incorporation or in an agreement authorized under W.S. 17-16-732.

(c) Repealed By Laws 1997, ch. 190, § 3.

17-16-802. Qualifications of directors.

The articles of incorporation or bylaws may prescribe qualifications for directors. A director need not be a resident of this state or a shareholder of the corporation unless the articles of incorporation or bylaws so prescribe.

17-16-803. Number and election of directors.

(a) A board of directors shall consist of one (1) or more individuals, with the number specified in or fixed in accordance with the articles of incorporation or bylaws.

(b) If a board of directors has power to fix or change the number of directors, the board may increase or decrease by thirty percent (30%) or less the number of directors last approved by the shareholders, but only the shareholders may increase or decrease by more than thirty percent (30%) the number of directors last approved by the shareholders.

(c) The articles of incorporation or bylaws may establish a variable range for the size of the board of directors by fixing a minimum and maximum number of directors. If a variable range is established, the number of directors may be fixed or changed from time to time within the minimum and maximum, by the shareholders or the board of directors. After shares are issued, only the shareholders may change the range for the size of the board or change from a fixed to a variable-range size board or vice versa.

(d) Directors are elected at the first annual shareholders' meeting and at each annual meeting thereafter unless their terms are staggered under W.S. 17-16-806.

17-16-804. Election of directors by certain classes of shareholders.

If the articles of incorporation authorize dividing the shares into classes, the articles may also authorize the election of all or a specified number of directors by the holders of one (1) or more authorized classes of shares. A class or classes of shares entitled to elect one (1) or more directors is a separate voting group for purposes of the election of directors.

17-16-805. Terms of directors generally.

(a) The terms of the initial directors of a corporation expire at the first shareholders' meeting at which directors are elected.

(b) The terms of all other directors expire at the next annual shareholders' meeting following their election unless their terms are staggered under W.S. 17-16-806.

(c) A decrease in the number of directors does not shorten an incumbent director's term.

(d) The term of a director elected to fill a vacancy expires at the next shareholders' meeting at which directors are elected.

(e) Despite the expiration of a director's term, he continues to serve until his successor is elected and qualifies or until there is a decrease in the number of directors.

17-16-806. Staggered terms for directors.

If there are three (3) or more directors, the articles of incorporation may provide for staggering their terms by dividing the total number of directors into two (2) or three (3) groups, with each group containing one-half (1/2) or one-third (1/3) of the total, as near as may be. In that event, the terms of directors in the first group expire at the first annual shareholders' meeting after their election, the terms of the second group expire at the second annual shareholders' meeting after their election, and the terms of the third group, if any, expire at the third annual shareholders' meeting after their election. At each annual shareholders' meeting held thereafter, directors shall be chosen for a term of two (2) years or three (3) years, as the case may be, to succeed those whose terms expire.

17-16-807. Resignation of directors.

(a) A director may resign at any time by delivering written notice to the board of directors, its chairman, or to the corporation.

(b) A resignation is effective when the notice is delivered unless the notice specifies a later effective date.

17-16-808. Removal of directors by shareholders.

(a) The shareholders may remove one (1) or more directors with or without cause unless the articles of incorporation provide that directors may be removed only for cause.

(b) If a director is elected by a voting group of shareholders, only the shareholders of that voting group may participate in the vote to remove him.

(c) If cumulative voting is authorized, a director may not be removed if the number of votes sufficient to elect him under cumulative voting is voted against his removal. If cumulative voting is not authorized, a director may be removed only if the number of votes cast to remove him exceeds the number of votes cast not to remove him.

(d) A director may be removed by the shareholders only at a meeting called for the purpose of removing him and the meeting notice shall state that the purpose, or one (1) of the purposes, of the meeting is removal of the director.

17-16-809. Removal of directors by judicial proceeding.

(a) The district court of the county where a corporation's principal office, or if none in this state, its registered office, is located may remove a director of the corporation from office in a proceeding commenced either by the corporation or by its shareholders holding at least ten percent (10%) of the outstanding shares of any class if the court finds that:

(i) The director engaged in fraudulent or dishonest conduct, or gross abuse of authority or discretion, with respect to the corporation; and

(ii) Removal is in the best interest of the corporation.

(b) The court that removes a director may bar the director from reelection for a period prescribed by the court.

(c) If shareholders commence a proceeding under subsection (a) of this section, they shall make the corporation a party defendant.

17-16-810. Vacancy on board.

(a) Unless the articles of incorporation provide otherwise, if a vacancy occurs on a board of directors, including a vacancy resulting from an increase in the number of directors:

(i) The shareholders may fill the vacancy;

(ii) The board of directors may fill the vacancy; or

(iii) If the directors remaining in office constitute fewer than a quorum of the board, they may fill the vacancy by the affirmative vote of a majority of all the directors remaining in office.

(b) If the vacant office was held by a director elected by a voting group of shareholders, only the holders of shares of that voting group are entitled to vote to fill the vacancy if it is filled by the shareholders.

(c) A vacancy that will occur at a specific later date, by reason of a resignation effective at a later date under W.S. 17-16-807(b) or otherwise, may be filled before the vacancy occurs but the new director may not take office until the vacancy occurs.

17-16-811. Compensation of directors.

Unless the articles of incorporation or bylaws provide otherwise, the board of directors may fix the compensation of directors.

17-16-820. Meetings.

(a) The board of directors may hold regular or special meetings within or outside of this state.

(b) Unless the articles of incorporation or bylaws provide otherwise, the board of directors may permit any or all directors to participate in a regular or special meeting by, or conduct the meeting through the use of, any means of communication by which all directors participating may communicate with each other during the meeting. A director participating in a meeting by this means is deemed to be present in person at the meeting.

17-16-821. Action without meeting.

(a) Unless the articles of incorporation or bylaws provide otherwise, action required or permitted by this act to be taken at a board of directors' meeting may be taken without a meeting if the action is taken by all members of the board. The action shall be evidenced by one (1) or more written consents describing the action taken, signed, either manually or in facsimile, by each director, and included in the minutes or filed with the corporate records reflecting the action taken.

(b) Action taken under this section is effective when the last director signs the consent, unless the consent specifies a different effective date.

(c) A consent signed under this section has the effect of a meeting vote and may be described as such in any document.

17-16-822. Notice of meeting.

(a) Unless the articles of incorporation or bylaws provide otherwise, regular meetings of the board of directors may be held without notice of the date, time, place or purpose of the meeting.

(b) Unless the articles of incorporation or bylaws provide for a longer or shorter period, special meetings of the board of directors shall be preceded by at least two (2) days notice of the date, time and place of the meeting. The notice need not describe the purpose of the special meeting unless required by the articles of incorporation or bylaws.

17-16-823. Waiver of notice.

(a) A director may waive any notice required by this act, the articles of incorporation, or bylaws before or after the date and time stated in the notice. Except as provided by subsection (b) of this section, the waiver shall be in writing, signed, either manually or in facsimile, by the director entitled to the notice, and filed with the minutes or corporate records.

(b) A director's attendance at or participation in a meeting waives any required notice to him of the meeting unless the director at the beginning of the meeting or promptly upon his arrival objects to holding the meeting or transacting business at the meeting and does not thereafter vote for or assent to action taken at the meeting.

17-16-824. Quorum and voting.

(a) Unless the articles of incorporation or bylaws require a greater number or unless otherwise specifically provided in this act, a quorum of a board of directors consists of:

(i) A majority of the fixed number of directors if the corporation has a fixed board size; or

(ii) A majority of the number of directors prescribed, or if no number is prescribed the number in office immediately before the meeting begins, if the corporation has a variable-range size board.

(b) The articles of incorporation or bylaws may authorize a quorum of a board of directors to consist of no fewer than one-third (1/3) of the fixed or prescribed number of directors determined under subsection (a) of this section.

(c) If a quorum is present when a vote is taken, the affirmative vote of a majority of directors present is the act of the board of directors unless the articles of incorporation or bylaws require the vote of a greater number of directors.

(d) The right to dissent or abstention is not available to a director who votes in favor of the action taken. A director who is present at a meeting of the board of directors or a committee of the board of directors when corporate action is taken is deemed to have assented to the action taken unless:

(i) He objects at the beginning of the meeting or promptly upon his arrival to holding the meeting or transacting business at the meeting;

(ii) His dissent or abstention from the action taken is entered in the minutes of the meeting; or

(iii) He delivers written notice of his dissent or abstention to the presiding officer of the meeting before its adjournment or to the corporation immediately after adjournment of the meeting.

17-16-825. Committees.

(a) Unless the articles of incorporation or bylaws provide otherwise, a board of directors may create one (1) or more committees and appoint members of the board of directors to serve on them. Each committee shall have one (1) or more members, who serve at the pleasure of the board of directors.

(b) The creation of a committee and appointment of members to it shall be approved by the greater of:

(i) A majority of all the directors in office when the action is taken; or

(ii) The number of directors required by the articles of incorporation or bylaws to take action under W.S. 17-16-824.

(c) W.S. 17-16-820 through 17-16-824, which govern meetings, action without meetings, notice and waiver of notice, and quorum and voting requirements of the board of directors, apply to committees and their members as well.

(d) To the extent specified by the board of directors or in the articles of incorporation or bylaws, each committee may exercise the authority of the board of directors under W.S. 17-16-801.

(e) A committee may not, unless specifically authorized by the board of directors:

(i) Authorize distributions;

(ii) Approve or propose to shareholders action that this act requires to be approved by shareholders;

(iii) Fill vacancies on the board of directors or on any of its committees;

(iv) Amend articles of incorporation pursuant to W.S. 17-16-1002;

(v) Adopt, amend or repeal bylaws;

(vi) Approve a plan of merger not requiring shareholder approval;

(vii) Authorize or approve reacquisition of shares, except according to a formula or method prescribed by the board of directors; or

(viii) Authorize or approve the issuance or sale or contract for sale of shares, or determine the designation and relative rights, preferences and limitations of a class or series of shares, except that the board of directors may authorize a committee or a senior executive officer of the corporation to do so within limits specifically prescribed by the board of directors.

(f) The creation of, delegation of authority to, or action by a committee does not alone constitute compliance by a director with the standards of conduct described in W.S. 17-16-830.

17-16-830. General standards for directors.

(a) A director shall discharge his duties as a director, including his duties as a member of a committee:

(i) In good faith;

(ii) With the care an ordinarily prudent person in a like position would exercise under similar circumstances; and

(iii) In a manner he reasonably believes to be in or at least not opposed to the best interests of the corporation.

(b) In discharging his duties a director is entitled to rely on information, opinions, reports or statements, including financial statements and other financial data, if prepared or presented by:

(i) One (1) or more officers or employees of the corporation whom the director reasonably believes to be reliable and competent in the matters presented;

(ii) Legal counsel, public accountants or other persons as to matters the director reasonably believes are within the person's professional or expert competence; or

(iii) A committee of the board of directors of which he is not a member if the director reasonably believes the committee merits confidence.

(c) A director is not acting in good faith if he has knowledge concerning the matter in question that makes reliance otherwise permitted by subsection (b) of this section unwarranted.

(d) A director is not liable for any action taken as a director, or any failure to take any action, if he performed the duties of his office in compliance with this section.

(e) For purposes of subsection (a) of this section, a director, in determining what he reasonably believes to be in or not opposed to the best interests of the corporation, shall consider the interests of the corporation's shareholders and, in his discretion, may consider any of the following:

(i) The interests of the corporation's employees, suppliers, creditors and customers;

(ii) The economy of the state and nation;

(iii) The impact of any action upon the communities in or near which the corporation's facilities or operations are located;

(iv) The long-term interests of the corporation and its shareholders, including the possibility that those interests may be best served by the continued independence of the corporation; and

(v) Any other factors relevant to promoting or preserving public or community interests.

17-16-831. Director conflict of interest.

(a) A conflict of interest transaction is a transaction with the corporation in which a director of the corporation has a direct or indirect interest. A conflict of interest transaction is not voidable by the corporation solely because of the director's interest in the transaction if any one (1) of the following is true:

(i) The material facts of the transaction and the director's interest were disclosed or known to the board of directors or a committee of the board of directors and the board of directors or committee authorized, approved or ratified the transaction;

(ii) The material facts of the transaction and the director's interest were disclosed or known to the shareholders entitled to vote and they authorized, approved or ratified the transaction; or

(iii) The transaction was fair to the corporation.

(b) For purposes of this section, a director of the corporation has an indirect interest in a transaction if:

(i) Another entity in which he has a material financial interest or in which he is a general partner is a party to the transaction; or

(ii) Another entity of which he is a director, officer or trustee is a party to the transaction and the transaction is or should be considered by the board of directors of the corporation.

(c) For purposes of paragraph (a)(i) of this section, a conflict of interest transaction is authorized, approved or ratified if it receives the affirmative vote of a majority of the directors on the board of directors or on the committee who have no direct or indirect interest in the transaction, but a transaction may not be authorized, approved or ratified under this section by a single director. If a majority of the directors who have no direct or indirect interest in the transaction vote to authorize, approve or ratify the transaction, a quorum is present for the purpose of taking action under this section. The presence of, or a vote cast by, a director with a direct or indirect interest in the transaction does not affect the validity of any action taken under paragraph (a)(i) of this section if the transaction is otherwise authorized, approved or ratified as provided in that paragraph.

(d) For purposes of paragraph (a)(ii) of this section, a conflict of interest transaction is authorized, approved or ratified if it receives the vote of a majority of the shares entitled to be counted under this subsection. Shares owned by or voted under the control of a director who has a direct or indirect interest in the transaction, and shares owned by or voted under the control of an entity described in paragraph (b)(i) of this section, may not be counted in a vote of shareholders to determine whether to authorize, approve or ratify a conflict of interest transaction under paragraph (a)(ii) of this section. The vote of those shares, however, is counted in determining whether the transaction is approved under other sections of this act. A majority of the shares, whether or not present, that are entitled to be counted in a vote on the transaction under this subsection constitutes a quorum for the purpose of taking action under this section.

17-16-832. Loans to directors.

(a) Except as provided by subsection (c) of this section, a corporation may not lend money to or guarantee the obligation of a director of the corporation unless:

(i) The particular loan or guarantee is approved by a majority of the votes represented by the outstanding voting shares of all classes, voting as a single voting group, except the votes of shares owned by or voted under the control of the benefited director; or

(ii) The corporation's board of directors determines that the loan or guarantee benefits the corporation and either approves the specific loan or guarantee or a general plan authorizing loans and guarantees.

(b) The fact that a loan or guarantee is made in violation of this section does not affect the borrower's liability on the loan.

(c) This section does not apply to loans and guarantees authorized by statute regulating any special class of corporations.

17-16-833. Liability for unlawful distributions.

(a) A director who votes for or assents to a distribution made in violation of W.S. 17-16-640 or the articles of incorporation is personally liable to the corporation for the amount of the distribution that exceeds what could have been distributed without violating W.S. 17-16-640 or the articles of incorporation if it is established that he did not perform his duties in compliance with W.S. 17-16-830. In any proceeding commenced under this section, a director has all of the defenses ordinarily available to a director.

(b) A director held liable under subsection (a) of this section for an unlawful distribution is entitled to contribution:

(i) From every other director who could be held liable under subsection (a) of this section for the unlawful distribution; and

(ii) From each shareholder for the amount the shareholder accepted knowing the distribution was made in violation of W.S. 17-16-640 or the articles of incorporation.

(c) A proceeding under this section is barred unless it is commenced within two (2) years after the date on which the effect of the distribution was measured under W.S. 17-16-640(e) or (g).

17-16-834. Repealed By Laws 1997, ch. 190, § 3.

17-16-840. Required officers.

(a) A corporation has the officers described in its bylaws or appointed by the board of directors in accordance with the bylaws.

(b) A duly appointed officer may appoint one (1) or more officers or assistant officers if authorized by the bylaws or the board of directors.

(c) The bylaws or the board of directors shall delegate to one (1) of the officers responsibility for preparing minutes of the directors' and shareholders' meetings and for authenticating records of the corporation.

(d) The same individual may simultaneously hold more than one (1) office in a corporation.

17-16-841. Duties of officers.

Each officer has the authority and shall perform the duties set forth in the bylaws or, to the extent consistent with the bylaws, the duties prescribed by the board of directors or by direction of an officer authorized by the board of directors to prescribe the duties of other officers.

17-16-842. Standards of conduct for officers.

(a) An officer with discretionary authority shall discharge his duties under that authority:

(i) In good faith;

(ii) With the care an ordinarily prudent person in a like position would exercise under similar circumstances; and

(iii) In a manner he reasonably believes to be in or at least not opposed to the best interests of the corporation.

(b) In discharging his duties an officer is entitled to rely on information, opinions, reports or statements, including financial statements and other financial data, if prepared or presented by:

(i) One (1) or more officers or employees of the corporation whom the officer reasonably believes to be reliable and competent in the matters presented; or

(ii) Legal counsel, public accountants or other persons as to matters the officer reasonably believes are within the person's professional or expert competence.

(c) An officer is not acting in good faith if he has knowledge concerning the matter in question that makes reliance otherwise permitted by subsection (b) of this section unwarranted.

(d) An officer is not liable for any action taken as an officer, or any failure to take any action, if he performed the duties of his office in compliance with this section.

(e) For purposes of subsection (a) of this section, an officer, in determining what he reasonably believes to be in or not opposed to the best interests of the corporation, shall consider the interests of the corporation's shareholders and, in his discretion, may consider any of the following:

(i) The interests of the corporation's employees, suppliers, creditors and customers;

(ii) The economy of the state and nation;

(iii) The impact of any action upon the communities in or near which the corporation's facilities or operations are located;

(iv) The long-term interests of the corporation and its shareholders, including the possibility that those interests may be best served by the continued independence of the corporation; and

(v) Any other factors relevant to promoting or preserving public or community interests.

17-16-843. Resignation and removal of officers.

(a) An officer may resign at any time by delivering notice to the corporation. A resignation is effective when the notice is delivered unless the notice specifies a later effective date. If a resignation is made effective at a later date and the corporation accepts the future effective date, its board of directors may fill the pending vacancy before the effective date if the board of directors provides that the successor does not take office until the effective date.

(b) A board of directors may remove any officer at any time with or without cause.

17-16-844. Contract rights of officers.

(a) The appointment of an officer does not itself create contract rights.

(b) An officer's removal does not affect the officer's contract rights, if any, with the corporation. An officer's resignation does not affect the corporation's contract rights, if any, with the officer.

17-16-850. Subarticle definitions.

(a) In this subarticle:

(i) "Corporation" includes any domestic or foreign predecessor entity of a corporation in a merger;

(ii) "Director" or "officer" means an individual who is or was a director or officer, respectively, of a corporation or who, while a director or officer of the corporation, is or was serving at the corporation's request as a director, officer, partner, trustee, employee or agent of another domestic or foreign corporation, partnership, joint venture, trust, employee benefit plan or other entity. A director or officer is considered to be serving an employee benefit plan at the corporation's request if his duties to the corporation also impose duties on, or otherwise involve services by, him to the plan or to participants in or beneficiaries of the plan. "Director" or "officer" includes, unless the context requires otherwise, the estate or personal representative of a director or officer;

(iii) "Disinterested director" means a director who, at the time of a vote referred to in W.S. 17-16-853(c) or a vote or selection referred to in W.S. 17-16-855(b) or (c), is not:

(A) A party to the proceeding; or

(B) An individual having a familial, financial, professional or employment relationship with the director whose indemnification or advance for expenses is the subject of the decision being made, which relationship would, in the circumstances, reasonably be expected to exert an influence on the director's judgment when voting on the decision being made.

(iv) "Expenses" includes counsel fees;

(v) "Liability" means the obligation to pay a judgment, settlement, penalty, fine (including an excise tax assessed with respect to an employee benefit plan), or reasonable expenses incurred with respect to a proceeding;

(vi) "Party" means an individual who was, is or is threatened to be made, a defendant or respondent in a proceeding;

(vii) "Proceeding" means any threatened, pending or completed action, suit or proceeding, whether civil, criminal, administrative, arbitrative or investigative and whether formal or informal.

17-16-851. Authority to indemnify.

(a) Except as otherwise provided in this section, a corporation may indemnify an individual who is a party to a proceeding because he is a director against liability incurred in the proceeding if:

(i) He conducted himself in good faith; and

(ii) He reasonably believed that his conduct was in or at least not opposed to the corporation's best interests; and

(iii) In the case of any criminal proceeding, he had no reasonable cause to believe his conduct was unlawful; or

(iv) He engaged in conduct for which broader indemnification has been made permissible or obligatory under a provision of the articles of incorporation, as authorized by W.S. 17-16-202(b)(v).

(b) A director's conduct with respect to an employee benefit plan for a purpose he reasonably believed to be in the interests of the participants in and beneficiaries of the plan is conduct that satisfies the requirement of paragraph (a)(ii) of this section.

(c) The termination of a proceeding by judgment, order, settlement, conviction, or upon a plea of nolo contendere or its equivalent is not, of itself, determinative that the director did not meet the standard of conduct described in this section.

(d) Unless ordered by a court under W.S. 17-16-854(a)(iii) a corporation may not indemnify a director under this section:

(i) In connection with a proceeding by or in the right of the corporation, except for reasonable expenses incurred in connection with the proceeding if it is determined that the director has met the standard of conduct under subsection (a) of this section; or

(ii) In connection with any proceeding with respect to conduct for which he was adjudged liable on the basis that he received a financial benefit to which he was not entitled.

(e) Repealed By Laws 1997, ch. 190, § 3.

17-16-852. Mandatory indemnification.

A corporation shall indemnify a director who was wholly successful, on the merits or otherwise, in the defense of any proceeding to which he was a party because he was a director of the corporation against reasonable expenses incurred by him in connection with the proceeding.

17-16-853. Advance for expenses.

(a) A corporation may, before final disposition of a proceeding, advance funds to pay for or reimburse the reasonable expenses incurred by a director who is a party to a proceeding because he is a director if he delivers to the corporation:

(i) A written affirmation of his good faith belief that he has met the standard of conduct described in W.S. 17-16-851 or that the proceeding involves conduct for which liability has been eliminated under a provision of the articles of incorporation as authorized by W.S. 17-16-202(b)(iv); and

(ii) His written undertaking to repay any funds advanced if he is not entitled to mandatory indemnification under W.S. 17-16-852 and it is ultimately determined that he has not met the standard of conduct described in W.S. 17-16-851.

(iii) Repealed By Laws 1997, ch. 190, § 3.

(b) The undertaking required by paragraph (a)(ii) of this section shall be an unlimited general obligation of the director but need not be secured and may be accepted without reference to the financial ability of the director to make repayment.

(c) Authorizations under this section shall be made:

(i) By the board of directors:

(A) If there are two (2) or more disinterested directors, by a majority vote of all the disinterested directors (a majority of whom shall for such purpose constitute a quorum) or by a majority of the members of a committee of two (2) or more disinterested directors appointed by such a vote; or

(B) If there are fewer than two (2) disinterested directors, by the vote necessary for action by the board in accordance with W.S. 17-16-824(c), in which authorization directors who do not qualify as disinterested directors may participate; or

(ii) By the shareholders, but shares owned by or voted under the control of a director who at the time does not qualify as a disinterested director may not be voted on the authorization.

17-16-854. Court-ordered indemnification and advance for expenses.

(a) A director who is a party to a proceeding because he is a director may apply for indemnification or an advance for expenses to the court conducting the proceeding or to another court of competent jurisdiction. After receipt of an application and after giving any notice it considers necessary, the court shall:

(i) Order indemnification if the court determines that the director is entitled to mandatory indemnification under W.S. 17-16-852;

(ii) Order indemnification or advance for expenses if the court determines that the director is entitled to indemnification or advance for expenses pursuant to a provision authorized by W.S. 17-16-858(a); or

(iii) Order indemnification or advance for expenses if the court determines, in view of all the relevant circumstances, that it is fair and reasonable:

(A) To indemnify the director; or

(B) To advance expenses to the director, even if he has not met the standard of conduct set forth in W.S. 17-16-851(a), failed to comply with W.S. 17-16-853 or was adjudged liable in a proceeding referred to in W.S. 17-16-851(d)(i) or (ii), but if he was adjudged so liable his indemnification shall be limited to reasonable expenses incurred in connection with the proceeding.

(b) If the court determines that the director is entitled to indemnification under paragraph (a)(i) of this section or to indemnification or advance for expenses under paragraph (a)(ii) of this section, it shall also order the corporation to pay the director's reasonable expenses incurred in connection with obtaining court-ordered indemnification or advance for expenses. If the court determines that the director is entitled to indemnification or advance for expenses under paragraph (a)(iii) of this section, it may also order the corporation to pay the director's reasonable expenses to obtain court-ordered indemnification or advance for expenses.

17-16-855. Determination and authorization of indemnification.

(a) A corporation may not indemnify a director under W.S. 17-16-851 unless authorized for a specific proceeding after a determination has been made that indemnification of the director is permissible because he has met the standard of conduct set forth in W.S. 17-16-851.

(b) The determination shall be made:

(i) If there are two (2) or more disinterested directors, by the board of directors by majority vote of all the disinterested directors (a majority of whom shall for such purpose constitute a quorum), or by a majority of the members of a committee of two (2) or more disinterested directors appointed by such a vote;

(ii) Repealed By Laws 1997, ch. 190, § 3.

(iii) By special legal counsel:

(A) Selected in the manner prescribed in paragraph (i) of this subsection; or

(B) If there are fewer than two (2) disinterested directors, selected by the board of directors (in which selection directors who do not qualify as disinterested directors may participate); or

(iv) By the shareholders, but shares owned by or voted under the control of a director who at the time does not qualify as a disinterested director may not be voted on the determination.

(c) Authorization of indemnification shall be made in the same manner as the determination that indemnification is permissible, except that if there are fewer than two (2) disinterested directors, authorization of indemnification shall be made by those entitled under paragraph (b)(iii) of this section to select special legal counsel.

17-16-856. Officers.

(a) A corporation may indemnify and advance expenses under this subarticle to an officer of the corporation who is a party to a proceeding because he is an officer of the corporation:

(i) To the same extent as a director; and

(ii) If he is an officer but not a director, to such further extent as may be provided by the articles of incorporation, the bylaws, a resolution of the board of directors or contract, except for:

(A) Liability in connection with a proceeding by or in the right of the corporation other than for reasonable expenses incurred in connection with the proceeding; or

(B) Liability arising out of conduct that constitutes:

(I) Receipt by him of a financial benefit to which he is not entitled;

(II) An intentional infliction of harm on the corporation or the shareholders; or

(III) An intentional violation of criminal law.

(iii) A corporation may also indemnify and advance expenses to a current or former officer, employee or agent who is not a director to the extent, consistent with public policy, that may be provided by its articles of incorporation, bylaws, general or specific action of its board of directors or contract.

(b) The provisions of paragraph (a)(ii) of this section shall apply to an officer who is also a director if the basis on which he is made a party to the proceeding is an act or omission solely as an officer.

(c) An officer of a corporation who is not a director is entitled to mandatory indemnification under W.S. 17-16-852, and may apply to a court under W.S. 17-16-854 for indemnification or an advance for expenses, in each case to the same extent to which a director may be entitled to indemnification or advance for expenses under those provisions.

17-16-857. Insurance.

A corporation may purchase and maintain insurance on behalf of an individual who is a director or officer of the corporation, or who, while a director or officer of the corporation, serves at the corporation's request as a director, officer, partner, trustee, employee or agent of another domestic or foreign corporation, partnership, joint venture, trust, employee benefit plan, or other entity, against liability asserted against or incurred by him in that capacity or arising from his status as a director or officer whether or not the corporation would have power to indemnify or advance expenses to him against the same liability under this subarticle.

17-16-858. Variation by corporate action; application of subarticle.

(a) A corporation may, by a provision in its articles of incorporation or bylaws or in a resolution adopted or a contract approved by its board of directors or shareholders, obligate itself in advance of the act or omission giving rise to a proceeding to provide indemnification in accordance with W.S. 17-16-851 or advance funds to pay for or reimburse expenses in accordance with W.S. 17-16-853. Any such obligatory provision shall be deemed to satisfy the requirements for authorization referred to in W.S. 17-16-853(c) and 17-16-855(c). Any provision that obligates the corporation to provide indemnification to the fullest extent permitted by law shall be deemed to obligate the corporation to advance funds to pay for or reimburse expenses in accordance with W.S. 17-16-853 to the fullest extent permitted by law, unless the provision specifically provides otherwise.

(b) Any provision pursuant to subsection (a) of this section shall not obligate the corporation to indemnify or advance expenses to a director of a predecessor of the corporation, pertaining to conduct with respect to the predecessor, unless otherwise specifically provided. Any provision for indemnification or advance for expenses in the articles of incorporation, bylaws, or a resolution of the board of directors or shareholders of a predecessor of the corporation in a merger or in a contract to which the predecessor is a party, existing at the time the merger takes effect, shall be governed by W.S. 17-16-1106(a)(iii).

(c) A corporation may, by provision in its articles of incorporation, limit any of the rights to indemnification or advance for expenses created by or pursuant to this subarticle.

(d) This subarticle does not limit a corporation's power to pay or reimburse expenses incurred by a director or officer in connection with his appearance as a witness in a proceeding at a time when he is not a party.

(e) This subarticle does not limit a corporation's power to indemnify, advance expenses to or provide or maintain insurance on behalf of an employee or agent.

17-16-859. Exclusivity of subarticle.

A corporation may provide indemnification or advance expenses to a director or an officer only as permitted by this subarticle.

ARTICLE 10
AMENDMENT OF ARTICLES OF INCORPORATION AND BYLAWS

17-16-1001. Authority to amend.

(a) A corporation may amend its articles of incorporation at any time to add or change a provision that is required or permitted in the articles of incorporation or to delete a provision not required in the articles of incorporation. Whether a provision is required or permitted in the articles of incorporation is determined as of the effective date of the amendment.

(b) A shareholder of the corporation does not have a vested property right resulting from any provision in the articles of incorporation, including provisions relating to management, control, capital structure, dividend entitlement or purpose, or duration of the corporation.

17-16-1002. Amendment by board of directors.

(a) Unless the articles of incorporation provide otherwise, a corporation's board of directors may adopt one (1) or more amendments to the corporation's articles of incorporation without shareholder action to:

(i) Extend the duration of the corporation if it was incorporated at a time when limited duration was required by law;

(ii) Delete the names and addresses of the initial directors;

(iii) Delete the name and address of the initial registered agent or registered office, if a statement of change is on file with the secretary of state;

(iv) Change each issued and unissued authorized share of an outstanding class into a greater number of whole shares if the corporation has only shares of that class outstanding;

(v) Change the corporate name by substituting the word "corporation," "incorporated," "company," "limited," or the abbreviation "corp.," "inc.," "co.," or "ltd.," for a similar word or abbreviation in the name, or by adding, deleting, or changing a geographical attribution for the name; or

(vi) Make any other change expressly permitted by this act to be made without shareholder action.

17-16-1003. Amendment by board of directors and shareholders.

(a) A corporation's board of directors may propose one (1) or more amendments to the articles of incorporation for submission to the shareholders.

(b) For the amendment to be adopted:

(i) The board of directors shall recommend the amendment to the shareholders unless the board of directors determines that because of conflict of interest or other special circumstances it should make no recommendation and communicates the basis for its determination to the shareholders with the amendment; and

(ii) The shareholders entitled to vote on the amendment shall approve the amendment as provided in subsection (e) of this section.

(c) The board of directors may condition its submission of the proposed amendment on any basis.

(d) The corporation shall notify each shareholder, whether or not entitled to vote, of the proposed shareholders' meeting in accordance with W.S. 17-16-705. The notice of meeting shall also state that the purpose, or one (1) of the purposes, of the meeting is to consider the proposed amendment and contain or be accompanied by a copy or summary of the amendment.

(e) Unless this act, the articles of incorporation, or the board of directors acting pursuant to subsection (c) of this section require a greater vote or a vote by voting groups, the amendment to be adopted shall be approved by:

(i) A majority of the votes entitled to be cast on the amendment by any voting group with respect to which the amendment would create dissenters' rights; and

(ii) The votes required by W.S. 17-16-725 and 17-16-726 by every other voting group entitled to vote on the amendment.

17-16-1004. Voting on amendments by voting groups.

(a) The holders of the outstanding shares of a class are entitled to vote as a separate voting group, if shareholder voting is otherwise required by this act, on a proposed amendment if the amendment would:

(i) Increase or decrease the aggregate number of authorized shares of the class;

(ii) Effect an exchange or reclassification of all or part of the shares of the class into shares of another class;

(iii) Effect an exchange or reclassification, or create the right of exchange, of all or part of the shares of another class into shares of the class;

(iv) Change the designation, rights, preferences, or limitations of all or part of the shares of the class;

(v) Change the shares of all or part of the class into a different number of shares of the same class;

(vi) Create a new class of shares having rights or preferences with respect to distributions or to dissolution that are prior, superior, or substantially equal to the shares of the class;

(vii) Increase the rights, preferences, or number of authorized shares of any class that, after giving effect to the amendment, have rights or preferences with respect to distributions or to dissolution that are prior, superior, or substantially equal to the shares of the class;

(viii) Limit or deny any existing preemptive right of all or part of the shares of the class; or

(ix) Cancel or otherwise affect rights to distributions or dividends that have accumulated but not yet been declared on all or part of the shares of the class.

(b) If a proposed amendment would affect a series of a class of shares in one (1) or more of the ways described in subsection (a) of this section, the shares of that series are entitled to vote as a separate voting group on the proposed amendment.

(c) If a proposed amendment that entitles two (2) or more series of shares to vote as separate voting groups under this section would affect those two (2) or more series in the same or a substantially similar way, the shares of all the series so affected shall vote together as a single voting group on the proposed amendment.

(d) A class or series of shares is entitled to the voting rights granted by this section although the articles of incorporation provide that the shares are nonvoting shares.

17-16-1005. Amendment before issuance of shares.

If a corporation has not yet issued shares, its incorporators or board of directors may adopt one (1) or more amendments to the corporation's articles of incorporation.

17-16-1006. Articles of amendment.

(a) A corporation amending its articles of incorporation shall deliver to the secretary of state for filing articles of amendment setting forth:

(i) The name of the corporation;

(ii) The text of each amendment adopted;

(iii) If an amendment provides for an exchange, reclassification, or cancellation of issued shares, provisions for implementing the amendment if not contained in the amendment itself;

(iv) The date of each amendment's adoption;

(v) If an amendment was adopted by the incorporators or board of directors without shareholder action, a statement to that effect and that shareholder action was not required; and

(vi) If an amendment was approved by the shareholders:

(A) The designation, number of outstanding shares, number of votes entitled to be cast by each voting group entitled to vote separately on the amendment, and number of votes of each voting group indisputably represented at the meeting; and

(B) Either the total number of votes cast for and against the amendment by each voting group entitled to vote separately on the amendment or the total number of undisputed votes cast for the amendment by each voting group and a statement that the number cast for the amendment by each voting group was sufficient for approval by that voting group.

17-16-1007. Restated articles of incorporation.

(a) A corporation's board of directors may restate its articles of incorporation at any time with or without shareholder action.

(b) The restatement may include one (1) or more amendments to the articles. If the restatement includes an amendment requiring shareholder approval, it shall be adopted as provided in W.S. 17-16-1003.

(c) If the board of directors submits a restatement for shareholder action, the corporation shall notify each shareholder, whether or not entitled to vote, of the proposed shareholders' meeting in accordance with W.S. 17-16-705. The notice shall also state that the purpose, or one (1) of the purposes, of the meeting is to consider the proposed restatement and contain or be accompanied by a copy of the restatement that identifies any amendment or other change it would make in the articles.

(d) A corporation restating its articles of incorporation shall deliver to the secretary of state for filing articles of restatement setting forth the name of the corporation and the text of the restated articles of incorporation together with a certificate setting forth:

(i) Whether the restatement contains an amendment to the articles requiring shareholder approval and, if it does not, that the board of directors adopted the restatement; or

(ii) If the restatement contains an amendment to the articles requiring shareholder approval, the information required by W.S. 17-16-1006.

(e) Duly adopted restated articles of incorporation supersede the original articles of incorporation and all amendments to them.

(f) The secretary of state may certify restated articles of incorporation, as the articles of incorporation currently in effect, without including the certificate information required by subsection (d) of this section.

17-16-1008. Amendment pursuant to court-ordered reorganization.

(a) A corporation's articles of incorporation may be amended without action by the board of directors or shareholders to carry out a plan of reorganization ordered or decreed by a court of competent jurisdiction under federal statute if the articles of incorporation after amendment contain only provisions required or permitted by W.S. 17-16-202.

(b) The individual or individuals designated by the court shall deliver to the secretary of state for filing articles of amendment setting forth:

(i) The name of the corporation;

(ii) The text of each amendment approved by the court;

(iii) The date of the court's order or decree approving the articles of amendment;

(iv) The title of the reorganization proceeding in which the order or decree was entered; and

(v) A statement that the court had jurisdiction of the proceeding under federal statute.

(c) Shareholders of a corporation undergoing reorganization do not have dissenters' rights except as and to the extent provided in the reorganization plan.

(d) This section does not apply after entry of a final decree in the reorganization proceeding even though the court retains jurisdiction of the proceeding for limited purposes unrelated to consummation of the reorganization plan.

17-16-1009. Effect of amendment.

An amendment to articles of incorporation does not affect a cause of action existing against or in favor of the corporation, a proceeding to which the corporation is a party, or the existing rights of persons other than shareholders of the corporation. An amendment changing a corporation's name does not abate a proceeding brought by or against the corporation in its former name.

17-16-1020. Amendment by board of directors or shareholders.

(a) A corporation's board of directors may amend or repeal the corporation's bylaws unless:

(i) The articles of incorporation or this act reserve this power exclusively to the shareholders in whole or part; or

(ii) The shareholders in amending or repealing a particular bylaw provide expressly that the board of directors may not amend or repeal that bylaw.

(b) A corporation's shareholders may amend or repeal the corporation's bylaws even though the bylaws may also be amended or repealed by its board of directors.

17-16-1021. Bylaw increasing quorum or voting requirement for shareholders.

(a) If authorized by the articles of incorporation, the shareholders may adopt or amend a bylaw that fixes a greater quorum or voting requirement for shareholders or voting groups of shareholders than is required by this act. The adoption or amendment of a bylaw that adds, changes or deletes a greater quorum or voting requirement for shareholders shall meet the same quorum requirement and be adopted by the same vote and voting groups required to take action under the quorum and voting requirement then in effect.

(b) A bylaw that fixes a greater quorum or voting requirement for shareholders under subsection (a) of this section may not be adopted, amended or repealed by the board of directors.

17-16-1022. Bylaw increasing quorum or voting requirement for directors.

(a) A bylaw that fixes a greater quorum or voting requirement for the board of directors may be amended or repealed:

(i) If originally adopted by the shareholders, only by the shareholders;

(ii) If originally adopted by the board of directors, either by the shareholders or by the board of directors.

(b) A bylaw adopted or amended by the shareholders that fixes a greater quorum or voting requirement for the board of directors may provide that it may be amended or repealed only by a specified vote of either the shareholders or the board of directors.

(c) Action by the board of directors under paragraph (a)(ii) of this section to adopt or amend a bylaw that changes the quorum or voting requirement for the board of directors shall meet the same quorum requirement and be adopted by the same vote required to take action under the quorum and voting requirement then in effect.

ARTICLE 11
MERGER, SHARE EXCHANGE, CONSOLIDATION AND CONVERSION

17-16-1101. Merger.

(a) One (1) or more corporations may merge into another corporation if the board of directors of each corporation adopts and, if required by W.S. 17-16-1103, its shareholders approve a plan of merger.

(b) The plan of merger shall set forth:

(i) The name of each corporation planning to merge and the name of the surviving corporation into which each other corporation plans to merge;

(ii) The terms and conditions of the merger; and

(iii) The manner and basis of converting the shares of each corporation into shares, obligations or other securities of the surviving or any other corporation or into cash or other property in whole or part.

(c) The plan of merger may set forth:

(i) Amendments to the articles of incorporation of the surviving corporation; and

(ii) Other provisions relating to the merger.

17-16-1102. Share exchange.

(a) A corporation may acquire all of the outstanding shares of one (1) or more classes or series of another corporation if the board of directors of each corporation adopts and, if required by W.S. 17-16-1103, its shareholders approve the exchange.

(b) The plan of exchange shall set forth:

(i) The name of the corporation whose shares will be acquired and the name of the acquiring corporation;

(ii) The terms and conditions of the exchange; and

(iii) The manner and basis of exchanging the shares to be acquired for shares, obligations or other securities of the acquiring or any other corporation or for cash or other property in whole or part.

(c) The plan of exchange may set forth other provisions relating to the exchange.

(d) This section does not limit the power of a corporation to acquire all or part of the shares of one (1) or more classes or series of another corporation through a voluntary exchange or otherwise.

17-16-1103. Action on plan.

(a) After adopting a plan of merger or share exchange, the board of directors of each corporation party to the merger, and the board of directors of the corporation whose shares will be acquired in the share exchange, shall submit the plan of merger, except as provided in subsection (g) of this section, or share exchange for approval by its shareholders.

(b) For a plan of merger or share exchange to be approved:

(i) The board of directors shall recommend the plan of merger or share exchange to the shareholders, unless the board of directors determines that because of conflict of interest or other special circumstances it should make no recommendation and communicates the basis for its determination to the shareholders with the plan; and

(ii) The shareholders entitled to vote shall approve the plan.

(c) The board of directors may condition its submission of the proposed merger or share exchange on any basis.

(d) The corporation shall notify each shareholder, whether or not entitled to vote, of the proposed shareholders' meeting in accordance with W.S. 17-16-705. The notice shall also state that the purpose, or one (1) of the purposes, of the meeting is to consider the plan of merger or share exchange and contain or be accompanied by a copy or summary of the plan.

(e) Unless this act, the articles of incorporation or the board of directors acting pursuant to subsection (c) of this section require a greater vote or a vote by voting groups, the plan of merger or share exchange to be authorized shall be approved by each voting group entitled to vote separately on the plan by a majority of all the votes entitled to be cast on the plan by that voting group.

(f) Separate voting by voting groups is required:

(i) On a plan of merger if the plan contains a provision that, if contained in a proposed amendment to articles of incorporation, would require action by one (1) or more separate voting groups on the proposed amendment under W.S. 17-16-1004; or

(ii) On a plan of share exchange by each class or series of shares included in the exchange, with each class or series constituting a separate voting group.

(g) Action by the shareholders of the surviving corporation on a plan of merger is not required if:

(i) The articles of incorporation of the surviving corporation will not differ, except for amendments enumerated in W.S. 17-16-1002, from its articles before the merger;

(ii) Each shareholder of the surviving corporation whose shares were outstanding immediately before the effective date of the merger will hold the same number of shares, with identical designations, preferences, limitations and relative rights, immediately after;

(iii) The number of voting shares outstanding immediately after the merger, plus the number of voting shares issuable as a result of the merger, either by the conversion of securities issued pursuant to the merger or the exercise of rights and warrants issued pursuant to the merger, will not exceed by more than twenty percent (20%) the total number of voting shares of the surviving corporation outstanding immediately before the merger; and

(iv) The number of participating shares outstanding immediately after the merger, plus the number of participating shares issuable as a result of the merger, either by the conversion of securities issued pursuant to the merger or the exercise of rights and warrants issued pursuant to the merger, will not exceed by more than twenty percent (20%) the total number of participating shares outstanding immediately before the merger.

(h) As used in subsection (g) of this section:

(i) "Participating shares" means shares that entitle their holders to participate without limitation in distributions; and

(ii) "Voting shares" means shares that entitle their holders to vote unconditionally in elections of directors.

(j) After a merger or share exchange is authorized, and at any time before articles of merger or share exchange are filed, the planned merger or share exchange may be abandoned, subject to any contractual rights, without further shareholder action, in accordance with the procedure set forth in the plan of merger or share exchange or, if none is set forth, in the manner determined by the board of directors.

17-16-1104. Merger of subsidiary.

(a) A parent corporation owning at least eighty percent (80%) of the outstanding shares of each class of a subsidiary corporation may merge the subsidiary into itself without approval of the shareholders of the parent or subsidiary.

(b) The board of directors of the parent shall adopt a plan of merger that sets forth:

(i) The names of the parent and subsidiary; and

(ii) The manner and basis of converting the shares of the subsidiary into shares, obligations or other securities of the parent or any other corporation or into cash or other property in whole or part.

(c) The parent shall mail a copy or summary of the plan of merger to each shareholder of the subsidiary who does not waive the mailing requirement in writing.

(d) The parent may not deliver articles of merger to the secretary of state for filing until at least thirty (30) days after the date it mailed a copy of the plan of merger to each shareholder of the subsidiary who did not waive the mailing requirement.

(e) Articles of merger under this section may not contain amendments to the articles of incorporation of the parent corporation, except for amendments enumerated in W.S. 17-16-1002.

17-16-1105. Articles of merger or share exchange.

(a) After a plan of merger or share exchange is approved by the shareholders, or adopted by the board of directors if shareholder approval is not required, the surviving or acquiring corporation shall deliver to the secretary of state for filing articles of merger or share exchange setting forth:

(i) The plan of merger or share exchange;

(ii) If shareholder approval was not required, a statement to that effect; and

(iii) If approval of the shareholders of one (1) or more corporations party to the merger or share exchange was required;

(A) The designation, number of outstanding shares, and number of votes entitled to be cast by each voting group entitled to vote separately on the plan as to each corporation; and

(B) Either the total number of votes cast for and against the plan by each voting group entitled to vote separately on the plan or the total number of undisputed votes cast for the plan separately by each voting group and a statement that the number cast for the plan by each voting group was sufficient for approval by that voting group.

(b) A merger or share exchange takes effect upon the effective date of the articles of merger or share exchange.

17-16-1106. Effect of merger or share exchange.

(a) When a merger takes effect:

(i) Every other corporation party to the merger merges into the surviving corporation and the separate existence of every corporation except the surviving corporation ceases;

(ii) The title to all real estate and other property owned by each corporation party to the merger is vested in the surviving corporation without reversion or impairment;

(iii) The surviving corporation has all liabilities of each corporation party to the merger;

(iv) A proceeding pending against any corporation party to the merger may be continued as if the merger did not occur or the surviving corporation may be substituted in the proceeding for the corporation whose existence ceased;

(v) The articles of incorporation of the surviving corporation are amended to the extent provided in the plan of merger; and

(vi) The shares of each corporation party to the merger that are to be converted into shares, obligations or other securities of the surviving or any other corporation or into cash or other property are converted, and the former holders of the shares are entitled only to the rights provided in the articles of merger or to their rights under article 13.

(b) When a share exchange takes effect, the shares of each acquired corporation are exchanged as provided in the plan, and the former holders of the shares are entitled only to the exchange rights provided in the articles of share exchange or to their rights under article 13.

17-16-1107. Merger or share exchange with foreign corporation.

(a) One (1) or more foreign corporations may merge or enter into a share exchange with one (1) or more domestic corporations if:

(i) In a merger, the merger is permitted by the law of the state or country under whose law each foreign corporation is incorporated and each foreign corporation complies with that law in effecting the merger;

(ii) In a share exchange, the corporation whose shares will be acquired is a domestic corporation, whether or not a share exchange is permitted by the law of the state or country under whose law the acquiring corporation is incorporated;

(iii) The foreign corporation complies with W.S. 17-16-1105 if it is the surviving corporation of the merger or acquiring corporation of the share exchange; and

(iv) Each domestic corporation complies with the applicable provisions of W.S. 17-16-1101 through 17-16-1104 and, if it is the surviving corporation of the merger or acquiring corporation of the share exchange, with W.S. 17-16-1105.

(b) Upon the merger or share exchange taking effect, the surviving foreign corporation of a merger and the acquiring foreign corporation of a share exchange is deemed:

(i) To appoint the secretary of state as its agent for service of process in a proceeding to enforce any obligation or the rights of dissenting shareholders of each domestic corporation party to the merger or share exchange; and

(ii) To agree that it will promptly pay to the dissenting shareholders of each domestic corporation party to the merger or share exchange the amount, if any, to which they are entitled under article 13.

(c) This section does not limit the power of a foreign corporation to acquire all or part of the shares of one (1) or more classes or series of a domestic corporation through a voluntary exchange or otherwise.

17-16-1110. Consolidation.

(a) Any two (2) or more domestic corporations may consolidate into a new corporation pursuant to a plan of consolidation approved in the manner provided in this act.

(b) The board of directors of each corporation shall, by a resolution adopted by each board, approve a plan of consolidation setting forth:

(i) The names of the corporations proposing to consolidate, and the name of the new corporation into which they proposed to consolidate, which is hereinafter designated as the new corporation;

(ii) The terms and conditions of the proposed consolidation;

(iii) The manner and basis of converting the shares of each corporation into shares or other securities or obligations of the new corporation or of any other corporation or, in whole or in part, into cash or other property;

(iv) With respect to the new corporation, all of the statements required to be set forth in articles of incorporation for corporations organized under this act; and

(v) Such other provisions with respect to the proposed consolidation as are deemed necessary or desirable.

17-16-1111. Approval by shareholders; abandonment of plan.

(a) The board of directors of each corporation, upon approving the plan of consolidation, shall, by resolution, direct that the plan be submitted to a vote at a meeting of shareholders, which may be either an annual or a special meeting. Written or printed notice shall be given to each shareholder of record whether or not entitled to vote at the meeting, not less than twenty (20) days before the meeting, in the manner provided in this act for the giving of notice of meetings of shareholders, and shall state that the purpose or one (1) of the purposes of the meeting is to consider the proposed plan of consolidation, whether the meeting be an annual or a special meeting. A copy of a summary of the plan of consolidation shall be included in or enclosed with the notice.

(b) At the shareholder's meeting for each corporation, a vote of the shareholders shall be taken on the proposed plan. The plan shall be approved upon receiving the affirmative vote of the holders of at least a majority of the shares entitled to vote. However, if any class of shares of each corporation is entitled to vote as a class, the plan shall be approved upon receiving the affirmative vote of the holders of at least a majority of the shares of each class of shares entitled to vote as a class. Any class of shares of each corporation shall be entitled to vote as a class if the plan contains any provision which, if contained in a proposed amendment to articles of incorporation, would entitle the class of shares to vote as a class.

(c) After approval by a vote of the shareholders of each corporation, and at any time prior to the filing of the articles of consolidation, the consolidation may be abandoned pursuant to provisions of the articles of consolidation, if any, set forth in the plan.

17-16-1112. Articles of consolidation.

(a) Upon approval, articles of consolidation shall be delivered to the secretary of state for filing. The articles of consolidation shall set forth:

(i) The plan of consolidation;

(ii) As to each corporation the shareholders of which were required to vote on the plan, the number of shares outstanding, and, if the shares of any class are entitled to vote as a class, the designation and number of outstanding shares of each class;

(iii) As to each corporation the shareholders of which were required to vote on the plan, the number of shares voted for and against the plan, respectively, and, if the shares of any class are entitled to vote as a class, the number of shares of each class voted for and against the plan respectively.

17-16-1113. Effect of consolidation.

(a) A consolidation becomes effective upon filing by the secretary of state, or on a later date, not more than thirty (30) days subsequent to filing the plan with the secretary of state, as shall be provided in the plan.

(b) When a consolidation takes effect:

(i) The several corporations party to the plan of consolidation are a single corporation, which is the new corporation provided for in the plan of consolidation;

(ii) The separate existence of all corporations party to the plan of consolidation except the new corporation ceases;

(iii) The new corporation has all the rights, privileges, immunities and powers and is subject to all the duties and liabilities of a corporation organized under this act;

(iv) The new corporation has all the rights, privileges, immunities and franchises, public or private, of each corporation party to the plan of consolidation. The title to all real estate and other property owned by each corporation party to the plan of consolidation is vested in the new corporation without reversion or impairment;

(v) The new corporation has all the liabilities and obligations of each corporation party to the plan of consolidation. Any claim existing or proceeding pending by or against any corporation party to the plan of consolidation may be continued as if the consolidation did not occur or the new corporation may be substituted for the corporation whose existence ceased. Neither the rights of creditors nor any liens upon the property of any corporation party to the plan of consolidation shall be impaired by the consolidation;

(vi) The statements set forth in the articles of consolidation and which are required or permitted to be set forth in the articles of incorporation of corporations organized under this act shall be deemed to be the original articles of incorporation of the new corporation;

(vii) The shares of each corporation party to the plan of consolidation that are to be converted into shares, obligations or other securities of the new corporation or into cash or other property are converted, and the former holders of the shares are entitled only to the rights provided in the plan of consolidation or to their rights under article 13 of this act.

17-16-1114. Consolidation of domestic and foreign corporations.

(a) One (1) or more foreign corporations and one (1) or more domestic corporations may be consolidated in the following manner, if the consolidation is permitted by the laws of the state under which each foreign corporation is organized:

(i) Each domestic corporation shall comply with the provisions of this act with respect to the consolidation of domestic corporations and each foreign corporation shall comply with the applicable provisions of the laws of the state under which it is organized;

(ii) If the new corporation in a consolidation is to be governed by the laws of any state other than Wyoming, it shall comply with the provisions of this act with respect to foreign corporations if it is to transact business in Wyoming, and in every case it shall file with the secretary of state of Wyoming:

(A) An agreement that it may be served with process in Wyoming in any proceeding for the enforcement of any obligation of any domestic corporation which is a party to such consolidation and in any proceeding for the enforcement of the rights of a dissenting shareholder of any such domestic corporation against the new corporation;

(B) An irrevocable appointment of the secretary of state of Wyoming as its agent to accept service of process in any such proceeding; and

(C) An agreement that it will promptly pay to the dissenting shareholders of any such domestic corporation the amount, if any, to which they shall be entitled under the provisions of this act with respect to the rights of dissenting shareholders.

17-16-1115. Conversion of corporation to limited liability company.

(a) A domestic corporation may be converted to a domestic limited liability company pursuant to this section.

(b) A foreign corporation may be converted to a domestic limited liability company pursuant to this section.

(c) The terms and conditions of a conversion of a corporation to a limited liability company shall be approved by all the shareholders or by a number or percentage specified in the articles of incorporation or bylaws, provided that any shareholders who will be liable to a greater extent after conversion, solely by reason of being an owner, shall approve the terms and conditions of the conversion.

(d) After the conversion is approved by the shareholders, the limited liability company shall file articles of organization which satisfy the requirements of W.S. 17-15-107 and include:

(i) A statement that the corporation was converted to a limited liability company;

(ii) Its former name;

(iii) The state of formation and the date of organization; and

(iv) A statement of the number of votes cast by the shareholders for and against conversion and if the vote is less than unanimous, the number or percentage required to approve the conversion under the articles of incorporation or bylaws.

(e) The conversion takes effect when the articles of organization are filed or at any later date specified in the articles.

17-16-1116. Effect of conversion.

(a) Upon conversion:

(i) All property owned by the corporation remains in the limited liability company;

(ii) All obligations of the converting corporation continue as obligations of the resulting limited liability company; and

(iii) An action or proceeding pending against the converting corporation may be continued as if the conversion had not occurred.

ARTICLE 12
SALE OF ASSETS

17-16-1201. Sale of assets in regular course of business and mortgage of assets.

(a) A corporation may, on the terms and conditions and for the consideration determined by the board of directors:

(i) Sell, lease, exchange, or otherwise dispose of all, or substantially all, of its property in the usual and regular course of business;

(ii) Mortgage, pledge, dedicate to the repayment of indebtedness, whether with or without recourse, or otherwise encumber any or all of its property whether or not in the usual and regular course of business; or

(iii) Transfer any or all of its property to a corporation all the shares of which are owned by the corporation.

(b) Unless the articles of incorporation require it, approval by the shareholders of a transaction described in subsection (a) of this section is not required.

17-16-1202. Sale of assets other than in regular course of business.

(a) A corporation may sell, lease, exchange, or otherwise dispose of all, or substantially all, of its property, with or without the good will, otherwise than in the usual and regular course of business, on the terms and conditions and for the consideration determined by the corporation's board of directors, if the board of directors proposes and its shareholders approve the proposed transaction.

(b) For a transaction to be authorized:

(i) The board of directors shall recommend the proposed transaction to the shareholders unless the board of directors determines that because of conflict of interest or other special circumstances it should make no recommendation and communicates the basis for its determination to the shareholders with the submission of the proposed transaction; and

(ii) The shareholders entitled to vote shall approve the transaction.

(c) The board of directors may condition its submission of the proposed transaction on any basis.

(d) The corporation shall notify each shareholder, whether or not entitled to vote, of the proposed shareholders' meeting in accordance with W.S. 17-16-705. The notice shall also state that the purpose, or one (1) of the purposes, of the meeting is to consider the sale, lease, exchange, or other disposition of all, or substantially all, the property of the corporation and contain or be accompanied by a description of the transaction.

(e) Unless the articles of incorporation or the board of directors, acting pursuant to subsection (c) of this section, require a greater vote or a vote by voting groups, the transaction to be authorized shall be approved by a majority of all the votes entitled to be cast on the transaction.

(f) After a sale, lease, exchange or other disposition of property is authorized, the transaction may be abandoned, subject to any contractual rights, without further shareholder action.

(g) A transaction that constitutes a distribution is governed by W.S. 17-16-640 and not by this section.

ARTICLE 13
DISSENTERS' RIGHTS

17-16-1301. Definitions.

(a) As used in this article:

(i) "Beneficial shareholder" means the person who is a beneficial owner of shares held in a voting trust or by a nominee as the record shareholder;

(ii) "Corporation" means the issuer of the shares held by a dissenter before the corporate action, or the surviving, new, or acquiring corporation by merger, consolidation, or share exchange of that issuer;

(iii) "Dissenter" means a shareholder who is entitled to dissent from corporate action under W.S. 17-16-1302 and who exercises that right when and in the manner required by W.S. 17-16-1320 through 17-16-1328;

(iv) "Fair value," with respect to a dissenter's shares, means the value of the shares immediately before the effectuation of the corporate action to which the dissenter objects, excluding any appreciation or depreciation in anticipation of the corporate action unless exclusion would be inequitable;

(v) "Interest" means interest from the effective date of the corporate action until the date of payment, at the average rate currently paid by the corporation on its principal bank loans, or, if none, at a rate that is fair and equitable under all the circumstances;

(vi) "Record shareholder" means the person in whose names shares are registered in the records of a corporation or the beneficial owner of shares to the extent of the rights granted by a nominee certificate on file with a corporation;

(vii) "Shareholder" means the record shareholder or the beneficial shareholder.

17-16-1302. Right to dissent.

(a) A shareholder is entitled to dissent from, and to obtain payment of the fair value of his shares in the event of, any of the following corporate actions:

(i) Consummation of a plan of merger or consolidation to which the corporation is a party if:

(A) Shareholder approval is required for the merger or the consolidation by W.S. 17-16-1103 or 17-16-1111 or the articles of incorporation and the shareholder is entitled to vote on the merger or consolidation; or

(B) The corporation is a subsidiary that is merged with its parent under W.S. 17-16-1104.

(ii) Consummation of a plan of share exchange to which the corporation is a party as the corporation whose shares will be acquired, if the shareholder is entitled to vote on the plan;

(iii) Consummation of a sale or exchange of all, or substantially all, of the property of the corporation other than in the usual and regular course of business, if the shareholder is entitled to vote on the sale or exchange, including a sale in dissolution, but not including a sale pursuant to court order or a sale for cash pursuant to a plan by which all or substantially all of the net proceeds of the sale will be distributed to the shareholders within one (1) year after the date of sale;

(iv) An amendment of the articles of incorporation that materially and adversely affects rights in respect of a dissenter's shares because it:

(A) Alters or abolishes a preferential right of the shares;

(B) Creates, alters or abolishes a right in respect of redemption, including a provision respecting a sinking fund for the redemption or repurchase, of the shares;

(C) Alters or abolishes a preemptive right of the holder of the shares to acquire shares or other securities;

(D) Excludes or limits the right of the shares to vote on any matter, or to cumulate votes, other than a limitation by dilution through issuance of shares or other securities with similar voting rights; or

(E) Reduces the number of shares owned by the shareholder to a fraction of a share if the fractional share so created is to be acquired for cash under W.S. 17-16-604.

(v) Any corporate action taken pursuant to a shareholder vote to the extent the articles of incorporation, bylaws, or a resolution of the board of directors provides that voting or nonvoting shareholders are entitled to dissent and obtain payment for their shares.

(b) A shareholder entitled to dissent and obtain payment for his shares under this article may not challenge the corporate action creating his entitlement unless the action is unlawful or fraudulent with respect to the shareholder or the corporation.

17-16-1303. Dissent by nominees and beneficial owners.

(a) A record shareholder may assert dissenters' rights as to fewer than all the shares registered in his name only if he dissents with respect to all shares beneficially owned by any one (1) person and notifies the corporation in writing of the name and address of each person on whose behalf he asserts dissenters' rights. The rights of a partial dissenter under this subsection are determined as if the shares as to which he dissents and his other shares were registered in the names of different shareholders.

(b) A beneficial shareholder may assert dissenters' rights as to shares held on his behalf only if:

(i) He submits to the corporation the record shareholder's written consent to the dissent not later than the time the beneficial shareholder asserts dissenters' rights; and

(ii) He does so with respect to all shares of which he is the beneficial shareholder or over which he has power to direct the vote.

17-16-1320. Notice of dissenters' rights.

(a) If proposed corporate action creating dissenters' rights under W.S. 17-16-1302 is submitted to a vote at a shareholders' meeting, the meeting notice shall state that shareholders are or may be entitled to assert dissenters' rights under this article and be accompanied by a copy of this article.

(b) If corporate action creating dissenters' rights under W.S. 17-16-1302 is taken without a vote of shareholders, the corporation shall notify in writing all shareholders entitled to assert dissenters' rights that the action was taken and send them the dissenters' notice described in W.S. 17-16-1322.

17-16-1321. Notice of intent to demand payment.

(a) If proposed corporate action creating dissenters' rights under W.S. 17-16-1302 is submitted to a vote at a shareholders' meeting, a shareholder who wishes to assert dissenters' rights shall deliver to the corporation before the vote is taken written notice of his intent to demand payment for his shares if the proposed action is effectuated and shall not vote his shares in favor of the proposed action.

(b) A shareholder who does not satisfy the requirements of subsection (a) of this section is not entitled to payment for his shares under this article.

17-16-1322. Dissenters' notice.

(a) If proposed corporate action creating dissenters' rights under W.S. 17-16-1302 is authorized at a shareholders' meeting, the corporation shall deliver a written dissenters' notice to all shareholders who satisfied the requirements of W.S. 17-16-1321.

(b) The dissenters' notice shall be sent no later than ten (10) days after the corporate action was taken, and shall:

(i) State where the payment demand shall be sent and where and when certificates for certificated shares shall be deposited;

(ii) Inform holders of uncertificated shares to what extent transfer of the shares will be restricted after the payment demand is received;

(iii) Supply a form for demanding payment that includes the date of the first announcement to news media or to shareholders of the terms of the proposed corporate action and requires that the person asserting dissenters' rights certify whether or not he acquired beneficial ownership of the shares before that date;

(iv) Set a date by which the corporation shall receive the payment demand, which date may not be fewer than thirty (30) nor more than sixty (60) days after the date the notice required by subsection (a) of this section is delivered; and

(v) Be accompanied by a copy of this article.

17-16-1323. Duty to demand payment.

(a) A shareholder sent a dissenters' notice described in W.S. 17-16-1322 shall demand payment, certify whether he acquired beneficial ownership of the shares before the date required to be set forth in the dissenters' notice pursuant to W.S. 17-16-1322(b)(iii), and deposit his certificates in accordance with the terms of the notice.

(b) The shareholder who demands payment and deposits his share certificates under subsection (a) of this section retains all other rights of a shareholder until these rights are cancelled or modified by the taking of the proposed corporate action.

(c) A shareholder who does not demand payment or deposit his share certificates where required, each by the date set in the dissenters' notice, is not entitled to payment for his shares under this article.

17-16-1324. Share restrictions.

(a) The corporation may restrict the transfer of uncertificated shares from the date the demand for their payment is received until the proposed corporate action is taken or the restrictions released under W.S. 17-16-1326.

(b) The person for whom dissenters' rights are asserted as to uncertificated shares retains all other rights of a shareholder until these rights are cancelled or modified by the taking of the proposed corporate action.

17-16-1325. Payment.

(a) Except as provided in W.S. 17-16-1327, as soon as the proposed corporate action is taken, or upon receipt of a payment demand, the corporation shall pay each dissenter who complied with W.S. 17-16-1323 the amount the corporation estimates to be the fair value of his shares, plus accrued interest.

(b) The payment shall be accompanied by:

(i) The corporation's balance sheet as of the end of a fiscal year ending not more than sixteen (16) months before the date of payment, an income statement for that year, a statement of changes in shareholders' equity for that year, and the latest available interim financial statements, if any;

(ii) A statement of the corporation's estimate of the fair value of the shares;

(iii) An explanation of how the interest was calculated;

(iv) A statement of the dissenter's right to demand payment under W.S. 17-16-1328; and

(v) A copy of this article.

17-16-1326. Failure to take action.

(a) If the corporation does not take the proposed action within sixty (60) days after the date set for demanding payment and depositing share certificates, the corporation shall return the deposited certificates and release the transfer restrictions imposed on uncertificated shares.

(b) If after returning deposited certificates and releasing transfer restrictions, the corporation takes the proposed action, it shall send a new dissenters' notice under W.S. 17-16-1322 and repeat the payment demand procedure.

17-16-1327. After-acquired shares.

(a) A corporation may elect to withhold payment required by W.S. 17-16-1325 from a dissenter unless he was the beneficial owner of the shares before the date set forth in the dissenters' notice as the date of the first announcement to news media or to shareholders of the terms of the proposed corporate action.

(b) To the extent the corporation elects to withhold payment under subsection (a) of this section, after taking the proposed corporate action, it shall estimate the fair value of the shares, plus accrued interest, and shall pay this amount to each dissenter who agrees to accept it in full satisfaction of his demand. The corporation shall send with its offer a statement of its estimate of the fair value of the shares, an explanation of how the interest was calculated, and a statement of the dissenter's right to demand payment under W.S. 17-16-1328.

17-16-1328. Procedure if shareholder dissatisfied with payment or offer.

(a) A dissenter may notify the corporation in writing of his own estimate of the fair value of his shares and amount of interest due, and demand payment of his estimate, less any payment under W.S. 17-16-1325, or reject the corporation's offer under W.S. 17-16-1327 and demand payment of the fair value of his shares and interest due, if:

(i) The dissenter believes that the amount paid under W.S. 17-16-1325 or offered under W.S. 17-16-1327 is less than the fair value of his shares or that the interest due is incorrectly calculated;

(ii) The corporation fails to make payment under W.S. 17-16-1325 within sixty (60) days after the date set for demanding payment; or

(iii) The corporation, having failed to take the proposed action, does not return the deposited certificates or release the transfer restrictions imposed on uncertificated shares within sixty (60) days after the date set for demanding payment.

(b) A dissenter waives his right to demand payment under this section unless he notifies the corporation of his demand in writing under subsection (a) of this section within thirty (30) days after the corporation made or offered payment for his shares.

17-16-1330. Court action.

(a) If a demand for payment under W.S. 17-16-1328 remains unsettled, the corporation shall commence a proceeding within sixty (60) days after receiving the payment demand and petition the court to determine the fair value of the shares and accrued interest. If the corporation does not commence the proceeding within the sixty (60) day period, it shall pay each dissenter whose demand remains unsettled the amount demanded.

(b) The corporation shall commence the proceeding in the district court of the county where a corporation's principal office, or if none in this state, its registered office, is located. If the corporation is a foreign corporation without a registered office in this state, it shall commence the proceeding in the county in this state where the registered office of the domestic corporation merged with or whose shares were acquired by the foreign corporation was located.

(c) The corporation shall make all dissenters, whether or not residents of this state, whose demands remain unsettled parties to the proceeding as in an action against their shares and all parties shall be served with a copy of the petition. Nonresidents may be served by registered or certified mail or by publication as provided by law.

(d) The jurisdiction of the court in which the proceeding is commenced under subsection (b) of this section is plenary and exclusive. The court may appoint one (1) or more persons as appraisers to receive evidence and recommend decision on the question of fair value. The appraisers have the powers described in the order appointing them, or in the amendment to it. The dissenters are entitled to the same discovery rights as parties in other civil proceedings.

(e) Each dissenter made a party to the proceeding is entitled to judgment for:

(i) The amount, if any, by which the court finds the fair value of his shares, plus interest, exceeds the amount paid by the corporation; or

(ii) The fair value, plus accrued interest, of his after-acquired shares for which the corporation elected to withhold payment under W.S. 17-16-1327.

17-16-1331. Court costs and counsel fees.

(a) The court in an appraisal proceeding commenced under W.S. 17-16-1330 shall determine all costs of the proceeding, including the reasonable compensation and expenses of appraisers appointed by the court. The court shall assess the costs against the corporation, except that the court may assess costs against all or some of the dissenters, in amounts the court finds equitable, to the extent the court finds the dissenters acted arbitrarily, vexatiously, or not in good faith in demanding payment under W.S. 17-16-1328.

(b) The court may also assess the fees and expenses of counsel and experts for the respective parties, in amounts the court finds equitable:

(i) Against the corporation and in favor of any or all dissenters if the court finds the corporation did not substantially comply with the requirements of W.S. 17-16-1320 through 17-16-1328; or

(ii) Against either the corporation or a dissenter, in favor of any other party, if the court finds that the party against whom the fees and expenses are assessed acted arbitrarily, vexatiously, or not in good faith with respect to the rights provided by this article.

(c) If the court finds that the services of counsel for any dissenter were of substantial benefit to other dissenters similarly situated, and that the fees for those services should not be assessed against the corporation, the court may award to these counsel reasonable fees to be paid out of the amounts awarded the dissenters who were benefited.

ARTICLE 14
DISSOLUTION

17-16-1401. Dissolution by incorporators or initial directors.

(a) A majority of the incorporators or initial directors of a corporation that has not issued shares or has not commenced business may dissolve the corporation by delivering to the secretary of state for filing articles of dissolution that set forth:

(i) The name of the corporation;

(ii) The date of its incorporation;

(iii) Either:

(A) That none of the corporation's shares has been issued; or

(B) That the corporation has not commenced business.

(iv) That no debt of the corporation remains unpaid;

(v) That the net assets of the corporation remaining after winding up have been distributed to the shareholders, if shares were issued; and

(vi) That a majority of the incorporators or initial directors authorized the dissolution.

17-16-1402. Dissolution by board of directors and shareholders.

(a) A corporation's board of directors may propose dissolution for submission to the shareholders.

(b) For a proposal to dissolve to be adopted:

(i) The board of directors shall recommend dissolution to the shareholders, unless the board of directors determines that because of conflict of interest or other special circumstances it should make no recommendation and communicates the basis for its determination to the shareholders; and

(ii) The shareholders entitled to vote shall approve the proposal to dissolve as provided in subsection (e) of this section.

(c) The board of directors may condition its submission of the proposal for dissolution on any basis.

(d) The corporation shall notify each shareholder, whether or not entitled to vote, of the proposed shareholders' meeting in accordance with W.S. 17-16-705. The notice shall also state that the purpose, or one (1) of the purposes, of the meeting is to consider dissolving the corporation.

(e) Unless the articles of incorporation or the board of directors, acting pursuant to subsection (c) of this section, require a greater vote or a vote by voting groups, the proposal to dissolve to be adopted shall be approved by a majority of all the votes entitled to be cast on that proposal.

17-16-1403. Articles of dissolution.

(a) At any time after dissolution is authorized, the corporation may dissolve by delivering to the secretary of state for filing articles of dissolution setting forth:

(i) The name of the corporation;

(ii) The date dissolution was authorized;

(iii) If dissolution was approved by the shareholders:

(A) The number of votes entitled to be cast on the proposal to dissolve; and

(B) Either the total number of votes cast for and against dissolution or the total number of undisputed votes cast for dissolution and a statement that the number cast for dissolution was sufficient for approval.

(iv) If voting by voting groups was required, the information required by paragraph (iii) of this subsection shall be separately provided for each voting group entitled to vote separately on the plan to dissolve.

(b) A corporation is dissolved upon the effective date of its articles of dissolution.

17-16-1404. Revocation of dissolution.

(a) A corporation may revoke its dissolution within one hundred twenty (120) days of the effective date of the dissolution.

(b) Revocation of dissolution shall be authorized in the same manner as the dissolution was authorized unless that authorization permitted revocation by action of the board of directors alone, in which event the board of directors may revoke the dissolution without shareholder action.

(c) After the revocation of dissolution is authorized, the corporation may revoke the dissolution by delivering to the secretary of state for filing articles of revocation of dissolution, together with a copy of its articles of dissolution, that set forth:

(i) The name of the corporation which shall satisfy the requirements of W.S. 17-16-401;

(ii) The effective date of the dissolution that was revoked;

(iii) The date that the revocation of dissolution was authorized;

(iv) If the corporation's board of directors or incorporators revoked the dissolution, a statement to that effect;

(v) If the corporation's board of directors revoked a dissolution authorized by the shareholders, a statement that revocation was permitted by action by the board of directors alone pursuant to that authorization; and

(vi) If shareholder action was required to revoke the dissolution, the information required by W.S. 17-16-1403(a)(iii) or (iv).

(d) Revocation of dissolution is effective upon the effective date of the articles of revocation of dissolution.

(e) When the revocation of dissolution is effective, it relates back to and takes effect as if the effective date of the dissolution and the corporation resumes carrying on its business as if dissolution had never occurred, except the corporation may be required to adopt some other name by amending its articles of incorporation in the manner provided by this act so its name satisfies the requirements of W.S. 17-16-401.

17-16-1405. Effect of dissolution.

(a) A dissolved corporation continues its corporate existence but may not carry on any business except that appropriate to wind up and liquidate its business and affairs, including:

(i) Collecting its assets;

(ii) Disposing of its properties that will not be distributed in kind to its shareholders;

(iii) Discharging or making provision for discharging its liabilities;

(iv) Distributing its remaining property among its shareholders according to their interests; and

(v) Doing every other act necessary to wind up and liquidate its business and affairs.

(b) Dissolution of a corporation does not:

(i) Transfer title to the corporation's property;

(ii) Prevent transfer of its shares or securities, although the authorization to dissolve may provide for closing the corporation's share transfer records;

(iii) Subject its directors or officers to standards of conduct different from those prescribed in article 8;

(iv) Change quorum or voting requirements for its board of directors or shareholders; change provisions for selection, resignation, or removal of its directors or officers or both; or change provisions for amending its bylaws;

(v) Prevent commencement of a proceeding by or against the corporation in its corporate name;

(vi) Abate or suspend a proceeding pending by or against the corporation on the effective date of dissolution; or

(vii) Terminate the authority of the registered agent of the corporation.

17-16-1406. Known claims against dissolved corporation.

(a) A dissolved corporation may dispose of the known claims against it by following the procedure described in this section.

(b) The dissolved corporation shall notify its known claimants in writing, by mail or private carrier or by personal delivery, of the dissolution at any time after its effective date. The written notice shall:

(i) Describe information that shall be included in a claim;

(ii) Provide a mailing address where a claim may be sent;

(iii) State the deadline, which may not be fewer than one hundred twenty (120) days from the effective date of the written notice, by which the dissolved corporation shall receive the claim; and

(iv) State that the claim will be barred if not received by the deadline.

(c) A claim against the dissolved corporation is barred:

(i) If a claimant who was given written notice under subsection (b) of this section does not deliver the claim to the dissolved corporation by the deadline; or

(ii) If a claimant whose claim was rejected by the dissolved corporation does not commence a proceeding to enforce the claim within ninety (90) days from the effective date of the rejection notice.

(d) For purposes of this section, "claim" does not include a contingent liability or a claim based on an event occurring after the effective date of dissolution.

17-16-1407. Unknown claims against dissolved corporation.

(a) A dissolved corporation may also publish notice of its dissolution and request that persons with claims against the corporation present them in accordance with the notice.

(b) The notice shall:

(i) Be published one (1) time in a newspaper of general circulation in the county where the dissolved corporation's principal office, or, if none in this state, its registered office, is or was last located;

(ii) Describe the information that shall be included in a claim and provide a mailing address where the claim may be sent; and

(iii) State that a claim against the corporation will be barred unless a proceeding to enforce the claim is commenced within four (4) years or the applicable statute of limitations, whichever is less, after the publication of the notice.

(c) If the dissolved corporation publishes a newspaper notice in accordance with subsection (b) of this section, the claim of each of the following claimants is barred unless the claimant commences a proceeding to enforce the claim against the dissolved corporation within four (4) years after the publication date of the newspaper notice:

(i) A claimant who did not receive written notice under W.S. 17-16-1406;

(ii) A claimant whose claim was timely sent to the dissolved corporation but not acted on; or

(iii) A claimant whose claim is contingent or based on an event occurring after the effective date of dissolution.

(d) A claim may be enforced under this section:

(i) Against the dissolved corporation, to the extent of its undistributed assets; or

(ii) If the assets have been distributed in liquidation, against a shareholder of the dissolved corporation to the extent of his pro rata share of the claim or the corporate assets distributed to him in liquidation, whichever is less, but a shareholder's total liability for all claims under this section may not exceed the total amount of assets distributed to him.

17-16-1420. Grounds for administrative dissolution.

(a) The secretary of state may commence a proceeding under W.S. 17-16-1421 to administratively dissolve a corporation if:

(i) The corporation is without a registered agent or registered office in this state for thirty (30) days or more;

(ii) The corporation does not notify the secretary of state within thirty (30) days that its registered agent or registered office has been changed, that its registered agent has resigned, or that its registered office has been discontinued;

(iii) The corporation's period of duration stated in its articles of incorporation expires;

(iv) The corporation does not deliver its annual reports or pay the annual license taxes to the secretary of state when due pursuant to W.S. 17-16-1630; or

(v) It is in the public interest and the corporation:

(A) Failed to provide records to the registered agent as required in W.S. 17-16-507;

(B) Has provided fraudulent information or has failed to correct false information upon request of the secretary of state on any filing under this act with the secretary of state; or

(C) Cannot be served by either the secretary of state or the registered agent at its address provided pursuant to W.S. 17-16-507.

17-16-1421. Procedure for and effect of administrative dissolution.

(a) If the secretary of state determines that one (1) or more grounds exist under W.S. 17-16-1420 for dissolving a corporation, he shall serve the corporation with written notice of his determination under W.S. 17-16-504, except for W.S. 17-16-1420(a)(iii) in which case dissolution is by choice and therefore automatic and W.S. 17-16-1420(a)(iv) in which case notice of the proposed dissolution shall be given only as provided in subsection (e) of this section.

(b) If the corporation does not correct each ground for dissolution or demonstrate to the reasonable satisfaction of the secretary of state that each ground determined by the secretary of state does not exist within sixty (60) days after service of the notice is perfected under W.S. 17-16-504, the secretary of state shall administratively dissolve the corporation by signing, either manually or in facsimile, a certificate of dissolution that recites the ground or grounds for dissolution and its effective date. The secretary of state shall file the original of the certificate and serve a copy on the corporation under W.S. 17-16-504. The provisions of subsection (e) of this section shall govern the procedures for dissolution pursuant to W.S. 17-16-1420(a)(iv).

(c) A corporation administratively dissolved under W.S. 17-16-1420 continues its corporate existence but may not carry on any business except that necessary to wind up and liquidate its business and affairs under W.S. 17-16-1405 and notify claimants under W.S. 17-16-1406 and 17-16-1407.

(d) The administrative dissolution of a corporation does not terminate the authority of its registered agent.

(e) Administrative dissolution of a corporation pursuant to W.S. 17-16-1420(a)(iv) shall be accomplished in accordance with the provisions of this subsection only. Prior to administratively dissolving a corporation pursuant to W.S. 17-16-1420(a)(iv), the secretary of state shall provide notice to the corporation at its last known mailing address by first class mail and publish once a week for two (2) consecutive weeks, in a newspaper of general circulation in the county in which the registered office of the corporation is located, notice that the corporation failed to comply with W.S. 17-16-1630. If the corporation does not correct the deficiency within sixty (60) days after the first date of publication the corporation shall be deemed dissolved. The effect of the dissolution shall be as provided in this section.

17-16-1422. Reinstatement following administrative dissolution.

(a) A corporation administratively dissolved under W.S. 17-16-1421 may apply to the secretary of state for reinstatement within two (2) years after the effective date of dissolution. Reinstatement may be denied by the secretary of state if the corporation has been the subject of secretary of state and law enforcement investigation pertaining to fraud or any other violation of state or federal law, or if there is other reason to believe the corporation was engaged in illegal operations. The application shall:

(i) Recite the name of the corporation and the effective date of its administrative dissolution;

(ii) State that the ground or grounds for dissolution either did not exist or have been eliminated;

(iii) Repealed By Laws 1999, ch. 196, § 2.

(iv) If the corporation was administratively dissolved for failing to deliver its annual report or pay the annual license taxes to the secretary of state when due pursuant to W.S. 17-16-1630, include payment of a sum equal to double the amount of fees and taxes then delinquent and a reinstatement certificate fee prescribed pursuant to W.S. 17-16-122.

(b) If the secretary of state determines that the application contains the information required by subsection (a) of this section and that the information is correct, he shall cancel the certificate of dissolution and prepare a certificate of reinstatement that recites his determination and the effective date of reinstatement, file the original of the certificate, and serve a copy on the corporation under W.S. 17-16-504.

(c) When the reinstatement is effective, it relates back to and takes effect as of the effective date of the administrative dissolution and the corporation resumes carrying on its business as if the administrative dissolution had never occurred.

(d) The corporation shall retain its registered corporate name during the two (2) year reinstatement period.

17-16-1423. Appeal from denial of reinstatement.

(a) If the secretary of state denies a corporation's application for reinstatement following administrative dissolution, he shall serve the corporation under W.S. 17-16-504 with a written notice that explains the reason or reasons for denial.

(b) The corporation may appeal the denial of reinstatement to the district court within thirty (30) days after service of the notice of denial is perfected. The corporation appeals by petitioning the court to set aside the dissolution and attaching to the petition copies of the secretary of state's certificate of dissolution, the corporation's application for reinstatement, and the secretary of state's notice of denial.

(c) The court may summarily order the secretary of state to reinstate the dissolved corporation or may take other action the court considers appropriate.

(d) The court's final decision may be appealed as in other civil proceedings.

17-16-1430. Grounds for judicial dissolution.

(a) The district court may dissolve a corporation:

(i) In a proceeding by the attorney general if it is established that:

(A) The corporation obtained its articles of incorporation through fraud; or

(B) The corporation has continued to exceed or abuse the authority conferred upon it by law.

(ii) In a proceeding by a shareholder if it is established that:

(A) The directors are deadlocked in the management of the corporate affairs, the shareholders are unable to break the deadlock, and irreparable injury to the corporation is threatened or being suffered, or the business and affairs of the corporation can no longer be conducted to the advantage of the shareholders generally, because of the deadlock;

(B) The directors or those in control of the corporation have acted, are acting, or will act in a manner that is illegal, oppressive or fraudulent;

(C) The shareholders are deadlocked in voting power and have failed, for a period that includes at least two (2) consecutive annual meeting dates, to elect successors to directors whose terms have expired; or

(D) The corporate assets are being misapplied or wasted.

(iii) In a proceeding by a creditor if it is established that:

(A) The creditor's claim has been reduced to judgment, the execution on the judgment returned unsatisfied, and the corporation is insolvent; or

(B) The corporation has admitted in writing that the creditor's claim is due and owing and the corporation is insolvent.

(iv) In a proceeding by the corporation to have its voluntary dissolution continued under court supervision.

17-16-1431. Procedure for judicial dissolution.

(a) Venue for a proceeding by the attorney general to dissolve a corporation lies in Laramie county district court. Venue for a proceeding brought by any other party named in W.S. 17-16-1430 lies in the county where a corporation's principal office, or, if none in this state, its registered office, is or was last located.

(b) It is not necessary to make shareholders parties to a proceeding to dissolve a corporation unless relief is sought against them individually.

(c) A court in a proceeding brought to dissolve a corporation may issue injunctions, appoint a receiver or custodian pendente lite with all powers and duties the court directs, take other action required to preserve the corporate assets wherever located, and carry on the business of the corporation until a full hearing can be held.

(d) Within ten (10) days of the commencement of a proceeding under W.S. 17-16-1430(a)(ii) to dissolve a corporation that has no shares listed on a national securities exchange or regularly traded in a market maintained by one (1) or more members of a national or affiliated securities association, the corporation must send to all shareholders, other than the petitioner, a notice stating that the shareholders are entitled to avoid the dissolution of the corporation by electing to purchase the petitioner's shares under W.S. 17-16-1434 and accompanied by a copy of W.S. 17-16-1434.

17-16-1432. Receivership or custodianship.

(a) A court in a judicial proceeding brought to dissolve a corporation may appoint one (1) or more receivers to wind up and liquidate, or one (1) or more custodians to manage, the business and affairs of the corporation. The court shall hold a hearing, after notifying all parties to the proceeding and any interested persons designated by the court, before appointing a receiver or custodian. The court appointing a receiver or custodian has exclusive jurisdiction over the corporation and all of its property wherever located.

(b) The court may appoint an individual or a domestic or foreign corporation authorized to transact business in this state as a receiver or custodian. The court may require the receiver or custodian to post bond, with or without sureties, in an amount the court directs.

(c) The court shall describe the powers and duties of the receiver or custodian in its appointing order, which may be amended from time to time. Among other powers:

(i) The receiver may:

(A) Dispose of all or any part of the assets of the corporation wherever located, at a public or private sale, if authorized by the court; and

(B) Sue and defend in his own name as receiver of the corporation in all Wyoming courts.

(ii) The custodian may exercise all of the powers of the corporation, through or in place of its board of directors or officers, to the extent necessary to manage the affairs of the corporation in the best interests of its shareholders and creditors.

(d) The court during a receivership may redesignate the receiver a custodian, and during a custodianship may redesignate the custodian a receiver, if doing so is in the best interests of the corporation, its shareholders and creditors.

(e) The court from time to time during the receivership or custodianship may order compensation paid and expense disbursements or reimbursements made to the receiver or custodian and his counsel from the assets of the corporation or proceeds from the sale of the assets.

17-16-1433. Decree of dissolution.

(a) If after a hearing the court determines that one (1) or more grounds for judicial dissolution described in W.S. 17-16-1430 exist, it may enter a decree dissolving the corporation and specifying the effective date of the dissolution, and the clerk of the court shall deliver a certified copy of the decree to the secretary of state, who shall file it.

(b) After entering the decree of dissolution, the court shall direct the winding up and liquidation of the corporation's business and affairs in accordance with W.S. 17-16-1405 and the notification of claimants in accordance with W.S. 17-16-1406 and 17-16-1407.

17-16-1434. Election to purchase in lieu of dissolution.

(a) In a proceeding under W.S. 17-16-1430(a)(ii) to dissolve a corporation that has no shares listed on a national securities exchange or regularly traded in a market maintained by one (1) or more members of a national or affiliated securities association, the corporation may elect or, if it fails to elect, one (1) or more shareholders may elect to purchase all shares owned by the petitioning shareholder at the fair value of the shares. An election pursuant to this section shall be irrevocable unless the court determines that it is equitable to set aside or modify the election.

(b) An election to purchase pursuant to this section may be filed with the court at any time within ninety (90) days after the filing of the petition under W.S. 17-16-1430(a)(ii) or at such later time as the court in its discretion may allow. If the election to purchase is filed by one (1) or more shareholders, the corporation shall, within ten (10) days thereafter, give written notice to all shareholders, other than the petitioner. The notice must state the name and number of shares owned by the petitioner and the name and number of shares owned by each electing shareholder and must advise the recipients of their right to join in the election to purchase shares in accordance with this section. Shareholders who wish to participate must file notice of their intention to join in the purchase no later than thirty (30) days after the effective date of the notice to them. All shareholders who have filed an election or notice of their intention to participate in the election to purchase thereby become parties to the proceeding and shall purchase in proportion to their ownership of shares as of the date the first election was filed, unless they otherwise agree or the court otherwise directs. After an election has been filed by the corporation or one (1) or more shareholders, the proceeding under W.S. 17-16-1430(a)(ii) may not be discontinued or settled, nor may the petitioning shareholder sell or otherwise dispose of his shares, unless the court determines that it would be equitable to the corporation and the shareholders, other than the petitioner, to permit such discontinuance, settlement, sale or other disposition.

(c) If, within sixty (60) days of the filing of the first election, the parties reach agreement as to the fair value in terms of purchase of the petitioner's shares, the court shall enter an order directing the purchase of petitioner's shares upon the terms and conditions agreed to by the parties.

(d) If the parties are unable to reach an agreement as provided for in subsection (c) of this section, the court, upon application of any party, shall stay the W.S. 17-16-1430(a)(ii) proceedings and determine the fair value of the petitioner's shares as of the day before the date on which the petition under W.S. 17-16-1430(a)(ii) was filed or as of such other date as the court deems appropriate under the circumstances.

(e) Upon determining the fair value of the shares, the court shall enter an order directing the purchase upon such terms and conditions as the court deems appropriate, which may include payment of the purchase price in installments, where necessary in the interest of equity, provision for security to assure payment of the purchase price and any additional costs, fees and expenses as may have been awarded, and, if the shares are to be purchased by the shareholders, the allocation of shares among them. In allocating petitioner's shares among holders of different classes of shares, the court should attempt to preserve the existing distribution of voting rights among holders of different classes insofar as practicable and may direct that the holders of a specific class or classes shall not participate in the purchase. Interest may be allowed at the rate and from the date determined by the court to be equitable, but if the court finds that the refusal of the petitioning shareholder to accept an offer of payment was arbitrary or otherwise not in good faith, no interest shall be allowed. If the court finds that the petitioning shareholder had probable grounds for relief under W.S. 17-16-1430(a)(ii)(B) or (D), it may award to the petitioning shareholder reasonable fees and expenses of counsel and of any experts employed by him.

(f) Upon entry of an order under subsection (c) or (e) of this section, the court shall dismiss the petition to dissolve the corporation under W.S. 17-16-1430, and the petitioning shareholder shall no longer have any rights or status as a shareholder of the corporation, except the right to receive the amounts awarded to him by the order of the court which shall be enforceable in the same manner as any other judgment.

(g) The purchase order pursuant to subsection (e) of this section shall be made within ten (10) days after the date the order becomes final unless before that time the corporation files with the court a notice of its intention to adopt articles of dissolution pursuant to W.S. 17-16-1402 and 17-16-1403, which articles must then be adopted and filed within fifty (50) days thereafter. Upon filing of such articles of dissolution, the corporation shall be dissolved in accordance with provisions of W.S. 17-16-1405 through 17-16-1407, and the order entered pursuant to subsection (e) of this section shall no longer be of any force or effect, except that the court may award the petitioning shareholder reasonable fees and expenses in accordance with the provisions of the last sentence of subsection (e) of this section and the petitioner may continue to pursue any claims previously asserted on behalf of the corporation.

(h) Any payment by the corporation pursuant to an order under subsection (c) or (e) of this section, other than an award of fees and expenses pursuant to subsection (e) of this section, is subject to the provisions of W.S. 17-16-640.

17-16-1440. Deposit with state treasurer.

Assets of a dissolved corporation that should be transferred to a creditor, claimant or shareholder of the corporation who cannot be found or who is not competent to receive them shall be reduced to cash and deposited with the state treasurer for safekeeping. When the creditor, claimant or shareholder furnishes satisfactory proof of entitlement to the amount deposited, the state treasurer shall pay him or his representative that amount.

ARTICLE 15
FOREIGN CORPORATIONS

17-16-1501. Authority to transact business required.

(a) A foreign corporation may not transact business in this state until it obtains a certificate of authority from the secretary of state.

(b) The following activities, among others, do not constitute transacting business within the meaning of subsection (a) of this section:

(i) Maintaining, defending or settling any proceeding;

(ii) Holding meetings of the board of directors or shareholders or carrying on other activities concerning internal corporate affairs;

(iii) Maintaining bank accounts;

(iv) Maintaining offices or agencies for the transfer, exchange and registration of the corporation's own securities or maintaining trustees or depositaries with respect to those securities;

(v) Selling through independent contractors;

(vi) Soliciting or obtaining orders, whether by mail or through employees or agents or otherwise, if the orders require acceptance outside this state before they become contracts;

(vii) Creating or acquiring indebtedness, mortgages and security interests in real or personal property;

(viii) Securing or collecting debts or enforcing mortgages and security interests in property securing the debts;

(ix) Owning, without more, real or personal property;

(x) Conducting an isolated transaction that is completed within thirty (30) days and that is not one in the course of repeated transactions of a like nature; or

(xi) Transacting business in interstate commerce.

(c) The list of activities in subsection (b) of this section is not exhaustive.

(d) A foreign corporation, foreign limited partnership or foreign limited liability company which is either an organizer, a manager or member of a company is not required to obtain a certificate of authority to undertake its duties in these capacities.

17-16-1502. Consequences of transacting business without authority.

(a) A foreign corporation transacting business in this state without a certificate of authority may not maintain a proceeding in any court in this state until it obtains a certificate of authority.

(b) The successor to a foreign corporation that transacted business in this state without a certificate of authority and the assignee of a cause of action arising out of that business may not maintain a proceeding based on that cause of action in any court in this state until the foreign corporation or its successor obtains a certificate of authority.

(c) A court may stay a proceeding commenced by a foreign corporation, its successor or assignee until it determines whether the foreign corporation or it [its] successor requires a certificate of authority. If it so determines, the court may further stay the proceeding until the foreign corporation or its successor obtains the certificate.

(d) A foreign corporation which transacts business in this state without a certificate of authority shall be liable to this state, for the years or parts thereof during which it transacted business in this state without a certificate of authority, in an amount equal to all fees and license taxes, plus interest of eighteen percent (18%), which would have been imposed by law upon such corporation had it duly applied for and received a certificate of authority to transact business in this state as required by this act and thereafter filed all reports required by law, and in addition shall be liable for a penalty in the amount of five thousand dollars ($5,000.00), reasonable audit expenses and reasonable attorney fees. The secretary of state may refuse to issue a certificate of authority until all taxes, fees, interest, expenses and penalties due under this section have been paid to him. The attorney general may collect all penalties and other sums due under this subsection.

(e) Notwithstanding subsections (a) and (b) of this section, the failure of a foreign corporation to obtain a certificate of authority does not impair the validity of its corporate acts or prevent it from defending any proceeding in this state.

17-16-1503. Application for certificate of authority.

(a) A foreign corporation may apply for a certificate of authority to transact business in this state by delivering an application to the secretary of state for filing. The application shall set forth:

(i) The name of the foreign corporation or, if its name is unavailable for use in this state, a corporate name that satisfies the requirements of W.S. 17-16-1506;

(ii) The name of the state or country under whose law it is incorporated;

(iii) Its date of incorporation and period of duration;

(iv) The street address of its principal office;

(v) The address of its registered office in this state and the name of its registered agent at that office;

(vi) The names and usual business addresses of its current directors and officers;

(vii) An estimate, expressed in dollars, of the value of the property of the corporation located and employed in the state of Wyoming;

(viii) A statement that the corporation accepts the constitution of the state of Wyoming in compliance with the requirement of article 10, section 5 of the Wyoming constitution; and

(ix) Such additional information as may be necessary or appropriate in order to enable the secretary of state to determine whether such corporation is entitled to a certificate of authority to transact business in this state and to determine and assess the fees and license taxes under the laws of this state.

(b) The foreign corporation shall deliver with the completed application a certificate of existence, or a document of similar import, dated not more than sixty (60) days prior to filing in Wyoming, duly authenticated by the secretary of state or other official having custody of corporate records in the state or country under whose law it is incorporated.

(c) The application for certificate of authority shall be accompanied by a written consent to appointment executed by the registered agent.

17-16-1504. Amended certificate of authority.

(a) A foreign corporation authorized to transact business in this state shall obtain an amended certificate of authority from the secretary of state if it changes:

(i) Its corporate name;

(ii) The period of its duration; or

(iii) The state or country of its incorporation.

(b) The requirements of W.S. 17-16-1503 for obtaining an original certificate of authority apply to obtaining an amended certificate under this section.

17-16-1505. Effect on certificate of authority.

(a) A certificate of authority authorizes the foreign corporation to which it is issued to transact business in this state subject, however, to the right of the state to revoke the certificate as provided in this act.

(b) A foreign corporation with a valid certificate of authority has the same but no greater rights and has the same but no greater privileges as, and except as otherwise provided by this act is subject to the same duties, restrictions, penalties and liabilities now or later imposed on, a domestic corporation of like character.

(c) This act does not authorize this state to regulate the organization or internal affairs of a foreign corporation authorized to transact business in this state.

17-16-1506. Corporate name of foreign corporation.

(a) If the corporate name of a foreign corporation does not satisfy the requirements of W.S. 17-16-401, the foreign corporation to obtain or maintain a certificate of authority to transact business in this state may use a fictitious name to transact business in this state if its real name is unavailable and it delivers to the secretary of state for filing a copy of the resolution of its board of directors, certified by its secretary, adopting the fictitious name.

(b) Except as authorized by subsections (c) and (d) of this section, the corporate name, including a fictitious name, of a foreign corporation shall not be the same as, or deceptively similar to the name of any trademark or service mark registered in this state and shall be distinguishable upon the records of the secretary of state from other business names as required by W.S. 17-16-401.

(c) A foreign corporation may apply to the secretary of state for authorization to use a name that is not distinguishable in accordance with the provisions of W.S. 17-16-401(c).

(i) Repealed By Laws 1996, ch. 80, § 3.

(ii) Repealed By Laws 1996, ch. 80, § 3.

(d) A foreign corporation may use in this state the name, including the fictitious name, of another domestic or foreign corporation that is used in this state if the other corporation is incorporated or authorized to transact business in this state and the foreign corporation has:

(i) Merged with the other corporation; or

(ii) Been formed by reorganization of the other corporation; or

(iii) Acquired all or substantially all of the assets, including the corporate name, of the other corporation.

(iv) Repealed By Laws 1996, ch. 80, § 3.

(e) If a foreign corporation authorized to transact business in this state changes its corporate name to one that does not satisfy the requirements of W.S. 17-16-401, it may not transact business in this state under the changed name until it adopts a name satisfying the requirements of W.S. 17-16-401 and obtains an amended certificate of authority under W.S. 17-16-1504.

17-16-1507. Registered office and registered agent of foreign corporation.

(a) Each foreign corporation authorized to transact business in this state shall continuously maintain in this state:

(i) A registered office that may be the same as any of its places of business; and

(ii) A registered agent, who may be:

(A) An individual who resides in this state and whose business office is identical with the registered office;

(B) A domestic corporation or not-for-profit domestic corporation whose business office is identical with the registered office; or

(C) A foreign corporation or foreign not-for-profit corporation authorized to transact business in this state whose business office is identical with the registered office.

17-16-1508. Change of registered office or registered agent of foreign corporation.

(a) A foreign corporation authorized to transact business in this state may change its registered office or registered agent by delivering to the secretary of state for filing a statement of change that sets forth:

(i) The name of the corporation;

(ii) The street address of its current registered office;

(iii) If the current registered office is to be changed, the street address of the new registered office;

(iv) The name of its current registered agent;

(v) If the current registered agent is to be changed, the name of the new registered agent and the new agent's written consent to the appointment executed by the registered agent, either on the statement or attached to it; and

(vi) That after the change or changes are made, the street addresses of its registered office and the business office of its registered agent will be identical.

(b) If a registered agent changes the street address of his business office, he may change the street address of the registered office of any foreign corporation for which he is the registered agent by notifying the corporation in writing of the change and signing, either manually or in facsimile, and delivering to the secretary of state for filing a statement of change that complies with the requirements of subsection (a) of this section and recites that the corporation has been notified of the change.

17-16-1509. Resignation of registered agent of foreign corporation.

(a) The registered agent of a foreign corporation may resign his agency appointment by signing and delivering to the secretary of state for filing the original and two (2) exact or conformed copies of a statement of resignation. The statement of resignation may include a statement that the registered office is also discontinued.

(b) After filing the statement, the secretary of state shall attach the filing receipt to one (1) copy and mail the copy and receipt to the registered office if not discontinued. The secretary of state shall mail the other copy to the foreign corporation at its principal office address shown in its most recent annual report.

(c) The agency appointment is terminated, and the registered office discontinued if so provided, on the thirty-first (31st) day after the date on which the statement was filed.

17-16-1510. Service on foreign corporation.

(a) The registered agent of a foreign corporation authorized to transact business in this state is the corporation's agent for service of process, notice or demand required or permitted by law to be served on the foreign corporation.

(b) A foreign corporation may be served by registered or certified mail, return receipt requested, addressed to the secretary of the foreign corporation at its principal office shown in its application for a certificate of authority or in its most recent annual report if the foreign corporation:

(i) Has no registered agent or its registered agent cannot with reasonable diligence be served;

(ii) Has withdrawn from transacting business in this state under W.S. 17-16-1520; or

(iii) Has had its certificate of authority revoked under W.S. 17-16-1531.

(c) Service is perfected under subsection (b) of this section at the earliest of:

(i) The date the foreign corporation receives the mail;

(ii) The date shown on the return receipt, if signed, either manually or in facsimile, on behalf of the foreign corporation; or

(iii) Five (5) days after its deposit in the United States mail, as evidence by the postmark, if mailed postpaid and correctly addressed.

(d) This section does not prescribe the only means, or necessarily the required means, of serving a foreign corporation.

17-16-1511. Merger of foreign corporation authorized to transact business in this state.

(a) Whenever a foreign corporation authorized to transact business in this state shall be a party to a statutory merger permitted by the laws of the state or country of incorporation, it shall, within thirty (30) days after a merger becomes effective, file with the secretary of state a current certificate of evidence issued by the proper officer of the state or country of incorporation which sets forth:

(i) The date of filing;

(ii) The names of each corporation involved and the states of incorporation; and

(iii) The name of the surviving corporation.

(b) It shall not be necessary for the corporation to procure either a new or amended certificate of authority to transact business in this state unless the name of the corporation is changed by merger or unless the corporation desires to pursue in this state other or additional purposes than those which it is then authorized to transact in this state.

17-16-1520. Withdrawal of foreign corporation.

(a) A foreign corporation authorized to transact business in this state may not withdraw from this state until it obtains a certificate of withdrawal from the secretary of state.

(b) A foreign corporation authorized to transact business in this state may apply for a certificate of withdrawal by delivering an application to the secretary of state for filing. The application shall set forth:

(i) The name of the foreign corporation and the name of the state or country under whose law it is incorporated;

(ii) That it is not transacting business in this state and that it surrenders its authority to transact business in this state;

(iii) That it revokes the authority of its registered agent to accept service on its behalf and appoints the secretary of state as its agent for service of process in any proceeding based on a cause of action arising during the time it was authorized to transact business in this state;

(iv) A mailing address to which the secretary of state may mail a copy of any process served on him under paragraph (iii) of this subsection; and

(v) A commitment to notify the secretary of state in the future of any change in its mailing address.

(c) After the withdrawal of the corporation is effective, service of process on the secretary of state under this section is service on the foreign corporation. Upon receipt of process, the secretary of state shall mail a copy of the process to the foreign corporation at the mailing address set forth under subsection (b) of this section.

17-16-1530. Grounds for revocation.

(a) The secretary of state may commence a proceeding under W.S. 17-16-1531 to revoke the certificate of authority of a foreign corporation authorized to transact business in this state if:

(i) The foreign corporation is without a registered agent or registered office in this state for thirty (30) days or more;

(ii) The foreign corporation does not inform the secretary of state under W.S. 17-16-1508 or 17-16-1509 that its registered agent or registered office has changed, that its registered agent has resigned, or that its registered office has been discontinued within thirty (30) days of the change, resignation or discontinuance;

(iii) An incorporator, director, officer or agent of the foreign corporation signed a document he knew was false in any material respect with intent that the document be delivered to the secretary of state for filing;

(iv) The corporation does not deliver its annual reports or pay the annual license taxes to the secretary of state when due pursuant to W.S. 17-16-1630; or

(v) It is in the public interest and the corporation:

(A) Has provided fraudulent information or has failed to correct false information upon request of the secretary of state on any filing under this act with the secretary of state; or

(B) Cannot be served by either the registered agent or by mail by the secretary of state acting as the agent for process.

17-16-1531. Procedure for and effect of revocation.

(a) If the secretary of state determines that one (1) or more grounds exist under W.S. 17-16-1530 for revocation of a certificate of authority, he shall serve the foreign corporation with written notice of his determination under W.S. 17-16-1510, except for revocation pursuant to W.S. 17-16-1530(a)(iv) in which case notice of the proposed revocation shall be given only as provided in subsection (f) of this section.

(b) If the foreign corporation does not correct each ground for revocation or demonstrate to the reasonable satisfaction of the secretary of state that each ground determined by the secretary of state does not exist within sixty (60) days after service of the notice is perfected under W.S. 17-16-1510, the secretary of state may revoke the foreign corporation's certificate of authority by signing, either manually or in facsimile, a certificate of revocation that recites the ground or grounds for revocation and its effective date. The secretary of state shall file the original of the certificate and serve a copy on the foreign corporation under W.S. 17-16-1510. The provisions of subsection (f) of this section shall govern the procedures for revocation pursuant to W.S. 17-16-1530(a)(iv).

(c) The authority of a foreign corporation to transact business in this state ceases on the date shown on the certificate revoking its certificate of authority.

(d) The secretary of state's revocation of a foreign corporation's certificate of authority appoints the secretary of state the foreign corporation's agent for service of process in any proceeding based on a cause of action which arose during the time the foreign corporation was authorized to transact business in this state. Service of process on the secretary of state under this subsection is service on the foreign corporation. Upon receipt of process, the secretary of state shall mail a copy of the process to the secretary of the foreign corporation at its principal office shown in its most recent annual report or in any subsequent communication received from the corporation stating the current mailing address of its principal office, or, if none are on file, in its application for a certificate of authority.

(e) Revocation of a foreign corporation's certificate of authority does not terminate the authority of the registered agent of the corporation.

(f) The revocation of a foreign corporation's certificate of authority pursuant to W.S. 17-16-1530(a)(iv) shall be accomplished in accordance with the provisions of this subsection only. Prior to revoking a foreign corporation's certificate of authority pursuant to W.S. 17-16-1530(a)(iv) the secretary of state shall provide notice to the corporation at its last known mailing address by first class mail and publish once a week for two (2) consecutive weeks, in a newspaper of general circulation in the county in which the registered office of the foreign corporation is located, notice that the corporation failed to comply with W.S. 17-16-1630. If the corporation does not correct the deficiency within sixty (60) days after the first date of publication the corporation's certificate of authority shall be deemed revoked. The effect of the revocation shall be as provided in this section with the authority of the foreign corporation to transact business in this state ceasing on the date the certificate is deemed revoked.

17-16-1532. Appeal from revocation.

(a) A foreign corporation may appeal the secretary of state's revocation of its certificate of authority pursuant to W.S. 16-3-114, within thirty (30) days after service of the certificate of revocation is perfected under W.S. 17-16-1510. The foreign corporation appeals by petitioning the court to set aside the revocation and attaching to the petition copies of its certificate of authority and the secretary of state's certificate of revocation.

(b) The court may summarily order the secretary of state to reinstate the certificate of authority or may take any other action the court considers appropriate.

(c) The court's final decision may be appealed as in other civil proceedings.

17-16-1533. Applicability of chapter 15 to foreign limited liability companies.

To the extent not inconsistent with the Wyoming Limited Liability Act, W.S. 17-15-101 through 17-15-144, a limited liability company organized in another jurisdiction may do business in Wyoming by complying with W.S. 17-16-1501 through 17-16-1510, 17-16-1520 and 17-16-1530 through 17-16-1532. The certificate of organization of a limited liability company organized in another jurisdiction may be revoked as provided in W.S. 17-16-1530 through 17-16-1532.

17-16-1534. Applicability of chapter 23 to foreign statutory trust companies.

To the extent not inconsistent with the Wyoming Statutory Trust Act, W.S. 17-23-101 through 17-23-302, a statutory trust as defined in W.S. 17-23-102(a)(v), which is organized in another jurisdiction may do business in Wyoming by complying with W.S. 17-16-1501 through 17-16-1510, 17-16-1520 and 17-16-1530 through 17-16-1532.

ARTICLE 16
RECORDS AND REPORTS

17-16-1601. Corporate records.

(a) A corporation shall keep as permanent records minutes of all meetings of its shareholders and board of directors, a record of all actions taken by the shareholders or board of directors without a meeting, and a record of all actions taken by a committee of the board of directors in place of the board of directors on behalf of the corporation.

(b) A corporation shall maintain appropriate accounting records.

(c) A corporation or its agent shall maintain a record of its shareholders, in a form that permits preparation of a list of the names and addresses of all shareholders, in alphabetical order by class of shares showing the number and class of shares held by each.

(d) A corporation shall maintain its records in written form or in another form capable of conversion into written form within a reasonable time.

(e) A corporation shall keep a copy of the following records at its principal office:

(i) Its articles or restated articles of incorporation and all amendments to them currently in effect;

(ii) Its bylaws or restated bylaws and all amendments to them currently in effect;

(iii) Resolutions adopted by its board of directors creating one (1) or more classes or series of shares, and fixing their relative rights, preferences and limitations, if shares issued pursuant to those resolutions are outstanding;

(iv) The minutes of all shareholders' meetings, and records of all action taken by shareholders without a meeting, for the past three (3) years;

(v) All written communications to shareholders generally within the past three (3) years, including the financial statements furnished for the past three (3) years under W.S. 17-16-1620;

(vi) A list of the names and business addresses of its current directors and officers; and

(vii) Its most recent annual report delivered to the secretary of state under W.S. 17-16-1630.

17-16-1602. Inspection of records by shareholders.

(a) A shareholder of a corporation is entitled to inspect and copy, during regular business hours at the corporation's principal office, any of the records of the corporation described in W.S. 17-16-1601(e) if he gives the corporation written notice of his demand at least five (5) business days before the date on which he wishes to inspect and copy.

(b) A shareholder who has been of record for at least six (6) months immediately preceding his demand and who shall be the holder of record of at least five percent (5%) of all the outstanding shares of a corporation is entitled to inspect and copy, during regular business hours at a reasonable location specified by the corporation, any of the following records of the corporation if the shareholder meets the requirements of subsection (c) of this section and gives the corporation written notice of his demand at least five (5) business days before the date on which he wishes to inspect and copy:

(i) Excerpts from minutes of any meeting of the board of directors, records of any action of a committee of the board of directors while acting in place of the board of directors on behalf of the corporation, minutes of any meeting of the shareholders, and records of action taken by the shareholders or board of directors without a meeting, to the extent not subject to inspection under W.S. 17-16-1602(a);

(ii) Accounting records of the corporation; and

(iii) The record of shareholders.

(c) A shareholder may inspect and copy the records described in subsection (b) of this section only if:

(i) His demand is made in good faith and for a proper purpose;

(ii) He describes with reasonable particularity his purpose and the records he desires to inspect; and

(iii) The records are directly connected with his purpose.

(iv) Repealed By Laws 1997, ch. 190, § 3.

(d) The right of inspection granted by this section may not be abolished or limited, but may be expanded, by a corporation's articles of incorporation or bylaws.

(e) This section does not affect:

(i) The right of a shareholder to inspect records under W.S. 17-16-720 or, if the shareholder is in litigation with the corporation, to the same extent as any other litigant; or

(ii) The power of a court, independently of this act, to compel the production of corporate records for examination.

(f) For purposes of this section, "shareholder" includes a beneficial owner whose shares are held in a voting trust or by a nominee on his behalf.

17-16-1603. Scope of inspection right.

(a) A shareholder's agent or attorney has the same inspection and copying rights as the shareholder he represents.

(b) The right to copy records under W.S. 17-16-1602 includes, if reasonable, the right to receive copies made by photographic, xerographic, or other means.

(c) The corporation may impose a reasonable charge, covering the costs of labor and material, for copies of any documents provided to the shareholder. The charge may not exceed the estimated cost of production or reproduction of the records.

(d) The corporation may comply with a shareholder's demand to inspect the record of shareholders under W.S. 17-16-1602(b)(iii) by providing him with a list of its shareholders that was compiled no earlier than the date of the shareholder's demand.

17-16-1604. Court-ordered inspection.

(a) If a corporation does not allow a shareholder who complies with W.S. 17-16-1602(a) to inspect and copy any records required by that subsection to be available for inspection, the district court of the county where the corporation's principal office, or, if none in this state, its registered office, is located may summarily order inspection and copying of the records demanded at the corporation's expense upon application of the shareholder.

(b) If a corporation does not within a reasonable time allow a shareholder to inspect and copy any other record, the shareholder who complies with W.S. 17-16-1602(b) and (c) may apply to the district court in the county where the corporation's principal office, or, if none in this state, its registered office, is located for an order to permit inspection and copying of the records demanded. The court shall dispose of an application under this subsection on an expedited basis.

(c) If the court orders inspection and copying of the records demanded, it shall also order the corporation to pay the shareholder's costs, including reasonable counsel fees, incurred to obtain the order unless the corporation proves that it refused inspection in good faith because it had a reasonable basis for doubt about the right of the shareholder to inspect the records demanded.

(d) If the court orders inspection and copying of the records demanded, it may impose reasonable restrictions on the use or distribution of the records by the demanding shareholder.

17-16-1620. Financial statements for shareholders.

(a) A corporation shall furnish, upon request, to its shareholders annual financial statements, which may be consolidated or combined statements of the corporation and one (1) or more of its subsidiaries, as appropriate, that include a balance sheet as of the end of the fiscal year, an income statement for that year, and a statement of changes in shareholders' equity for the year unless that information appears elsewhere in the financial statements. If financial statements are prepared for the corporation on the basis of generally accepted accounting principles, the annual financial statements shall also be prepared on that basis. If detailed financial statements are not prepared for the corporation on an annual basis, then a copy of its federal income tax return will satisfy the requirements of this section.

(b) If the annual financial statements are reported upon by a public accountant, his report shall accompany them. If not, the statements shall be accompanied by a statement of the president or the person responsible for the corporation's accounting records:

(i) Stating his reasonable belief whether the statements were prepared on the basis of generally accepted accounting principles and, if not, describing the basis of preparation; and

(ii) Describing any respects in which the statements were not prepared on a basis of accounting consistent with the statements prepared for the preceding year.

(c) A corporation shall mail, upon request, the annual financial statements to each shareholder within one hundred twenty (120) days after the close of each fiscal year. Thereafter, on written request from a shareholder who was not mailed the statements, the corporation shall mail him the latest financial statements.

17-16-1621. Other reports to shareholders.

(a) If a corporation indemnifies or advances expenses to a director under W.S. 17-16-851 through 17-16-854 in connection with a proceeding by or in the right of the corporation, the corporation shall report the indemnification or advance in writing to the shareholders with or before the notice of the next shareholders' meeting.

(b) If a corporation issues or authorizes the issuance of shares for promissory notes or for promises to render services in the future, the corporation shall report in writing to the shareholders the number of shares authorized or issued, and the consideration received by the corporation, with or before the notice of the next shareholders' meeting.

17-16-1630. Filing of reports and payment of tax required; amount of tax; exemptions; records.

(a) Every corporation organized under the laws of this state and every foreign corporation which obtains the right to transact and carry on business within this state (except banks, insurance companies and savings and loan associations) shall file with the secretary of state on or before the first day of the month of registration of every year a certification, under the penalty of perjury, by its treasurer or other fiscal agent setting forth its capital, property and assets located and employed in the state of Wyoming. The statement shall give the names and addresses of its officers and directors and the address of its principal office. On or before the first day of the month of registration of every year the corporation shall pay to the secretary of state in addition to all other statutory taxes and fees a license tax based upon the sum of its capital, property and assets reported, of fifty dollars ($50.00) or two-tenths of one mill on the dollar ($.0002), whichever is greater.

(i) Repealed By Laws 2000, Ch. 35, § 2.

(ii) Repealed By Laws 2000, Ch. 35, § 2.

(iii) Repealed By Laws 2000, Ch. 35, § 2.

(iv) Repealed By Laws 2000, Ch. 35, § 2.

(v) Repealed By Laws 2000, Ch. 35, § 2.

(b) The provisions of W.S. 17-16-1630(a) shall be modified as follows:

(i) Repealed By Laws 2000, Ch. 35, § 2.

(ii) Any corporation engaged in the public calling of carrying goods, passengers or information interstate is not required to comply with the provisions of W.S. 17-16-1630(a) except to the extent of capital, property and assets used in intrastate business in this state;

(iii) The value of all mines and mining claims from which gold, silver and other precious metals, soda, saline, coal, mineral oil or other valuable deposit, is or shall be produced is deemed equivalent to the assessed value of the gross product thereof, for the previous year;

(iv) The assessed value of any property shall be its actual value.

(c) Financial information in the annual report shall be current as of the end of the corporation's fiscal year immediately preceding the date the annual report is executed on behalf of the corporation. All other information in the annual report shall be current as of the date the annual report is executed on behalf of the corporation.

(d) If an annual report does not contain the information required by this section, the secretary of state shall promptly notify the reporting domestic or foreign corporation in writing and return the report to it for correction.

(e) Every corporation registered or authorized to do business in the state of Wyoming shall preserve for three (3) years at its principal place of business, suitable records and books as may be necessary to determine the amount of tax for which it is liable for under this act. All records and books shall be available for examination by the secretary of state or his designee during regular business hours except as arranged by mutual consent.

(f) In addition to other fees provided under this section, each corporation shall pay one hundred dollars ($100.00) to the secretary of state for initial incorporation or qualification to do business in Wyoming.

17-16-1631. Repealed By Laws 1997, ch. 192, § 3.

17-16-1632. Repealed By Laws 1997, ch. 192, § 3.

17-16-1633. Repealed By Laws 1997, ch. 192, § 3.

ARTICLE 17
DOMESTICATION AND CONTINUANCE OF FOREIGN CORPORATIONS; TRANSFER OF DOMESTIC CORPORATIONS

17-16-1701. Domestication of foreign corporations.

Any corporation incorporated under the laws of any of the several states of the United States for any purpose except acting as an insurer as defined in W.S. 26-1-102(a)(xvi), or acting as a financial institution as described by W.S. 13-1-101(a)(ix) may become a domestic corporation of this state by delivering or causing to be delivered to the secretary of state articles of domestication. Upon filing the articles of domestication, the secretary of state shall issue to the foreign corporation a certificate of domestication which shall continue the corporation as if it had been incorporated under this act. The articles of domestication, upon being filed by the secretary of state, constitute the articles of the domesticated foreign corporation and it shall thereafter have all the powers and privileges and be subjected to all the duties and limitations granted and imposed upon domestic corporations under the provisions of the Wyoming Business Corporation Act. A corporation does not become a resident for the purpose of W.S. 16-6-101 through 16-6-118 solely because it becomes a domestic corporation under this section.

17-16-1702. Application for certificate of domestication; articles of domestication.

(a) A foreign corporation, in order to procure a certificate of domestication shall file articles of domestication with the secretary of state, which articles shall include and set forth:

(i) A certified copy of its original articles of incorporation and all amendments thereto or its equivalent basic corporate charter or other authorization, and a certificate of good standing not more than thirty (30) days old;

(ii) The name of the corporation and the jurisdiction under the laws of which it is incorporated;

(iii) The date of incorporation and the period of duration of the corporation;

(iv) The address of the principal office of the corporation and the jurisdiction under the laws of which it is incorporated;

(v) The address of the proposed registered office of the corporation in this state, and the name of its proposed registered agent in this state at that address;

(vi) The purpose or purposes of the corporation which it proposes to pursue in the transaction of business in this state;

(vii) The names and addresses of the directors and officers of the corporation;

(viii) A statement of the aggregate number of shares or other ownership units which the corporation has authority to issue, itemized by classes, par value of shares, shares without par value and series, if any, within a class;

(ix) A statement of the aggregate number of issued shares or other ownership units itemized by classes, par value of shares, shares without par value and series, if any, within a class;

(x) A statement that the corporation accepts the constitution of this state in compliance with the requirement of article 10, section 5 of the Wyoming constitution;

(xi) Any additional information as may be necessary or appropriate to enable the secretary of state to determine whether the corporation is entitled to a certificate of domestication evidencing its authority to transact business in this state, and to determine and assess the fees and license taxes under the laws of this state.

17-16-1710. Continuance of foreign corporations.

(a) Subject to subsection (b) of this section, any corporation incorporated for any purpose except acting as an insurer as defined in W.S. 26-1-102(a)(xvi), or acting as a financial institution as described by W.S. 13-1-101(a)(ix) under the laws of any jurisdiction other than this state may, if the jurisdiction will acknowledge the corporation's termination of domicile in the foreign jurisdiction, apply to the secretary of state for registration under this act, thus continuing the foreign corporation in Wyoming as if it had been incorporated in this state. The secretary of state may issue a certificate of registration upon receipt of an application supported by articles of continuance as provided by this act together with the statements, information and documents set out in subsection (c) of this section. The certificate of registration may then be issued subject to any limitations and conditions and may contain any provisions as may appear proper to the secretary of state.

(b) The secretary of state shall cause notice of issuance of a certificate of registration to be given forthwith to the proper officer of the jurisdiction in which the corporation was previously incorporated.

(c) The articles of continuance filed by a foreign corporation with the secretary of state shall contain:

(i) A certified copy of its original articles of incorporation and all amendments thereto or its equivalent basic corporate charter or other authorization;

(ii) The name of the corporation and the jurisdiction under the laws of which it is incorporated;

(iii) The date of incorporation and the period of duration of the corporation;

(iv) The address of the principal office of the corporation;

(v) The address of the proposed registered office of the corporation in this state and the name of its proposed registered agent in this state at the address;

(vi) The purpose or purposes of the corporation which it proposes to pursue in the transaction of business in this state;

(vii) The names and respective business addresses of the directors and officers of the corporation;

(viii) A statement of the aggregate number of shares or other ownership units which the corporation has authority to issue, itemized by classes, par value of shares, shares without par value and series, if any, within a class;

(ix) A statement of the aggregate number of issued shares or other ownership units itemized by classes, par value of shares, shares without par value and series, if any, within a class;

(x) Such additional information concerning capital structure or financial status as the secretary of state deems necessary to establish fees;

(xi) A statement that the corporation accepts the constitution of this state in compliance with the requirements of article 10, section 5 of the Wyoming constitution;

(xii) Any additional information necessary or appropriate to enable the secretary of state to determine whether the corporation is entitled to a certificate of registration evidencing its authority to transact business in the state and to determine and to assess any fees and taxes under the laws of this state;

(xiii) Any additional information permitted in articles of incorporation under W.S. 17-16-202.

(d) The application shall be executed by the corporation by its president or other officer, director, trustee, manager or person performing functions equivalent to those of a president and who is authorized to execute the application on behalf of the corporation and shall be verified by the officer signing the application.

(e) The provisions of the articles of continuance may, without expressly so stating, vary from the provisions of the corporation's articles of incorporation or equivalent basic corporate charter or other authorization, if the variation is one which a corporation incorporated under the Wyoming Business Corporation Act could effect by way of amendment to its articles of incorporation. Upon issuance of a certificate of continuance by the secretary of state, the articles of continuance shall be deemed to be the articles of incorporation of the continued corporation. The corporation may elect to incorporate by reference in the articles of continuance its basic corporate charter or other authorization which had been adopted by the corporation in the foreign jurisdiction, in order to permit the same to continue to act as the articles of incorporation of the corporation, provided, however, that such basic corporate charter or other authorization shall be deemed amended to the extent necessary to make the same conform to the laws of Wyoming and to the provisions of the articles of continuance.

(f) Except for the purpose of W.S. 16-6-101 through 16-6-118, the existence of any corporation heretofore or hereafter issued a certificate of continuation under this act shall be deemed to have commenced on the date the corporation commenced its existence in the jurisdiction in which the corporation was first formed, incorporated or otherwise came into being. The laws of Wyoming shall apply to a corporation continuing under this act to the same extent as if the corporation had been incorporated under the laws of Wyoming from and after the issuance of a certificate of continuation under this act by the secretary of state to the corporation. When a foreign corporation is continued as a corporation under this act, such continuance shall not affect the corporation's ownership of its property or liability for any existing obligations, causes of action, claims, pending or threatened prosecutions or civil or administrative actions, convictions, rulings, orders, judgments, or any other characteristics or aspects of the corporation and its existence.

(g) A share of stock of a foreign corporation issued before the corporation's continuance in Wyoming is deemed to have been issued in compliance with the Wyoming Business Corporation Act and the provisions of the articles of continuance, irrespective of whether the share is fully paid and nonassessable, and irrespective of any designation, rights, privileges, restrictions or conditions set out on or referred to in the certificate representing the share, and irrespective of whether the certificate is in registered or bearer form. Continuance under this act does not deprive a stockholder of any right or privilege that he claims under, or relieve the stockholder of any liability in respect of, an issued share.

(h) As used in this section, the term "corporation" shall include any incorporated organization, foundation, trust, association, or similar entity which appears to the secretary of state to possess characteristics sufficiently similar to those of a corporation organized under the Wyoming Business Corporation Act.

(j) This act applies to all corporations continued in Wyoming on the effective date of this act. The repeal of any statute or part thereof by this act shall have such effect as is provided in W.S. 17-16-1803.

17-16-1720. Transfer of a Wyoming corporation to another jurisdiction.

(a) A corporation incorporated or continued under this act may, if authorized by resolution duly adopted by a vote of two-thirds (2/3) of the holders of the issued shares of each class of stock of the corporation, whether or not entitled to vote on any other issue, and by the laws of any other jurisdiction, apply to the proper officer of the other jurisdiction for a certificate of registration, and to the secretary of state of this state for a certificate of transfer.

(b) The secretary of state shall require that the corporation maintain within the state an agent for service of process for at least one (1) year after the transfer is effected and shall impose any conditions he considers appropriate for the protection of creditors and stockholders, including the provision of notice to the public of the application described in subsection (a) of this section, the provision of a bond or a deposit of funds in an appropriate depository located in Wyoming and subject to the jurisdiction of the courts of Wyoming, and if such conditions are not met, the secretary of state may refuse to issue a certificate of transfer.

(c) The secretary of state, upon compliance by the applicant and the secretary with subsections (a) and (b) of this section and receipt of payment of the special toll charge prescribed by subsection (e) of this section shall immediately transmit a notice of issuance of a certificate of transfer to the proper officer of the jurisdiction to which the corporation is transferred.

(d) Upon issuance of a certificate of transfer, the corporation shall be continued as if it had been incorporated under the laws of the other jurisdiction and becomes a corporation under the laws of the other jurisdiction upon issuance by such jurisdiction of a certificate of registration.

(e) Every corporation organized, domesticated or continued under the laws of this state in order to receive a certificate of transfer pursuant to subsection (c) of this section shall pay to the secretary of state, in addition to all other statutory taxes and fees, a special toll charge equal to the percentage of the net actual value of its assets, wherever located, as follows, but in no case shall any special toll charge be less than one thousand dollars ($1,000.00):

(i) Upon the first one million dollars ($1,000,000.00)............................one percent (1%);

(ii) Upon the second million dollars ($2,000,000.00)...........nine-tenths of one percent (0.9%);

(iii) Upon the third million dollars ($3,000,000.00)..........eight-tenths of one percent (0.8%);

(iv) Upon the fourth million dollars ($4,000,000.00)..........seven-tenths of one percent (0.7%);

(v) Upon the fifth million dollars ($5,000,000.00)............six-tenths of one percent (0.6%);

(vi) Upon the sixth million dollars ($6,000,000.00)...........five-tenths of one percent (0.5%);

(vii) Upon the seventh million dollars ($7,000,000.00)...........four-tenths of one percent (0.4%);

(viii) Upon the eighth million dollars ($8,000,000.00)..........three-tenths of one percent (0.3%);

(ix) Upon the ninth million dollars ($9,000,000.00)........two-tenths of one percent (0.2%); and

(x) Upon the tenth million dollars ($10,000,000.00) and each additional million dollars or fraction thereof...........one-tenth of one percent (0.1%).

(f) The secretary of state shall determine the net actual value of the assets of a corporation liable for the special toll charge imposed by subsection (e) of this section. The secretary of state shall withhold issuance of a certificate of transfer until payment of the special toll charge is made or guaranteed in a form satisfactory to the secretary of state.

ARTICLE 18
TRANSITION PROVISIONS

17-16-1801. Application to existing domestic corporations.

(a) Except as provided in subsection (b) of this section, this act applies to domestic corporations in existence on its effective date that were incorporated under any general statute of this state providing for incorporation of corporations for profit if power to amend or repeal the statute under which the corporation was incorporated was reserved.

(b) For corporations incorporated in Wyoming prior to the effective date of this act, the cumulative voting and shareholder preemptive rights provisions contained in former W.S. 17-1-123 and 17-1-130 are continued for a period of four (4) years from the effective date of this act unless the corporation amends its articles of incorporation to provide otherwise.

17-16-1802. Applications to qualified foreign corporations.

A foreign corporation authorized to transact business in this state on the effective date of this act is subject to this act but is not required to obtain a new certificate of authority to transact business under this act.

17-16-1803. Saving provisions.

(a) Except as provided in subsection (b) of this section, the repeal of a statute by this act does not affect:

(i) The operation of the statute or any action taken under it before its repeal;

(ii) Any ratification, right, remedy, privilege, obligation or liability acquired, accrued or incurred under the statute before its repeal;

(iii) Any violation of the statute, or any penalty, forfeiture or punishment incurred because of the violation, before its repeal; or

(iv) Any proceeding, reorganization or dissolution commenced under the statute before its repeal, and the proceeding, reorganization or dissolution may be completed in accordance with the statute as if it had not been repealed.

(b) If a penalty or punishment imposed for violation of a statute repealed by this act is reduced by this act, the penalty or punishment if not already imposed shall be imposed in accordance with this act.

CHAPTER 17 : CLOSE CORPORATION SUPPLEMENT

ARTICLE 1
PROVISIONS

17-17-101. Short title.

This chapter shall be known and may be cited as the "Wyoming Statutory Close Corporation Supplement."

17-17-102. Application of Wyoming Business Corporation Act and the provisions of W.S. 17-3-101 through 17-3-104.

(a) The Wyoming Business Corporation Act applies to statutory close corporations to the extent not inconsistent with the provisions of this chapter.

(b) This chapter applies to a professional corporation organized under W.S. 17-3-101 through 17-3-104 whose articles of incorporation contain the statement required by W.S. 17-17-103(a), except insofar as W.S. 17-3-101 through 17-3-104 contain inconsistent provisions.

(c) This chapter does not repeal or modify any statute or rule of law that is or would apply to a corporation that is organized under the Wyoming Business Corporation Act and the provisions of W.S. 17-3-101 through 17-3-104 and that does not elect to become a statutory close corporation under W.S. 17-17-103.

17-17-103. Definition and election of statutory close corporation status.

(a) A statutory close corporation is a corporation whose articles of incorporation contain a statement that the corporation is a statutory close corporation.

(b) A corporation having thirty-five (35) or fewer shareholders may become a statutory close corporation by amending its articles of incorporation to include the statement required by subsection (a) of this section. For corporations formed prior to January 1, 1990, the amendment shall be approved by all of the holders of the votes of each class or series of shares of the corporation, whether or not otherwise entitled to vote on amendments. For corporations formed on or after January 1, 1990, the amendment must be approved by the holders of at least two-thirds (2/3) of the votes of each class or series of shares of the corporation, voting as separate voting groups, whether or not otherwise entitled to vote on amendments. If the amendment is adopted, a shareholder who voted against the amendment is entitled to assert dissenters' rights under W.S. 17-16-1301 through 17-16-1331.

17-17-110. Notice of statutory close corporations status on issued shares.

(a) The following statement must appear conspicuously on each share certificate issued by a statutory close corporation: The rights of shareholders in a statutory close corporation may differ materially from the rights of shareholders in other corporations. Copies of the articles of incorporation and bylaws, shareholders' agreements, and other documents, any of which may restrict transfers and affect voting and other rights, may be obtained by a shareholder on written request to the corporation.

(b) Within a reasonable time after the issuance or transfer of uncertificated shares, the corporation shall send to the shareholders a written notice containing the information required by subsection (a) of this section.

(c) The notice required by this section satisfies all requirements of this chapter and of W.S. 17-16-627 that notice of share transfer restrictions be given.

(d) A person claiming an interest in shares of a statutory close corporation which has complied with the notice requirement of this section is bound by the documents referred to in the notice. A person claiming an interest in shares of a statutory close corporation which has not complied with the notice requirement of this section is bound by any documents of which he, or a person through whom he claims, has knowledge or notice.

(e) A corporation shall provide to any shareholder upon his written request and without charge copies of provisions that restrict transfer or affect voting or other rights of shareholders appearing in articles of incorporation, bylaws, or shareholders' or voting trust agreements filed with the corporation.

17-17-111. Share transfer prohibition.

(a) An interest in shares of a statutory close corporation may not be voluntarily or involuntarily transferred, by operation of law or otherwise, except to the extent permitted by the articles of incorporation or under W.S. 17-17-112 or pursuant to a buy-sell agreement entered into by all the shareholders.

(b) Except to the extent the articles of incorporation provide otherwise, this section does not apply to a transfer:

(i) To the corporation or to any other holder of the same class or series of shares;

(ii) To members of the shareholder's immediate family, or to a trust, all of whose beneficiaries are members of the shareholder's immediate family, which immediate family consists of his spouse, parents, lineal descendants, including adopted children and stepchildren, and the spouse of any lineal descendant, and brothers and sisters;

(iii) That has been approved in writing by all of the holders of the corporation's shares having general voting rights;

(iv) To a personal representative upon the death of a shareholder or to a trustee or receiver as the result of a bankruptcy, insolvency, dissolution or similar proceeding brought by or against a shareholder;

(v) By merger, consolidation or share exchange under W.S. 17-16-1101 through 17-16-1114, or an exchange of existing shares for other shares of a different class or series in the corporation;

(vi) By a pledge as collateral for a loan that does not grant the pledgee any voting rights possessed by the pledgor; or

(vii) Made after termination of the corporation's status as a statutory close corporation.

17-17-112. Share transfer after first refusal by corporation.

(a) A person desiring to transfer shares of a statutory close corporation subject to the transfer prohibition of W.S. 17-17-111 must first offer them to the corporation by obtaining an offer to purchase the shares for cash from a third person who is eligible to purchase the shares under subsection (b) of this section. The offer by the third person must be in writing and state the offeror's name and address, the number and class, or series, of shares offered, the offering price per share, and the other terms of the offer.

(b) A third person is eligible to purchase the shares if:

(i) He is eligible to become a qualified shareholder under any federal or state tax statute the corporation has adopted and he agrees in writing not to terminate his qualification without the approval of the remaining shareholders; and

(ii) His purchase of the shares will not impose a personal holding company tax or similar federal or state penalty tax on the corporation.

(c) The person desiring to transfer shares shall deliver the offer to the corporation, and by doing so offers to sell the shares to the corporation on the terms of the offer. Within twenty (20) days after the corporation receives the offer, the corporation shall call a special shareholders' meeting, to be held not more than forty (40) days after the call, to decide whether the corporation should purchase all, but not less than all, of the offered shares. The offer must be approved by the affirmative vote of the holders of a majority of votes entitled to be cast at the meeting, excluding votes in respect of the shares covered by the offer.

(d) The corporation must deliver to the offering shareholder written notice of acceptance within seventy-five (75) days after receiving the offer or the offer is rejected. If the corporation makes a counteroffer, the shareholder must deliver to the corporation written notice of acceptance within fifteen (15) days after receiving the counteroffer or the counteroffer is rejected. If the corporation accepts the original offer or the shareholder accepts the corporation's counteroffer, the shareholder shall deliver to the corporation duly endorsed certificates for the shares, or instruct the corporation in writing to transfer the shares if uncertificated, within twenty (20) days after the effective date of the notice of acceptance. The corporation may specifically enforce the shareholder's delivery or instruction obligation under this subsection.

(e) A corporation accepting an offer to purchase shares under this section may allocate some or all of the shares to one (1) or more of its shareholders or to other persons if all the shareholders voting in favor of the purchase approve the allocation. If the corporation has more than one (1) class or series of shares, however, the remaining holders of the class or series of shares being purchased are entitled to a first option to purchase the shares not purchased by the corporation in proportion to their shareholdings or in some other proportion agreed to by all the shareholders participating in the purchase.

(f) If an offer to purchase shares under this section is rejected, the offering shareholder, for a period of one hundred twenty (120) days after the corporation received his offer, is entitled to transfer to the third person offeror all, but not less than all, of the offered shares in accordance with the terms of his offer to the corporation.

17-17-113. Attempted share transfer in breach of prohibition.

(a) An attempt to transfer shares in a statutory close corporation in violation of a prohibition against transfer binding on the transferee is ineffective.

(b) An attempt to transfer shares in a statutory close corporation in violation of a prohibition against transfer that is not binding on the transferee, either because the notice required by W.S. 17-17-110 was not given or because the prohibition is held unenforceable by a court, gives the corporation an option to purchase the shares from the transferee for the same price and on the same terms that he purchased them. To exercise its option, the corporation must give the transferee written notice within thirty (30) days after they are presented for registration in the transferee's name. The corporation may specifically enforce the transferee's sale obligation upon exercise of its purchase option.

17-17-114. Compulsory purchase of shares after death of shareholder.

(a) This section, and W.S. 17-17-115 through 17-17-117, apply to a statutory close corporation only if so provided in its articles of incorporation. If these sections apply, the personal representative of the estate or the surviving joint tenant of a deceased shareholder may require the corporation to purchase or cause to be purchased all, but not less than all, of the decedent's shares or jointly owned shares or to be dissolved.

(b) The provisions of W.S. 17-17-115 through 17-17-117 may be modified only if the modification is set forth or referred to in the articles of incorporation.

(c) An amendment to the articles of incorporation to provide for application of W.S. 17-17-115 through 17-17-117, or to modify or delete the provisions of these sections, must be approved by the holders of at least two-thirds (2/3) of the votes of each class or series of shares of the statutory close corporation, voting as separate voting groups, whether or not otherwise entitled to vote on amendments. If the corporation has no shareholders when the amendment is proposed, it must be approved by at least two-thirds (2/3) of the subscribers for shares, if any, or, if none, by all of the incorporators.

(d) A shareholder who votes against an amendment to modify or delete the provisions of W.S. 17-17-115 through 17-17-117 is entitled to dissenters' rights under W.S. 17-16-1301 through 17-16-1331 if the amendment upon adoption terminates or substantially alters his existing rights under these sections to have his shares purchased.

(e) A shareholder may waive his and his estate's rights under W.S. 17-17-115 through 17-17-117 by a signed writing.

(f) W.S. 17-17-115 through 17-17-117 do not prohibit any other agreement providing for the purchase of shares upon a shareholder's death, nor do they prevent a shareholder from enforcing any remedy he has independent of these sections.

17-17-115. Exercise of compulsory purchase right.

(a) A person entitled and desiring to exercise the compulsory purchase right described in W.S. 17-17-114 must deliver a written notice to the corporation, within one hundred twenty (120) days after the death of the shareholder, describing the number and class or series of shares beneficially owned by the decedent and requesting that the corporation offer to purchase the shares.

(b) Within twenty (20) days after the effective date of the notice, the corporation shall call a special shareholders' meeting, to be held not more than forty (40) days after the call, to decide whether the corporation should offer to purchase the shares. A purchase offer must be approved by the affirmative vote of the holders of a majority of votes entitled to be cast at the meeting, excluding votes in respect of the shares covered by the notice.

(c) The corporation must deliver a purchase offer to the person requesting it within seventy-five (75) days after the effective date of the request notice. A purchase offer must be accompanied by the corporation's balance sheet as of the end of a fiscal year ending not more than sixteen (16) months before the effective date of the request notice, an income statement for that year, a statement of changes in shareholders' equity for that year, and the latest available interim financial statements, if any. The person must accept the purchase offer in writing within fifteen (15) days after receiving it or the offer is rejected.

(d) A corporation agreeing to purchase shares under this section may allocate some or all of the shares to one (1) or more of its shareholders or to other persons if all the shareholders voting in favor of the purchase offer approve the allocation. If the corporation has more than one (1) class or series of shares, however, the remaining holders of the class or series of shares being purchased are entitled to a first option to purchase the shares not purchased by the corporation in proportion to their shareholdings or in some other proportion agreed to by all the shareholders participating in the purchase.

(e) If price and other terms of a compulsory purchase of shares are fixed or are to be determined by the articles of incorporation, bylaws, or a written agreement, the price and terms so fixed or determined govern the compulsory purchase unless the purchaser defaults, in which event the buyer is entitled to commence a proceeding for dissolution under W.S. 17-17-116.

17-17-116. Court action to compel purchase.

(a) If an offer to purchase shares made under W.S. 17-17-115 is rejected, or if no offer is made, the person exercising the compulsory purchase right may commence a proceeding against the corporation to compel the purchase in the district court of the county where the corporation's principal office, or, if none in this state, its registered office, is located. The corporation at its expense shall notify in writing all of its shareholders, and any other person the court directs, of the commencement of the proceeding. The jurisdiction of the court in which the proceeding is commenced under this subsection is plenary and exclusive.

(b) The court shall determine the fair value of the shares subject to compulsory purchase in accordance with the standards set forth in W.S. 17-17-142 together with terms for the purchase. Upon making these determinations the court shall order the corporation to purchase or cause the purchase of the shares or empower the person exercising the compulsory purchase right to have the corporation dissolved.

(c) After the purchase order is entered, the corporation may petition the court to modify the terms of purchase and the court may do so if it finds that changes in the financial or legal ability of the corporation or other purchaser to complete the purchase justify a modification.

(d) If the corporation or other purchaser does not make a payment required by the court's order within thirty (30) days of its due date, the seller may petition the court to dissolve the corporation and, absent a showing of good cause for not making the payment, the court shall do so.

(e) A person making a payment to prevent or cure a default by the corporation or other purchaser is entitled to recover the payment from the defaulter.

17-17-117. Court costs and other expenses.

(a) The court in a proceeding commenced under W.S. 17-17-116 shall determine the total costs of the proceeding, including the reasonable compensation and expenses of appraisers appointed by the court and of counsel and experts employed by the parties. Except as provided in subsection (b) of this section, the court shall assess these costs equally against the corporation and the party exercising the compulsory purchase right.

(b) The court may assess all or a portion of the total costs of the proceeding:

(i) Against the person exercising the compulsory purchase right if the court finds that the fair value of the shares does not substantially exceed the corporation's last purchase offer made before commencement of the proceeding and that the person's failure to accept the offer was arbitrary, or otherwise not in good faith; or

(ii) Against the corporation if the court finds that the fair value of the shares substantially exceeds the corporation's last sale offer made before commencement of the proceeding and that the offer was arbitrary, or otherwise not made in good faith.

17-17-120. Shareholder agreements.

(a) All the shareholders of a statutory close corporation may agree in writing to regulate the exercise of the corporate powers and the management of the business and affairs of the corporation or the relationship among the shareholders of the corporation.

(b) An agreement authorized by this section is effective although:

(i) It eliminates a board of directors;

(ii) It restricts the discretion or powers of the board or authorizes director proxies or weighted voting rights;

(iii) Its effect is to treat the corporation as a partnership; or

(iv) It creates a relationship among the shareholders or between the shareholders and the corporation that would otherwise be appropriate only among partners.

(c) If the corporation has a board of directors, an agreement authorized by this section restricting the discretion or powers of the board relieves directors of liability imposed by law, and imposes that liability on each person in whom the board's discretion or power is vested, to the extent that the discretion or powers of the board of directors are governed by the agreement.

(d) A provision eliminating a board of directors in an agreement authorized by this section is not effective unless the articles of incorporation contain a statement to that effect as required by W.S. 17-17-121.

(e) A provision entitling one (1) or more shareholders to dissolve the corporation under W.S. 17-17-133 is effective only if a statement of this right is contained in the articles of incorporation.

(f) To amend an agreement authorized by this section, all the shareholders must approve the amendment in writing unless the agreement provides otherwise.

(g) Subscribers for shares may act as shareholders with respect to an agreement authorized by this section if shares are not issued when the agreement was made.

(h) This section does not prohibit any other agreement between or among shareholders in a statutory close corporation.

17-17-121. Elimination of board of directors.

(a) A statutory close corporation may operate without a board of directors if its articles of incorporation contain a statement to that effect.

(b) An amendment to articles of incorporation eliminating a board of directors must be approved by all the shareholders of the corporation, whether or not otherwise entitled to vote on amendments, or if no shares have been issued, by all the subscribers for shares, if any, or if none, by all the incorporators.

(c) While a corporation is operating without a board of directors as authorized by subsection (a) of this section:

(i) All corporate powers shall be exercised by or under the authority of, and the business and affairs of the corporation managed under the direction of, the shareholders;

(ii) Unless the articles of incorporation provide otherwise:

(A) Action requiring director approval or both director and shareholder approval is authorized if approved by the shareholders; and

(B) Action requiring a majority or greater percentage vote of the board of directors is authorized if approved by the majority or greater percentage of the votes of shareholders entitled to vote on the action.

(iii) A shareholder is not liable for his act or omission, although a director would be, unless the shareholder was entitled to vote on the action;

(iv) A requirement by a state or the United States that a document delivered for filing contain a statement that specified action has been taken by the board of directors is satisfied by a statement that the corporation is a statutory close corporation without a board of directors and that the action was approved by the shareholders; and

(v) The shareholders by resolution may appoint one (1) or more shareholders to sign documents as "designated directors."

(d) An amendment to articles of incorporation deleting the statement eliminating a board of directors must be approved by the holders of at least two-thirds (2/3) of the votes of each class or series of shares of the corporation, voting as separate voting groups, whether or not otherwise entitled to vote on amendments. The amendment must also specify the number, names and addresses of the corporation's directors or describe who will perform the duties of a board under W.S. 17-16-801.

17-17-122. Bylaws.

(a) A statutory close corporation need not adopt bylaws if provisions required by law to be contained in bylaws are contained in either the articles of incorporation or a shareholder agreement authorized by W.S. 17-17-120.

(b) If a corporation does not have bylaws when its statutory close corporation status terminates under W.S. 17-17-131, the corporation shall immediately adopt bylaws under W.S. 17-16-206.

17-17-123. Annual meeting.

(a) The annual meeting date for a statutory close corporation is the last business day of the third month following the close of the business year unless its articles of incorporation, bylaws, or a shareholder agreement authorized by W.S. 17-17-120 fixes a different date.

(b) A statutory close corporation need not hold an annual meeting unless one (1) or more shareholders deliver written notice to the corporation requesting a meeting at least thirty (30) days before the meeting date determined under subsection (a) of this section.

17-17-124. Execution of documents in more than one capacity.

Notwithstanding any law to the contrary, an individual who holds more than one (1) office in a statutory close corporation may execute, acknowledge or verify in more than one (1) capacity any document required to be executed, acknowledged or verified by the holders of two (2) or more offices.

17-17-125. Limited liability.

The failure of a statutory close corporation to observe the usual corporate formalities or requirements relating to the exercise of its corporate powers or management of its business and affairs is not a ground for imposing personal liability on the shareholders for liabilities of the corporation.

17-17-130. Merger, consolidation, share exchange and sale of assets.

(a) A plan of merger, consolidation or share exchange that:

(i) If effected would terminate statutory close corporation status must be approved by the holders of at least two-thirds (2/3) of the votes of each class or series of shares of the statutory close corporation, voting as separate voting groups, whether or not the holders are otherwise entitled to vote on the plan;

(ii) If effected would create the surviving or new corporation as a statutory close corporation must be approved by the holders of at least two-thirds (2/3) of the votes of each class or series of shares of the surviving corporation, voting as separate voting groups, whether or not the holders are otherwise entitled to vote on the plan.

(b) A sale, lease, exchange, mortgage, encumbrance or other disposition of all or substantially all of the property, with or without the good will, of a statutory close corporation, if not made in the usual and regular course of business, must be approved by the holders of at least two-thirds (2/3) of the votes of each class or series of shares of the corporation, voting as separate voting groups, whether or not the holders are otherwise entitled to vote on the transaction.

17-17-131. Termination of statutory close corporation status.

(a) A statutory close corporation may terminate its statutory close corporation status by amending its articles of incorporation to delete the statement that it is a statutory close corporation. If the statutory close corporation has elected to operate without a board of directors under W.S. 17-17-121, the amendment must either comply with W.S. 17-16-801 or delete the statement dispensing with the board of directors from its articles of incorporation.

(b) An amendment terminating statutory close corporation status must be approved by the holders of at least two-thirds (2/3) of the votes of each class or series of shares of the corporation, voting as separate voting groups, whether or not the holders are otherwise entitled to vote on amendments.

(c) If an amendment to terminate statutory close corporation status is adopted, each shareholder who voted against the amendment is entitled to assert dissenters' rights under W.S. 17-16-1301 through 17-16-1331.

17-17-132. Effect of termination of statutory close corporation status.

(a) A corporation that terminates its status as a statutory close corporation is thereafter subject to all provisions of the Wyoming Business Corporation Act and, if incorporated under W.S. 17-3-101 through 17-3-104, to all provisions of those statutes.

(b) Termination of statutory close corporation status does not affect any right of a shareholder or of the corporation under an agreement or the articles of incorporation unless this chapter, the Wyoming Business Corporation Act, or another law of this state invalidates the right.

17-17-133. Shareholder option to dissolve corporation.

(a) The articles of incorporation of a statutory close corporation may authorize one (1) or more shareholders, or the holders of a specified number or percentage of shares of any class or series, to dissolve the corporation at will or upon the occurrence of a specified event or contingency. The shareholder or shareholders exercising this authority must give written notice of the intent to dissolve to all the other shareholders. Sixty (60) days after the effective date of the notice, the corporation shall begin to wind up and liquidate its business and affairs and file articles of dissolution under W.S. 17-16-1403 through 17-16-1407.

(b) Unless the articles of incorporation provide otherwise, an amendment to the articles of incorporation to add, change or delete the authority to dissolve described in subsection (a) of this section must be approved by the holders of all the outstanding shares, whether or not otherwise entitled to vote on amendments, or if no shares have been issued, by all the subscribers for shares, if any, or if none, by all the incorporators.

17-17-140. Court action to protect shareholders.

(a) Subject to satisfying the conditions of subsections (c) and (d) of this section, a shareholder of a statutory close corporation may petition the district court for any of the relief described in W.S. 17-17-141 through 17-17-143 if:

(i) The directors or those in control of the corporation have acted, are acting, or will act in a manner that is illegal, oppressive, fraudulent or unfairly prejudicial to the petitioner, whether in his capacity as shareholder, director or officer of the corporation;

(ii) The directors or those in control of the corporation are deadlocked in the management of the corporation's affairs, the shareholders are unable to break the deadlock, and the corporation is suffering or will suffer irreparable injury or the business and affairs of the corporation can no longer be conducted to the advantage of the shareholders generally because of the deadlock; or

(iii) There exists one (1) or more grounds for judicial dissolution of the corporation under W.S. 17-16-1430.

(b) A shareholder must commence a proceeding under subsection (a) of this section in the district court of the county where the corporation's principal office, or, if none in this state, its registered office, is located. The jurisdiction of the court in which the proceeding is commenced is plenary and exclusive.

(c) If a shareholder has agreed in writing to pursue a nonjudicial remedy to resolve disputed matters, he may not commence a proceeding under this section with respect to the matters until he has exhausted the nonjudicial remedy.

(d) If a shareholder has dissenters' rights under this chapter or W.S. 17-16-1301 through 17-16-1331 with respect to proposed corporate action, he must commence a proceeding under this section before he is required to give notice of his intent to demand payment under W.S. 17-16-1321 or to demand payment under W.S. 17-16-1323 or the proceeding is barred.

(e) Except as provided in subsections (c) and (d) of this section, a shareholder's right to commence a proceeding under this section and the remedies available under W.S. 17-17-141 through 17-17-143 are in addition to any other right or remedy he may have.

17-17-141. Ordinary relief.

(a) If the court finds that one (1) or more of the grounds for relief described in W.S. 17-17-140(a) exist, it may order such relief as it deems appropriate including one (1) or more of the following types of relief:

(i) The performance, prohibition, alteration or setting aside of any action of the corporation or of its shareholders, directors, or officers or of any other party to the proceeding;

(ii) The cancellation or alteration of any provision in the corporation's articles of incorporation or bylaws;

(iii) The removal from office of any director or officer;

(iv) The appointment of any individual as a director or officer;

(v) An accounting with respect to any matter in dispute;

(vi) The appointment of a custodian to manage the business and affairs of the corporation;

(vii) The appointment of a provisional director who has all the rights, powers and duties of a duly elected director to serve for the term and under the conditions prescribed by the court;

(viii) The payment of dividends; or

(ix) The award of damages to any aggrieved party.

(b) If the court finds that a party to the proceeding acted arbitrarily, or otherwise not in good faith, it may award one (1) or more other parties their reasonable expenses, including counsel fees and the expenses of appraisers or other experts, incurred in the proceeding.

17-17-142. Extraordinary relief; share purchase.

(a) If the court finds that the ordinary relief described in W.S. 17-17-141(a) is or would be inadequate or inappropriate, it may order the corporation dissolved under W.S. 17-17-143 unless the corporation or one (1) or more of its shareholders purchases all the shares of the shareholder for their fair value and on terms determined under subsection (b) of this section.

(b) If the court orders a share purchase, it shall:

(i) Determine the fair value of the shares, considering among other relevant evidence the going concern value of the corporation, any agreement among some or all of the shareholders fixing the price or specifying a formula for determining share value for any purpose, the recommendations of appraisers, if any, appointed by the court, and any legal constraints on the corporation's ability to purchase the shares;

(ii) Specify the terms of the purchase, including if appropriate terms for installment payments, subordination of the purchase obligation to the rights of the corporation's other creditors, security for a deferred purchase price, and a covenant not to compete or other restriction on the seller;

(iii) Require the seller to deliver all his shares to the purchaser upon receipt of the purchase price or the first installment of the purchase price;

(iv) Provide that after the seller delivers his shares he has no further claim against the corporation, its directors, officers or shareholders, other than a claim to any unpaid balance of the purchase price and a claim under any agreement with the corporation or the remaining shareholders that is not terminated by the court; and

(v) Provide that if the purchase is not completed in accordance with the specified terms, the corporation is to be dissolved under W.S. 17-17-143.

(c) After the purchase order is entered, any party may petition the court to modify the terms of the purchase and the court may do so if it finds that changes in the financial or legal ability of the corporation or other purchaser to complete the purchase justify a modification.

(d) If the corporation is dissolved because the share purchase was not completed in accordance with the court's order, the selling shareholder has the same rights and priorities in the corporation's assets as if the sale had not been ordered.

17-17-143. Extraordinary relief; dissolution.

(a) The court may dissolve the corporation if it finds:

(i) There are one (1) or more grounds for judicial dissolution under W.S. 17-16-1430; or

(ii) All other relief ordered by the court under W.S. 17-17-141 or 17-17-142 has failed to resolve the matters in dispute.

(b) In determining whether to dissolve the corporation, the court shall consider among other relevant evidence the financial condition of the corporation but may not refuse to dissolve solely because the corporation has accumulated earnings or current operating profits.

17-17-150. Application to existing corporations.

This chapter applies to all corporations electing statutory close corporation status under W.S. 17-17-103 after its effective date.

17-17-151. Reservation of power to amend or repeal.

The legislature has power to amend or repeal all or part of this chapter at any time and all corporations subject to this chapter are governed by the amendment or repeal.

CHAPTER 25 : CLOSE LIMITED LIABILITY COMPANY SUPPLEMENT

17-25-101. Short title.

This chapter shall be known and may be cited as the "Wyoming Close Limited Liability Company Supplement."

17-25-102. Application of Wyoming Limited Liability Company Act.

(a) The Wyoming Limited Liability Company Act applies to close limited liability companies to the extent not inconsistent with the provisions of this chapter and the powers provided the secretary of state by W.S. 17-15-137 shall apply to this supplement.

(b) This chapter does not repeal or modify any statute or rule of law that is or would apply to a limited liability company that is organized under the Wyoming Limited Liability Company Act that does not elect to become a close limited liability company.

17-25-103. Definition and election of close limited liability company status.

(a) A close limited liability company is a limited liability company whose articles of organization contain a statement that the company is a close limited liability company.

(b) A limited liability company formed under W.S. 17-15-101 through 17-15-144 may convert to a close limited liability company by amending its articles of organization to include the statement required by subsection (a) of this section.

(c) A statement in substantially the following form shall appear conspicuously in the operating agreement and on any certificates of ownership in a close limited liability company:

NOTICE OF RESTRICTIONS ON TRANSFERS AND WITHDRAWALS

The rights of members in a close limited liability company may differ materially from the rights of members in other limited liability companies. The Close Limited Liability Company Supplement, articles of organization, and operating agreement of a close limited liability company may restrict transfer of ownership interests, withdrawal or resignation from the company, return of capital contributions and dissolution of the company.

17-25-104. Formation.

Any person may form a close limited liability company which shall have one (1) or more members by signing and delivering one (1) original and one (1) exact or conformed copy of the articles of organization to the secretary of state for filing. The person forming the close limited liability company need not be a member of the company.

17-25-105. Articles of organization.

The articles of organization of a close limited liability company shall include a statement that the company is a close limited liability company and shall set forth the matters required by W.S. 17-15-107(a) except paragraphs (viii) and (x).

17-25-106. Management.

Management of a close limited liability company shall be vested in its members which, unless otherwise provided in the operating agreement, shall be in proportion to the division of profits and losses among members. If provision is made for it in the articles of organization, management of the company may be vested in a manager or managers who shall be appointed in the articles of organization or operating agreement or elected by the members in the manner prescribed by the operating agreement of the company. The manager or managers, or persons appointed by the manager or managers, shall also hold the offices and have the responsibilities accorded to them by the members and set out in the operating agreement of the company.

17-25-107. Withdrawal of members and return of members' contributions to capital.

(a) A member may only withdraw from a close limited liability company upon the terms and conditions set forth in the operating agreement. If no terms and conditions for withdrawal of a member are set forth in the company's operating agreement, a member may withdraw only with the consent of all other members of the company.

(b) A member shall not receive out of close limited liability company property any part of his or its contribution to capital unless:

(i) All liabilities of the company, except liabilities to members on account of their contributions to capital, have been paid or there remains property of the company sufficient to pay them; and

(ii) All members consent to such return of contributions to capital;

(iii) The company is dissolved; or

(iv) The articles of organization or operating agreement of the company otherwise provide for the return of contributions to capital.

(c) In the absence of a statement in the articles of organization to the contrary or the consent of all members of the close limited liability company, a member, irrespective of the nature of his or its contribution, has only the right to demand and receive cash in return for his or its contribution to capital.

(d) A member of a close limited liability company may not have the company dissolved for a failure to return his or its contribution to capital.

17-25-108. Dissolution.

(a) A close limited liability company organized under this chapter shall be dissolved upon the occurrence of any of the following events:

(i) When the period fixed for the duration of the company expires;

(ii) By the unanimous written agreement of all members; or

(iii) At the time or upon the occurrence of events specified in the operating agreement.

(b) As soon as possible following the occurrence of any of the events specified in subsection (a) of this section causing the dissolution of a close limited liability company, the company shall execute a statement of intent to dissolve in the form prescribed by the secretary of state.

17-25-109. Applicability of flexible limited liability company.

The flexible limited liability company provisions of W.S. 17-15-144 shall not apply to a close limited liability company organized under this chapter.

CHAPTER 26 : CONVERSION

17-26-101. Conversion of entities.

(a) Any entity, domestic or foreign, may convert to any other entity, domestic or foreign, pursuant to this section. As used in this section, "entity" means any entity authorized to be formed under this title and organized under the laws of this state or the laws of another state that are the functional equivalent.

(b) A domestic entity may be converted into any form of foreign entity recognized in that foreign jurisdiction pursuant to this section.

(c) A foreign entity may be converted into a domestic entity if the conversion is authorized pursuant to the articles of incorporation, articles of organization, certificate of limited partnership, articles of association, registration statement or other document of similar import filed or recorded by or for an entity in the jurisdiction in which the entity is formed.

(d) The converting domestic or foreign entity shall approve the terms and conditions of the conversion in accord with the documents enumerated in subsection (c) of this section.

(e) After the conversion is approved, the newly converted domestic entity shall file the appropriate document of organization as enumerated in subsection (c) of this section and include:

(i) Information that clearly names and identifies the converting entity and the newly converted entity;

(ii) The state of original formation and the date of original organization; and

(iii) Proof that conversion is approved by the owners or members of the converting entity in accordance with the authority given the converting entity.

(f) The conversion takes effect when the appropriate document of organization enumerated in subsection (c) of this section is filed or at any later date specified in the document.

(g) Upon conversion, all property owned by the converting entity remains in the newly converted entity. All obligations of the converting entity continue as obligations of the newly converted entity. Any action or proceeding pending against the converting entity may be continued as if the conversion had not occurred.

About the Author

Kathleen Spitzer is a corporate, real estate and asset protection attorney practicing in Jackson Hole, Wyoming. She graduated Magna Cum Laude from the College of the Holy Cross in Worcester, Massachusetts and received her J.D. from the Northwestern School of Law of Lewis and Clark College in Portland, Oregon. In law school, she was editor-in-chief of the law journal, Animal Law.

Kathleen is a member of the Wyoming, Idaho and Oregon State Bar Associations and has extensive knowledge in corporate, business and real estate law matters. An avid real estate investor herself, Kathleen specializes in helping individuals understand the complexities of business structures and assisting entrepreneurs in protecting their assets and limiting their liability exposure.

Kathleen is on the board of the Family Safety Network in Driggs, Idaho. She enjoys winter sports and mountain biking and lives in the Jackson Hole area with her husband and daughter.